Studying School Subjects

The Falmer Press Teachers' Library

The Falmer Press Teachers' Library Series: 10

Studying School Subjects

Ivor F. Goodson and
Colin J. Marsh

 The Falmer Press

(A member of the Taylor & Francis Group)
London • Washington, D.C.

UK   Falmer Press, 1 Gunpowder Square, London, EC4A 3DE
USA Falmer Press, Taylor & Francis Inc., 1900 Frost Road, Suite 101, Bristol, PA 19007

First published in 1996

A catalogue record for this book is available from the British Library

Library of Congress Cataloging-in-Publication Data are available on request

ISBN 0-7507-0588-4 cased
ISBN 0-7507-0589-2 paper

Jacket design by Caroline Archer

Typeset in 10/12pt Times by
Graphicraft Typesetters Ltd., Hong Kong.

Printed in Great Britain by Biddles Ltd., Guildford and King's Lynn on paper which has a specified pH value on final paper manufacture of not less than 7.5 and is therefore 'acid free'.

Every effort has been made to contact copyright holders for their permission to reprint material in this book. The publishers would be grateful to hear from any copyright holder who is not here acknowledged and will undertake to rectify any errors or omissions in future editions of this book.

Contents

Preface

In recent decades school subjects have rapidly emerged as a major focus of inquiry for a range of educational studies. As a result, there is a need for introductory texts in this area of work.

In some areas of inquiry a number of collections or introductions are already available. In the sociology of school knowledge, for instance, Michael Young's edited collection *Knowledge and Control* provides a pioneering collection of studies; his work is excellently complemented by Geoff Whitty's *Sociology of School Knowledge*. More recently Bernstein, in *Structuring a Pedagogic Discourse* and *Pedagogy, Symbolic Control and Identity*, provides generative lines of inquiry for those studying school subjects. Dowling's work in secondary school mathematics provides an example of just how generative these insights might prove.

Work on school texts has similarly been summarized and introduced in number of works. Michael Apple's *Teachers and Texts* and *Official Knowledge* provides accessible introductions to this field of inquiry.

Yet, a wide range of work has emerged which employs a socio-historical approach to school subjects and which also studies the historical emergence of subject traditions and subject departments. To date, there is no summarizing text to introduce new students to this work. Hence, we decided to develop a guidebook to this range of work and to do so in ways that provide a student with sampled highlights from some of the more exemplary works in the field. So the book is a mix of introductions: to sources, to concepts and to methods. In doing so we hope new studies will be undertaken which will broaden and deepen our understandings of school subjects; for these social inventions remain at the centre of the formal educational sector.

September 1996

References

APPLE, M.W. (1986) *Teachers and Texts: A Political Economy of Class and Gender Relations in Education*, New York, Routledge & Kegan Paul

APPLE, M.W. (1993) *Official Knowledge: Democratic Education in a Conservative Age*, New York, Routledge

BERNSTEIN, B. (1996) *Pedagogy, Symbolic Control and Identity*, London, Taylor & Francis

BERNSTEIN, B. (1990) *The Structuring of Pedagogic Discourse* (Vol. IV of Class, codes and control), London and New York, Routledge

DOWLING, P. (1993) A Language for the Sociological Description of Pedagogic Texts with Particular Reference to the Secondary School Mathematics Scheme SMP, 11–6, dissertation, University of London

WHITTY, G. (1985) *Sociology and School Knowledge*, London, Methuen

YOUNG, M.F.D. (Ed) (1971) *Knowledge and Control: New Directions for the Sociology of Education*, London, Collier-Macmillan

Acknowledgments

A wide range of people have helped in putting together this introductory volume. Most importantly the researchers at the RUCCUS Educational Research Unit at the University of Western Ontario, particularly research assistants Monica Muckenfuss, Chris Anstead and Jane King.

Many colleagues have been generous in responding to particular chapters: Dr Barry Cooper, Professor Gary McCulloch, Professor Judith Little, Professor Bill Green, Professor Peter Medway and Dr Leslie Siskin — Our thanks to them.

The difficulty of a book of this sort is that it is addressing a kind of moving target — especially at this time of rapid restructuring in curriculum matters; new initiatives such as the Dearing Report in Britain came out after the book went to press, likewise with major reports in the USA and Canada. Hence, there have been some valuable displays of understanding from the publishers, Falmer Press who have, as always, been patient and persistent 'beyond the call of duty'. Thanks to Malcolm Clarkson and Jackie Day in particular.

The authors and publishers would like to thank the following for permission to reproduce their material:

The Struggle for the American Curriculum 1893 - 1959 by Kliebard, H, Published by Routledge.
English and Englishness by Doyle, B, Published by Routledge.
Howson, A.G, History of Mathematics Education in England, Published by Cambridge University Press.

Chapter 1

Introduction: Studying School Subjects

Why Study School Subjects?

In many parts of the world there is now evidence of a basic reconstitution within the school curriculum. Sometimes this is presented as the reestablishment of the 'traditional' over the 'progressive'; the 'basic' over the 'esoteric' or 'idiosyncratic'; the 'rigorous' over the 'experimental'. In the early 1980s, US Secretary of Education, William Bennett, wishfully caught the flavour of this gathering reconstitution which grew in global scale through the 1990s:

> The national debate on education is now focused on truly important matters: mastering the basics-math, history, science, and English; insisting on high standards and expectations; ensuring discipline in the classroom; conveying a grasp of our moral and political principles; and nurturing the character of our young. (Bennett, 1990, quoted in Apple, 1990a, p. 379)

Curriculum theory has had too little to say about the historical or political dimensions of this change. The concern of most curriculum specialists has been on how to implement the changes, on how to train subject teachers or how to develop 'pedagogic content knowledge'. Abjectly the curriculum theorist has too often played the part of the facilitator of political will: 'ours not to reason why, ours but to do or die'.

The historical amnesia of so much curriculum theory is both a symptom and a cause of this intellectual and political posture. As we shall see the failure to study school subjects historically and sociologically has many causes but whatever the causes the result is that 'subjects' have become a normative aspect of schooling, treated as taken-for granted 'givens'. In fact, however, nothing could be further from the truth; by 'studying school subjects' we rapidly come to understand them as the most quintessential of social and political constructions. School subjects by this view are social constructions that intersect with patterns of social relations and social structure and are intimately implicated in the reproduction thereof and in processes of cultural transmission.

How can it be that the form of social construction that sits at the heart of schooling worldwide has remained so substantially unscrutinized? If we begin by accepting that school subjects themselves are an important source for study a number of problems arise. 'The subject' is an elusive and multifaceted phenomenon because it is defined, redefined and negotiated at a number of levels and in a number of arenas. In our scrutiny it would be impossible to arbitrate over which points in the ongoing negotiations were critical. Also, the terrain differs substantially according to local or national structures and patterns. In such a shifting and multi-layered terrain, it is plainly problematic to try to define common ground for this study.

A good deal of the most important scholarship on the school curriculum, certainly on curriculum as a social construction, emerged seriously in the 1960s and early 1970s. This was, however, a period of change, expansion and experimentation everywhere in the Western world, and nowhere more so than in the world of schooling in general, and curriculum in particular. For critical curriculum scholarship to happen during such times was both encouraging and, in a sense, symptomatic. The emergence of a field of study of curriculum as social construction and as ideology was an important new direction. However, while itself symptomatic of a period of social questioning and criticism, this burgeoning of critical scholarship was not without its negative side. This negative side had two important aspects. Firstly, influential scholars in the field often took a value position which assumed that schooling should be reformed root and branch; 'revolutionized'; 'the maps of learning redrawn'. Secondly, this scholarship took place at a time when a wide range of curriculum reform movements were seeking to do precisely this — to revolutionize school curricula. On both grounds, therefore, it was unlikely that such scholars would wish to focus upon, let alone concede, the areas of stability that may have existed within the school curriculum. Their concern was not so much with what existed, what was *there*, but with what *ought* to be there.

Yet the areas of stability and universality with regard to school subjects are nothing less than astounding; they provide an antidote to the optimistic 'change assumptions' of the curriculum scholars of the sixties and seventies and now to the new 'change' and 'restructuring' optimists of the 1990s. Recent research offers a further reminder that national and local proponents of subject change face a 'world culture' of school subjects. In *School Knowledge for the Masses*, Meyer, Kamens and Benavot (1993) have reviewed the spread of school subjects as a *world movement* associated with modernisation. Much of their data is located at the primary level, even so, the universal characteristics of 'core' school subjects are shared throughout the world. Without exception in the wide range of countries they reviewed the same short list of basic subjects were granted unquestioned pre-eminence, normally in the period 1890–1910. If anything, their work reminds us of the aberrant nature of curriculum reform aspirations in the sixties and seventies and shows that the contemporary reconstitution of traditional school subjects follows the trends of a long-lasting world movement. Throughout the Western world there is exhortation, but also evidence, about this 'return to basics', this reinscription of traditional subjects. In England, for instance, the new National Curriculum defines a range of subjects to be taught as a 'core' curriculum in all schools. The subject categories thereby instated bear an uncanny resemblance to the list generally defined as secondary school subjects in the 1904 Regulations. In this sense, the National Curriculum reflects a new movement to reconstitute the school subjects first launched in the world movement of the 1890–1910 period.

New Directions for Studying School Subjects

In studying school subjects, our scholarly inquiry has now arrived at a new stage. Initial work in the early twentieth century provided some important precursors to the work of studying subjects as social construction; sociologists of knowledge like Bernstein and Young, Giroux and Apple, then played a vital role in rescuing and reasserting the validity of this intellectual project; in the process however, some of the necessary focus on historical and empirical circumstances has been lost. The task now being undertaken is to reexamine the role of sociological and historical methods in the study of curriculum and to rearticulate a mode of study for extending an understanding of the social history of the school curriculum and, in this work, particularly school subjects.

In fact, Young later came to acknowledge the somewhat static determinism of his earlier writing in *Knowledge and Control* and to argue that historical work should be an essential ingredient of the study of school knowledge. He wrote of the need to understand the 'historical emergence and persistence of particular conventions (school subjects for example).' By failing to situate the problems of contemporary education historically we are again limited from understanding issues of politics and control. He concluded that 'one crucial way of reformulating and transcending the limits within which we work is to see . . . how such limits are not given or fixed but produced through the conflicting actions and interests of men in history' (Young, 1977, pp. 248–9). Elsewhere, Goodson has called for us to develop a social constructionist perspective on studying school subjects (see Goodson, 1990, pp. 299–312).

The study of the written curriculum of school subjects should afford a range of insights into schooling. But it is very important to stress that such inquiry must be allied to other kinds of study: in particular studies of school process, of school departments, of school texts and discourses, and of the history of pedagogy. Schooling is composed of the interlinked matrix of these, and indeed other, vital ingredients.

One of the important reasons for studying school subjects is that they create justificatory discourses or 'regimes of truth' for the organization of school knowledge. Much of the work on school subject matter and content knowledge assumes that classroom practitioners can reorganize and redirect school knowledge in ways that are more pedagogically sensitive. However, studying school subjects as dominant discourses implies that they, themselves, set parameters for practice. In this sense, the preactive definition of school subjects is a crucial part of understanding 'the terms of engagement' within the schooling. Much of the work on school subject matter assumes degrees of autonomy on behalf of school teachers which is denied by the power of preactive school subject definition. The very forms and discourses of school subject knowledge definition provide important parameters for any subsequent redefinition. In this sense, to understand school subject knowledge is to begin to study the nature of schooling; it is also to begin to understand the limits on the growing focus on 'practice'. To focus and embrace practice is to accept a whole range of preactive decisions about schooling. 'Practice' in this way, in sublimal form, exhorts us to accept the limits of political feasibility.

The link between subject knowledge and subject pedagogy is a crucial line of inquiry; so too is the link between subject knowledge and subject assessment. In addition, more broadly conceived notions of curriculum will have to be explored: the hidden curriculum, the curriculum conceived of as topics and activities and most important of all the primary and pre-school curriculum. Further work must be undertaken on comparative studies of the school curriculum. As work begins to explore the way in which school subject content relates to the parameters of practice we shall begin to see in a more grounded way how the world of schooling is structured.

This book is entitled *Studying School Subjects* but like any title it may mislead. Because the focus is on the scholarly study of school subjects as constructed social phenomena, it does not adopt the more recognizable pattern of 'studying school subjects' so familiar to school students and teachers. More specifically the book does not look at how school subject knowledge is negotiated in the classroom. This is perhaps the most crucial dimension in understanding school subjects. But we have taken the view that this dimension cannot be fully elucidated until the neglected area of study of school subjects, their *'preactive' definition*, is undertaken. The definition of subject knowledge which precedes interactive negotiation and redefinition in the classroom and which is currently the site of such considerable political activity must be studied in it's own right.

The current wave of reconstitution of school subjects indicates the importance of the preactive definition of school knowledge whether this be conducted at national or local level, or at school or department level. In the end our studies of such preactive definition must illuminate the crucial relationship between these preactive definitions of subjects and their interactive realisation in school classrooms. But for the moment so neglected is the study of the preactive definition of school subjects that no such marriage of methodologies could be consummated. *Studying School Subjects* is therefore the precursor to investigating the links between school subject knowledge and classroom pedagogy and activity; and indeed between broader political purposes and educational objectives.

The work of the past two decades or so has provided an initial intellectual grounding for a more broad-based and sustained project of studying school subjects. This book seeks to further this initial, somewhat narrow, intellectual base, which is largely monographic in form, towards a much wider range of studies which embrace all aspects of school subjects. As a result, we have tried to provide some introduction to the 'feel' and quality of sources for the study of school subjects by providing quotes at some length, from some of the major works in the area. The concern is to provide an introductory text for those undertaking the study of school subjects and to point out in preliminary manner the major areas of inquiry for such work.

Chapter 2 briefly discusses school subjects as cultural and historical phenomena, as a way of providing a contextual background to the inquiry chapters. What then follows are a series of sections which cover the main foci for studying school subjects. Hence chapter 3 discusses school case studies and looks at a number of case studies of this sort which provide examples of this form of inquiry.

Chapter 4 discusses in some detail the study of subject 'traditions' and concludes that just as there are important differences within subject boundaries of the same order as the differences between subjects, so also there are major 'traditions' which exist with varying degrees of articulation and allegiance, *within* most school subjects.

Chapter 5 discusses the organizational vehicle which carries school subjects in most secondary schools namely the 'subject department'. This is a neglected area of study but one of growing importance in this era of educational restructuring.

Chapters 6, 7 and 8 provide an introduction to work on the social histories of three subjects: science, mathematics and English. Historical study of these three 'core' subjects is well advanced and provides exemplars for future work on other subjects.

In chapters 9 and 10 more sociological studies in the school subject are presented. Studies of patterns of stability and change are reviewed and the reader is introduced to some explanatory frameworks that have emerged in this work.

Reflections and Issues

1 To what extent do you consider that school subjects have remained stable and universal over time? With reference to a school subject that you currently teach or are most familiar with, how has it changed over the decades, if at all? Which individuals/groups/interests do you think have been responsible for the changes, or lack of changes?

2 Is it legitimate to separate out preactive definitions of subjects from their interactive realisation in classrooms? What are some advantages in focusing upon preactive definitions prior to seeking relationships with interactive experiences in the classrooms? What are some of the problems in following this line of research?

3 In terms of the subject(s) you currently teach or are most familiar with, explore the relationship between the subject's content and form and how it is taught. How can these relationships be justified? Are some of the links changing, and if so, in what direction and why?

Suggested Reading

Useful articles includes:

Apple, M.W. (1990) 'The politics of official knowledge in the United States', *Journal of Curriculum Studies*, **22**, 4.

Goodson, I.F. (1990) 'Studying curriculum: Towards a social constructionist perspective', *Journal of Curriculum Studies*, **22**, 4.

Goodson, I.F. (1997) 'Becoming a school subject', in Goodson, I.F. with Anstead, C.J. and Mangan, J.M. *Subject Knowledge: Readings for the Study of School Subjects*, London and Washington, DC: Falmer Press.

Useful books include:

Apple, M.W. (1990) *Ideology and Curriculum*. 2nd Edition. London: Routledge.

Goodson, I.F. (1995) *The Making of Curriculum: Collected Essays*, 2nd Edition, London and Washington, DC: Falmer Press, especially for a more detailed discussion of 'preactive' and 'interactive' curriculum categories.

Goodson, I.F. (Ed) (1988) *International Perspectives in Curriculum History*, London: Routledge, 2nd Edition.

Goodson, I.F. (1993) *School Subjects and Curriculum Change*, 3rd Edition, London and Washington, DC: Falmer Press.

Kliebard, H. (1986) *The Struggle for the American Curriculum 1893–1958*, London and Washington, DC: Falmer Press.

Messer-Davidow, E. *et al* (Ed) (1993) *Knowledges: Historical and Critical Studies in Disciplinarity*, Charlottesville and London: University Press of Virginia.

Meyer, J.W., Kamens, D.H. and Benavot, A. (1993) *School Knowledge for the Masses*, London and Washington, DC: Falmer Press.

Tomkins, G.S. (1986) *A Common Countenance: Stability and Change in the Canadian Curriculum*, Scarborough: Prentice-Hall.

Chapter 2

School Subjects: The Context of Cultural Inventions

The State's involvement, sponsorship, funding and control of mass education developed first in Western Europe and this model was later utilized in patterns of national development throughout the world. 'Yet most comprehensive studies of education almost entirely overlook the historical origins of state systems of schooling . . . thereby ignoring the sociological significance of the successful institutionalization of this social innovation' (Ramirez and Boli, 1987, p. 2). The State's involvement in schooling intersects crucially with the economic history of Western Europe. While some of the early models for state systems pre-date the Industrial Revolution, it seems probable that the succession of the domestic/putter out system by the factory system was something of a watershed. The factory system, in breaking-up existing family patterns, opened up the socialization of the young to penetration by state systems of schooling. Yet Ramirez and Boli stress the sheer universality of mass state-sponsored education and hence they argue that the state's compelling interest in education:

> was not solely a response to the needs of an industrialized economy, to class or status conflicts, or to unique historical conjunctures in particular countries, such as the character of the central bureaucracy in Prussia, the revolutions and reactions in France, the power of the peasantry in Sweden, or the extension of the franchise to the working classes in England. (*ibid*)

The common feature uniting the wide range of initiatives by states to fund and manage mass schooling was, they argue, the endeavour of constructing a national polity; the power of the nation — state, it was judged, would be unified through the participation of the State's subjects in national projects. Central in this socialization into national identity was the project of mass State schooling. The sequence followed by those states promoting this national project of mass schooling were strikingly similar. Initially there was the promulgation of a national interest in mass education; this was followed by legislation to make schooling compulsory for all. To organize the system of mass schools, state departments or ministries of education were formed. State authority was then exercised over all schools — both those 'autonomous' schools already existing and newly proliferating schools specifically organized or opened by the State. These state agencies began to exert their control over schooling by defining the school curriculum and by mandating school subject content knowledge. The link between schools, and an essentially 'meritocratic' view of the social order was discernable at the time of the Reformation. Alongside the industrialization of Europe and the progressive embourgeoisement of society this pattern was refined and promoted:

> with the embourgeoisement of much of European society during the nine-teenth century, the significance of schooling as a general means of occu-pational success and social mobility became broadly institutionalized. In this way, there was an economic and social ideology that supported uni-versal education and that complemented the political ideology of state-directed schooling for purposes of national progress. Though this 'human capital' theory of progress, which facilitated linkages between the state and school, originated among the bourgeoisie, the bourgeois classes fought against the expansion of schooling in the nineteenth century. However the economic success of the bourgeoisie so greatly aided the organizational and extractive powers of the state that it was unable to contain the drive toward universal public education. (*ibid*, pp. 13–14)

The achievement of universal public education, especially where organized in 'common schools', did not, however, mark the final stage in the institutionalization of fair and equitable democratic schooling. The school curriculum may be employed not only to designate but also to differentiate and this power was to be substantially explored in the era of universal public education and of common schooling.

In one of the first countries to industrialize, Britain, the demand for universal public education was developing considerably by the mid-nineteenth century — it formed an important plank in the populist agitations of the Chartists in the 1840s. Reviewing formal school knowledge, Bernstein (1971) has argued that pedagogy, curriculum, and evaluation comprise the three message systems through which formal state education is realized in the contemporary period (p. 47). The general connection between 'class' pedagogies and a curriculum based on sequence and prescription had begun to emerge earlier, from the sixteenth century onwards, but in the 1850s the third prong of Bernstein's trilogy of 'message systems' began to develop with the inauguration of the first university examination boards setting examinations for schools. The centennial report of the University of Cambridge Local Examinations Syndicate states that 'the establishment of these examinations was the universities' response to petitions that they should help in the development of 'schools for the middle class.'[1]

By the mid-nineteenth century, the power of curriculum to differentiate, was being institutionalized. The birth of secondary *examinations* and the institutional-ization of curriculum *differentiation* were almost exactly contemporaneous. For instance the Taunton Report classified secondary schooling into three grades de-pending on the time spent in school. Taunton asserted:

> The difference in time assigned makes some difference in the very nature of education itself; if a boy cannot remain at school beyond the age of 14

it is useless to begin teaching him such subjects as required a longer time for their proper study; if he can continue until 18 or 19, it may be expedient to postpone some studies that would otherwise be commenced earlier.[2]

The Taunton Report noted that 'these instructions correspond roughly but by no means exactly to the gradations of society'. In 1868, schooling until 18 or 19 was for the sons of men with considerable incomes independent of their own exertions, or professional men, and men in business whose profits put them on the same level. These received a mainly classical curriculum. The second grade, up to 16, was for sons of the 'mercantile classes'. Their curriculum was less classical in orientation and had a certain practical orientation. The third grade, until 14, was for the sons of 'the smaller tenant farmer, the small tradesmen (and) the superior artisans'. Their curriculum was based on the three 'Rs' but carried out to a very good level. These gradations cover secondary schooling. Meanwhile most of the working class remained in elementary schools where they were taught rudimentary skills in the three 'Rs'. By this time the curriculum functioned as a major identifier of, and mechanism for, social differentiation. This power to designate and differentiate established a conclusive place for curriculum in the epistemology of schooling.

The link with earlier religious notions of education, and indeed differentiation, can be discerned in other parts of the world. In the convict colonies in Australia in the late eighteenth century educational structures were developed to provide elementary education for the lower orders of society and to upgrade the moral fibre of many of the parents. Writing in New South Wales in March 1792, Reverend R. Johnson stated that:

> I have long wished that some method could be hit upon for such of the convicts as wished and wanted to be instructed to read — great numbers of them both of men and women, I believe and fear know not a letter of the alphabet — from the great success that has attended the Sunday schools in England, I should think and hope that if a similar plan was adopted and pursued here . . . would be a means, and that a great one, of bringing some of these unhappy wretches to a better way of thinking.[3]

Reading and spelling were considered to be required for the lower classes. Not so essential, as deemed by the ruling officials, were other subjects such as writing and arithmetic. Because the overriding goal was to provide moral training for the children, it was necessary to incorporate a religious emphasis in all subjects. Thus, the Bible was used to teach reading. Children were required to recite the catechism and passages from the Bible.

The notion of intelligence subject to 'discipline' was continuous with early Calvinist dogma. The intellect disciplined by the moral sense and will to carry out Christian tasks; not knowledge for intrinsic education but knowledge to carry out moral and religious missions. This notion of disciplined intelligence drew on the philosophy called 'Scottish Common Sense' for its justification. Hence, from the early Calvinist origins in Scotland notions of discipline as curriculum were carried to other parts of the world. Tomkins (1986) has argued that Scottish Common Sense 'dominated philosophical thought in the English-speaking world during most of the nineteenth century and strongly influenced American college curricula'. He states 'its influence was even stronger and more long-lasting in Canada' (p. 35).

That the link between these notions of discipline and differentiation was sustained from Calvinist origins can be clearly confirmed in the work of Egerton Ryerson, the most influential architect of the Canadian public education system. Ryerson fully embraced notions of disciplined intelligence but for him it was crucially linked with two distinctly different types of curriculum. The first of these was an essentially preparatory level 'requisite for the ordinary duties of life'. This curriculum comprised the study of English language and literature, mathematics, natural science and 'the outlines of mental and moral philosophy, evidences of Christianity, geography and history'. The social curriculum was devised for those planning 'professional pursuits' after going to college: in most cases, the clergy, law, politics and business. The main components were classics, mathematics and the physical sciences, moral science, rhetoric and *belles lettres* and theology.[4]

In the USA, the theory of mental discipline was of considerable influence in the mid-nineteenth century. But Kliebard (1986) judges that by the 1890s the theory was 'starting to unravel as a consequence of increased awareness of social transformation' (p. 8). At the same time the struggle for the American curriculum, particularly in relation to the early Republican dreams of the common school, intensified.

In 1892 the National Education Associated appointed a so-called 'Committee of Ten' to look into the issue of uniform college entrance requirements. The Chairman of the Committee was Charles W. Eliot, President of Harvard, an advocate of mental discipline but also a humanist with a concern for educational reform. The Report of the Committee laid down important ground rules for the school curriculum and was later seen as symptomatic of the 'crass domination exercised by the college over the high school'. In fact the domination served in time to facilitate curriculum differentiation:

> The academic subjects that the Committee saw as appropriate for the general education of all students were seen by many later reformers as appropriate only for that segment of the high school population that was destined to go on to college. In fact, subjects like French and algebra came to be called college-entrance subjects, a term practically unknown in the nineteenth century. Even subjects like English became differentiated with standard literary works prescribed for those destined for college, while popular works and 'practical' English were provided for the majority. (*ibid*, pp. 15–16)

The dreams of the common school were then coming under severe strain because the Republican common core had essentially come to be viewed by some as a preparatory mode for subsequent university education. The expanding universities were thereby seen as sources of cultural property and of individual occupational mobility (see chapter 6, pp. 000–000).

In fact, in most Western state systems of education, by the end of the nineteenth century, the universities had been placed at the apex of accreditation. In some countries like Britain this was formalized into 'Type 1' schooling for university and professional preparation, with other types of schools for other types of people; in Canada Egerton Ryerson promoted a belief in one curriculum for university preparation and one for 'everyday life', and in the USA the dream of the common school for all began to come under pressure from groups who began to develop the case for different curricula for different destinations.

But if differentiation was a growing feature of internal school curricula it is important to assess the commonalities of mass schooling that were in evidence by the end of the nineteenth century. This is significant because certain apparent 'givens' such as *school subjects* have already entered our account. A sequencing of curriculum for 'forms' or 'classes' had emerged in the late middle ages and were certainly a feature of much of state schooling by the nineteenth century. A system of 'forms' or 'classes' is not however, a classroom system. The distinction is a vital one to grasp. For instance, English public schools in the nineteenth century were often organized into 'forms' and had a formal pattern of curriculum but there were *not* classrooms as such, nor subjects as such, there was not, in short, a classroom system as such. Hence the public schools followed 'no common pattern of education, though they agreed on the taking of Latin and Greek as the main component of the curriculum'. Each public school 'evolved its own unique form of organization with idiosyncratic vocabularies to describe them'. The curriculum sometimes depended on the learning of common texts but such texts might not be 'taught' in any collective manner — rather, pupils would work through them at their own individual pace. Further 'where students were divided into 'forms' (a term referring originally to the benches on which they sat) this was done in rough and ready manner for the convenience of teaching and not with the idea of establishing a hierarchy of ability or a sequence of learning' (Reid, 1985, p. 296).

In the state system of schooling inaugurated in Britain in the late nineteenth century however, a 'classroom system' was rapidly institutionalized. In a sense we can see the classroom system as a standardized invention which essentially drives out the more idiosyncratic and individualized forms of schooling. The classroom system is in this sense a system for mass schooling to be administered by local and national bureaucracies. Hamilton (1980) judges that by dawn of the twentieth century:

> the batch production rhetoric of the 'classroom system' (for example lessons, subjects, timetables, standardization, streaming) had become so pervasive that it successfully achieved a normative status — creating the standards against which all subsequent educational innovations came to be judged. (p. 282)

In Britain the dominant political economy of State schooling by the beginning of the twentieth century combined the trilogy of pedagogy, curriculum and evaluation. The last of the pieces in the trilogy was the establishment of university examination boards, and here the side-effects on curriculum were to be both pervasive and long-lasting. The classroom system inaugurated a world of timetables and compartmentalized lessons; the curriculum manifestation of this systemic change was the school subject. If 'class and curriculum' entered educational discourse when schooling was transformed into a mass activity in Britain, 'classroom system and school subject' emerged at the stage at which that mass activity became a State-organized system. And in spite of the many alternative ways of conceptualizing and organizing curriculum the convention of the subject retains its supremacy. In the modern era we are essentially dealing with the *curriculum as subject*.

While this system was inaugurated in Britain in the 1850s, it was established on the present footing with the definition of the Secondary Regulations in 1904 which list the main subjects followed by the establishment of a subject-based 'School Certificate' in 1917. From this date curriculum conflict began to resemble the existing situation in focusing on the definition and evaluation of *examinable* knowledge. Hence the School Certificate subjects rapidly became the overriding concern of grammar schools and the academic subjects it examined soon established ascendancy on these schools' timetables. The Norwood Report of 1943 stated that:

> a certain sameness in the curriculum of schools resulted from the double necessity of finding a place for the many subjects competing for time in the curriculum and the need to teach these subjects in such a way and to such a standard as will ensure success in the School Certificate examination.[5]

The normative character of the system is clear and as a result of 'these necessities' the curriculum had 'settled down into an uneasy equilibrium, the demands of specialists and subjects being widely adjusted and compensated' (*ibid*). The extent to which university examination boards thereby influenced the curriculum through examination subjects is evident. The academic subject-centred curriculum was in fact strengthened in the period following the 1944 Education Act. In 1951 the introduction of the General Certificate of Education allowed subjects to be taken separately at the Ordinary ('O') level (in the School Certificate blocks of 'main' subjects had to be passed); and the introduction of an Advanced ('A') level increased subject specialization and enhanced the link between 'academic' examinations and university 'disciplines'. The academic subjects which dominated 'O' and especially 'A' level examinations were then closely linked to university definitions; but even more crucially they were linked to patterns of resource allocation. Academic 'subjects' claiming close connections to university 'disciplines' were for the 'able' students. From the beginning it was assumed that such students required 'more staff, more highly paid staff and more money for equipment and books' (Byrne, 1974, p. 29). The crucial and sustained line between 'academic' subjects and preferential resources and status was therefore established.

But if this system was predominant with regard to staffing and resources for academic subjects in grammar schools, the implications for the other schools (and styles of curriculum) should not be forgotten. Echoing Taunton, the Norwood Report had discovered that schooling had created distinctive groups of pupils of which needed to be treated 'in a way appropriate to itself'. This time the social and class basis of differentiation remained the same but the rationale and mechanism for differentiation was significantly different. Before, the argument had focused on time spent at school; now the emphasis was on different 'mentalities' each recognizing a different curriculum. First, 'the pupil who is interested in learning for its own sake, who can grasp an argument or follow a piece of connected reasoning'. Such pupils 'educated by the curriculum commonly associated with grammar schools have entered the learned professions or have taken up higher administrative or business posts'.[6] The second group whose interests lie in the field of applied science or applied arts were to go to technical schools (which never developed very far). Thirdly were the pupils who deal 'more easily with concrete things than with ideas'. The curriculum would 'make a direct appeal to interests, which it would awaken by practical touch with affairs'.[7] A practical curriculum then for a manual occupational future.

We see then the emergence of a definite pattern of *prioritizing* of pupils through curriculum; what emerges Goodson (1985) has called elsewhere 'the triple alliance between academic subjects, academic examinations and able pupils' (p. 33). Working through patterns of resource allocation, this means a process of pervasive 'academic drift' afflicts sub-groups promoting school subjects. Hence subjects as diverse as woodwork and metalwork, physical education, art, technical studies, bookkeeping, needlework and domestic science have pursued status improvements by arguing for enhanced academic examinations and qualifications. Likewise, schools defined as different from grammar schools, the technical schools and secondary modern schools also were ultimately drawn into the process of academic drift, both ending up competing for success through academic subject-based styles of examination.

The conflict and compromises around the school curriculum and within school subjects represent at once a *fragmentation* and an *internalization* of the struggles over schooling. Fragmentation is evident because conflicts take place through a range of compartmentalized subjects; internalization occurs because these conflicts now take place within school and subject boundaries. We shall see later how these struggles are partially expressed through and encapsulated in more general traditions at work within schooling.

Britain during the first half of the twentieth system saw the organization of a state system of mass schooling where three different types of schools were built on the foundations of differentiated curriculum. The continuities since the Taunton Report of 1868 are readily discernible.

In Australia a system of mass schooling was initiated by the establishing of Education Acts with their hegemonic demands (Seddon, 1989, pp. 155–73) for each state (Victoria was the first colony in 1872 and Western Australia the last in 1893) whereby free, compulsory and secular education was provided by centralized State Education Departments responsible to a Minister in each State government. The result was a minimal, academic curriculum which continued well into the next century, as noted by Freeman Butts (1955):

Everywhere I went I found a uniform hierarchy of schools, a hierarchy of courses, and a hierarchy of subjects. The fundamental assumption of each was that the traditional academic disciplines are more to be valued than the non-academic studies.

A succession of Education Acts in Britain in the 1870s and 80s had some influence upon curriculum practices in the respective Australian state systems. The Devonshire Commission (1872–75) recommended that natural science be included in the curriculum, the Samuelson Commission (1882–84) emphasized manual and technical instruction for boys, while the Cross Commission (1886–88) recommended a widened range of subjects for boys and girls, namely:

The three Rs, needlework for girls, and linear drawing for boys, singing, English, English history, geography (especially of the British Empire), and common objects in the lower standards, leading to an understanding of elementary science in the higher standards. (Gordon and Lawton, 1978, p. 17)

In the USA building on different origins and a distinct social structure, a different intersection of division of curriculum and division of labour can be distinguished emerging from the original common school plan. In their 1893 Report the Committee of Ten had specifically ruled out any preparation for 'life' or future occupations as an underpinning rationale. Their concern, as we have seen, was exclusively with academic training, in academic disciplines of study. The brief of the Committee was to define a school curriculum in line with the admissions policies of the universities. We have argued this close linking of the school curriculum to the universities' left opponents of the hegemony of academic subjects (who were often also opponents of the common school) with vital ammunition. To present the common school as closely linked to universities was to implicitly leave the common school as without vocational purposes beyond that of the professional preparation of the elite. This central contradiction allowed a coalition of forces to lead the attack both on the hegemonic academic curriculum and also therefore on the common curriculum and the common school. Hence by 1917 vocational education for occupations for which the majority were destined, came to be seen 'as such an urgent necessity as to require federal aid'.

The significance of the success of vocational education was not simply that a new subject had been added, nor that a major new curriculum option had been created, but that many existing subjects, particularly at the secondary level, were becoming infused with criteria drawn from vocational education. This became evident in the increasing popularity of such courses as business mathematics and business English as legitimate substitutes for traditional forms of these subjects. In very visible ways, the whole curriculum for all but the college-bound was becoming vocationalized. (Kliebard, 1986, p. 129)

John Dewey, at this time, immediately saw the differentiating potential of vocational education. Dewey aimed his writing against the pro-vocational writing of one of the leading advocates of vocationalizing, David Snedden, Commissioner of Education in Massachusetts (and sometimes adjunct professor at Teachers' College, Columbia University). In 1915 Dewey summarized Snedden's view as 'the identification of education with acquisition of specialized skill in the management of machines at the expense of an industrial intelligence based on science and a knowledge of social problems and conditions' (p. 42). Dewey was clear on the effects of such a vocationalism and in a phrase, with echoes back to the Calvinist origins of curriculum disciplines and differentiations, argued that vocational education was likely to become 'an instrument in accomplishing the feudal dogma of social predestination' (Dewey, 1916, p. 372). Clearly we are a long way from the common school of the republic — and travelling fast in another direction of social and cultural production and reproduction.

> Hence in the 'scant three decades' since the Committee of Ten recommendations: direct training for one's future occupational role had emerged as a major, if not the predominant element in the high school curriculum for that segment of school population whose 'probable destiny' did not include attendance in colleges. (Kliebard, 1986, pp. 149–50)

In this sense vocational education was 'the most successful innovation in the twentieth century' in the USA in that 'none other approaches it in the range of support it received and the extent to which it became implemented into the curriculum of American schools'.

> On one level the success of vocational education can be attributed to the fact that it acted as a kind of magic mirror in which the powerful interest groups of the period could see their own reflected ways of reforming what was increasingly regarded as a curriculum out of tune with the times. (*ibid*, p. 150)

Of course this judgment is in a sense circular. Powerful interest groups in particular helped create 'a climate of public opinion' which they could then respond to with their favoured remedy. Also the remedy was that of only *certain* powerful interest groups — the universities were plainly ambivalent about the change. One would need more scholarly investigation of the views of the labour unions, immigrant and radical groups. These were groups with some power at the time, with their own associations and media. Plainly, some influential groups were more powerful than others and at this time pursued their objectives with considerable vigour and success.

Interestingly the American remedy differed from that in Britain and elsewhere where vocational education was seldom pursued through separate vocational schools — the rhetoric of the common school was perhaps as important to democratic imagery as it clearly was to the historic intentions of the founders of the American republic. Hence the political compromise which emerged was the common school structure with differentiation internalized:

> The comprehensive high school established itself as the typical, if not the quintessential, American educational institution, with curricular tracking, both formal and informal, attending to the differentiating function that social efficiency educators considered so critical. (*ibid*, p. 151)

Not just social efficiency educators it would seem but the powerful interest groups which Kliebard mentions but fails to identify. No doubt further work in this specific area would do a great deal to elucidate the peculiar potency of social efficiency curriculum reforms. Certainly Ross Finney's vision of the social order related to social efficiency goals was clear. The pattern of curriculum differentiation was for him, closely akin to a pattern of social differentiation based on leadership and followership which 'leads us again to the notion of a graduated hierarchy of intelligence and enlightenment'.

> At the apex of such a system must be the experts, who are pushing forward research in highly specialized sections of the front. Behind them are such men and women as the colleges should produce, who are familiar with the findings of the experts and are able to relate part with part. By these relatively independent leaders of thought, progressive change and constant readjustment will be provided for. Back of these are the high school graduates, who are somewhat familiar with the vocabulary of those above them, have some feeling of acquaintance with the various fields, and a respect for expert knowledge. Finally, there are the duller masses, who mouth the catchwords of those in front of them, imagine that they understand, and follow by imitation. (Finney, 1990, quoted in Apple, 1990b, p. 77)

Essentially the story of American schooling at this stage seems to be one of common purposes vitiated by internalized differentiation and subject fragmentation. This internalization of conflict is nowhere clearer than in the internal history of school subjects. For like the common school label the school subject label survived — the rhetoric, at least, remained the same. For the full story we have to open the covers and look inside. The story of the American high school curriculum is therefore paradoxical — stability of categories combined with unstable internal properties. Kliebard captures this complexity well in reviewing the struggle for the American curriculum in the years 1893–1958:

> The one fortress that proved virtually impregnable was the school subject. The subject as the basic unit in the curriculum successfully resisted the more ambitious efforts to replace it with anything like functional areas of living or projects arising from student interest . . .

But subject labels alone may be misleading. Some of the reforms advanced by the various interest groups were accomplished within the overall context of the subject organization of the curriculum. To be sure, not all the changes may be regarded as signs of progress, but modest successes were achieved in restructuring, integrating and modernizing the subjects that comprise the curriculum. The subjects survived but in an altered form. (Kliebard, 1986, p. 269)

In Britain the last twenty-five years of reform in schooling provide a different testimony on the fate of common school movements. For the common school, the comprehensive school, came late to Britain after centuries of aspiration and struggle. In 1965 the Labour government began systematic reorganization of the tripartite system (grammar, technical and secondary modern schools) into a unified system of comprehensive schools for all (from age 10/11 to age 16/18). From the beginning of comprehensive schools it was possible to discern the influence of what Kliebard has called 'powerful interest groups'. For instance the House of Commons motion which led to comprehensive reorganization was worded this way:

This House, conscious of the need to raise educational standards at all levels, and regretting that the realization of this objective is impeded by the separation of children into different types of schools, notes with approval the efforts of local authorities to reorganize secondary education on comprehensive lines which will preserve all that is valuable in grammar school education for those children who now receive it and make it available to more children. (DES, 1965, p. 1)

As we have noted the grammar schools were essentially the gateway to the universities and to professional life. The examinations they taught towards arose out of the universities' response to petitions that they should help in the development of 'schools for the middle classes'. Hence the House of Commons motion pays homage to one particular tradition in British secondary schooling the tradition for the training of the privileged minority drawn primarily from the middle class. In phrasing the motion for the birth of the common school in these terms there was the implication that the favouring of these groups could be sustained in the common school era, though perhaps now extended to more children. But plainly a grammar school curriculum preparing pupils for the universities and professional life could *never* provide a basic common curriculum for a common school, unless of course *all* pupils intended to pass through university to the professions. The irony of the motion had then to be grasped as essentially a statement of obeisance to the powerful interest groups in British society. So it was to prove.

The British common school was from the beginning built on grounds which favoured the grammar school curriculum of the elite minority. This opened the way for internal differentiation and subject fragmentation behind the doors of the common school. As early as 1969, just four years after the House of Commons motion, a British sociologist warned that inside the common school a 'curriculum for inequality' was in action. Shipman (1971) spoke ironically of the intended convergencies of curriculum development coming from the introduction of new courses into:

> a school that is still clearly divided into two sections, one geared to a system of external examinations, the other less constrained. The former is closely tied to the universities and is within established academic traditions. The latter has a short history and is still in its formative stages. (pp. 101–2)

Shipman was clear that the problem was not of the intrinsic character of the two types of curriculum but the division into two separate sections which 'may be producing a new means of sustaining old divisions'. Two different traditions produced 'two nations' of pupils:

> one is firmly planted in revered academic traditions, is adapted to teaching from a pool of factual knowledge and has clearly defined, if often irrelevant subject boundaries. The other is experimental, looking to America rather than our own past for inspiration, focuses on contemporary problems, groups subjects together and rejects formal teaching methods. One emphasises a schooling within a framework of external examinations the other attempts to align school work to the environment of children. (*ibid*, p. 104)

But in juxtaposing the academic tradition with what we call in chapter 4, the pedagogic tradition, Shipman was leaving out a third continuing element in the British secondary school. For it was not only 'aligning school work to the environment of the child' as there had always been a utilitarian tradition concerned to prepare the child for the environment of work. This utilitarian strain was, we noted, the tendency which, in the guise of vocational education, helped shatter the notion of unified purpose in the American common school. So in Britain it became the focus of those concerned with the results of the comprehensive school. It was in fact a Labour Prime Minister, James Callaghan, who in 1976, masterminded a 'great debate' on education. The priorities became clear in a speech he gave at Ruskin College, Oxford in October 1976. 'No new policies were proposed but the government had now established that educational standards, and the relationship of education to the economy, were to be as much of a priority as comprehensive reform in solution.'[8] Hence a decade after its inception the comprehensive reform of schooling was placed alongside the need for education to serve the economy.

In the following decade any question of equal concern for comprehensive reform and education for the economy rapidly vanished. With the election of Margaret Thatcher in 1979 the comprehensive idea came under attack from a variety of sources — but again, the need for more vocational education was the main rationale provided for confirming internal differentiation. The government launched a Technical and Vocational Initiative (TVEI) funded by central government to restructure the internal curriculum of the secondary schools. In addition an Assisted

Places Scheme was funded to sponsor private and direct grant schools, traditionally the preserve of the middle and upper classes. In the latter school the traditional academic curriculum predominated, while in the state schools more vocational education was rapidly pursued. The British experience reads in certain specific ways like a rapidly compressed re-run of the history of the American common school. Powerful interest groups have sought to erode the possibility of the common school and to reestablish and enhance differentiation through the promotion of vocational initiatives. In Britain the history of secondary schooling may now be returning full circle with moves to formally re-introduce 'selection' practices for secondary schools (Narayan and Frugill, 1996, p. 18). Significantly, the new National Curriculum which has been legislated for the public sector schools has not been extended to the private 'public schools' (see chapter 9). Again, as is happening in different ways in the United States, this is taking place alongside a reconstitution of the social configuration of schooling. The school subject provides a microcosm wherein the history of the social forces which underpin the patterns of curriculum and schooling might be scrutinized and analyzed.

Reflections and Issues

1 Explain the apparent contradiction of a growing differentiation of school curricula yet an increasing commonality of mass schooling in the USA and the UK by the end of the nineteenth century.

2 In terms of your teaching experience, do you consider that students are prioritised through curriculum? To what extent do you consider that this affects historically disadvantaged groups such as women, ethnic minorities and other groups? Are you aware of subjects that have obtained status improvements by emphasizing academic orientations?

3 Do you agree that the promotion of vocational initiatives in the UK recently has enhanced differentiation within schools? Provide examples of some vocational policies or structures that have fostered differentiation of students.

Suggested Reading

There are several useful articles including:

Hamilton, D. (1980) 'Adam Smith and the moral economy of the classroom system', *Journal of Curriculum Studies*, **12**, 4.

Ramirez, F.O. and Boli, J. (1987) 'The political construction of mass schooling: European origins and worldwide institutionalism', *Sociology of Education*, **60**, January.

Goodson, I.F. (1995) 'The Context of Cultural Invention: Learning and Curriculum.' In Cookson, P. and Schneider, B. (Eds) *Transforming Schools*, New York and London: Garland Press.

Useful books include:

Boli, J. (1989) *New Citizens for a New Society — The Institutional Origins of Mass School-ing in Sweden*, Oxford: Pergamon Press.

Goodson, I.F. (1995) *The Making of Curriculum: Collected Essays*, 2nd Edition, London and Washington, DC: Falmer Press.

Goodson, I.F. (1994) *Studying Curriculum: Cases and Methods*, Buckingham: Open Univer-sity Press/New York: Teachers College Press/Toronto: OISE Press.

Goodson, I.F. (Ed)(1985) *Social Histories of the Secondary Curriculum: Subjects for Study*, Lewes: Falmer Press.

Hamilton, D. (1989) *Towards a Theory of Schooling*. London and Washington, DC: Falmer Press.

Kliebard, H.M. (1986) *The Struggle for the American Curriculum 1893–1958*, Boston and London: Routledge and Kegan Paul.

Kliebard, H.M. (1992) *Forging the American Curriculum: Essays in Curriculum History and Theory*. New York and London: Routledge Chapman and Hall.

Young, M.F.D. (Ed) (1971) *Knowledge and Control*, London: Macmillan.

Notes

1 University of Cambridge Local Examinations Syndicate (1958) Centennial Report, Cam-bridge, p. 1.
2 The Taunton Report (1868) Schools Inquiry Commission, p. 587.
3 Reverend R. Johnson's report in 1792, as cited in Turney (1975).
4 *Ibid*. Quotes from Ryerson come from McKillop (1979).
5 The Norwood Report (1943) *Board of Education: Curriculum and Examinations in Secondary Schools*, London, HMSO.
6 *Ibid*, p. 2.
7 *Ibid*, p. 4.
8 Callaghan, the Rt Hon James (1976) speech, Ruskin College, Oxford, 18 October.

Chapter 3

Subjects and Schooling:
Four School Case Studies

School histories provide vital evidence of the patterning of curriculum within the school and in this chapter we look briefly at four case studies of schools. Then, in the following chapter, we shall look at curriculum differentiation as it is expressed through different 'traditions' within school subjects.

In comparing the place of school subjects in the functioning of schooling historical studies allow us to pursue the 'position' of the school with regard to the state, the economy and the general social structure. To trace this through we have to concentrate on the changing functions of the school, the relationship between the school and the economy and, finally, the relationship between the school and university sectors. These aspects impinge with different force and relevance in different local and national conditions. As we began to see in the previous chapter, the commonalities and distinctions between Britain, the USA, Australia and Canada are especially instructive.

Four School Case Studies: England, USA, Australia and Canada

By reviewing four case studies of schools in England, the USA, Australia and Canada, it is possible to discern some of the changes in the function and position of the school in different milieux; we can then go on to relate this to the history of school subjects.

Hightown Grammar School (England)

Hightown Grammar School in Northern England was established in 1906 and achieved full grammar school status in 1932. Lacey (1970) judges that in the period 1906–1921 the school essentially acted as a 'finishing school' for the local job market. Academic qualifications and examination results were not then the primary concern of the school for the goal of the school and its pupils was not an academic or professional career but a secure job in local industry.

> The school was used as a jumping-off place, one of higher status than the
> ordinary or higher elementary school, from which it was possible to obtain

the best clerical, commercial, technical and trade apprenticeships in local industry. For this purpose a two-year course was often as good as a three-year course. Given the conditions in local industry, academic qualifications were to a large extent ignored in favour of a 'secondary school boy' with a good family. (p. 15)

In the period from 1923 onwards Lacey discerned a noticeable change of emphasis in the school's priorities, as evidenced in the Headmasters' reports. From this date there were detailed reports on results in examinations, school certificates and, later, high school certificates. Hence,

an increased number of boys were able to exploit the 'prestige' route to universities. The importance the school attached to academic success at this time can be gauged by the fact that when a sixth-former won the first State scholarship, in the 1930s, the whole school was given a day's holiday.

By 1945 the community was beginning to view the school as the gateway to the universities and to professional life (*ibid*, p. 21).

By 1945 then, Hightown Grammar was a 'professionalizing school', Lacey notes three developments:

1 The recognition by parents that the educational system provided the most promising avenues for career advancement. This led to increased competition for grammar school places in the only school generally available with an established and direct route to further education — in particular to the universities.
2 The gradual assumption on the part of the grammar school teachers that the school's *main* function was to send its pupils into future education, and in particular to the universities.
3 Awareness by the Hightown education authorities of factors 1 and 2 above, and hence the realization that they could achieve a prominent reputation in the educational field by investing in a larger, successful grammar school. (*ibid*, pp. 26–7)

The emphasis on an academic style of curriculum was clearly evidenced at the time of Lacey's fieldwork in the 1960s. There were a hierarchy of subjects which were reflected by the cash allowances to the positions of responsibility as heads of department:

£450   English, maths
£355   History, geography, French, chemistry
£260   Biology, physics
£165   Art, music, handicrafts
£100   Physical education, economics

This shows a clear gradation from the 'academic' subjects down to the creative, manual and physical subjects (the only exception, economics, had a low rating because it was a minority choice, with small numbers of pupils) (*ibid*, p. 159).

The link to university and professional preparation and the academic orientation of the grammar school was then clearly established after 1945. But the desirability and privilege of grammar school education in contributing to pupils' career choices did not go unnoticed. By the 1960s there was a powerful lobby arguing for the abolition of grammar schools (who catered for only 20 per cent or so of the school population) and their replacement by comprehensive schools for all pupils. This equalitarian impulse sought to counteract the fact that the grammar schools, with primarily middle class clienteles, had essentially become arenas for the sponsorship of privilege for a minority. In 1965, the Government issued a circular on 'comprehensive reorganization' and within a decade, most grammar schools had disappeared to be replaced by all-ability comprehensive schools. Differentiation by type of schools was thereby abolished. But as we saw the struggle over purpose and over differentiation now moved inside the school and further, was often internalized in the conflicts within school subjects.

Central High School (USA)

In the United States the story unfolds in a different manner and different sequence for the common school had been an integral part of the early blueprint for the new republic. Equal opportunity and equal access to a common curriculum were judged to be fundamental prerequisites for the building of a democratic republic of peoples in the new American State. Horace Mann (1957) articulated the vision of the Common School:

> The development of the common nature; the cultivation of the germs of intelligence, uprightness, benevolence, truth that belongs to all — these are the principal, the aim, the end — while special preparations for the field or the shop, for the forum or the desk, for the land or the sea are but incidents. (p. 12)

Mann's view of the American common school in the 1840s was quite clear: it should have as its purpose the same general education for all students. This meant specifically that it should never differentiate its curriculum towards vocational ends. To do so would be to renege on the democratic vision of the republic.

David Labaree has studied an 'exemplary' high school, Central High School in Philadelphia, since its foundation in 1838. In fact it assumed a prominent, indeed pre-eminent role in the schooling of the town from that date, being the only public high school for boys up until 1885. During most of the nineteenth century Central's curriculum stressed practical value although 'the high school's practical curriculum was actually an academic curriculum with a practical bend' (Labaree, 1986, p. 44) and 'to the modern eye, Central's practical curriculum appears heavily academic and allowed little choice. Indeed from 1856 to 1889 there was no choice at all:

everyone took the same classes' (Labaree, 1984, p. 560). The practical orientation comprised vocational courses taking up 12 per cent of the pupil's schedule; this was however a significant modification of the normally dominant classical and liberal education courses. The combination of practical and (predominantly) academic courses were then taught as a common curriculum to all students up until 1889.

The common curriculum does not, however, mean that Central High was a 'school of the republic' open equally to all. This was most clearly the case in regard to the school's admission policy: only those pupils who gained a high score on the entrance examination were admitted. Central's pupils were then the high achievers and 'because of economic pressures, most of them were middle class. Working class families could ill afford to send a potential wage earner to high school' (Labaree, 1956, p. 49). (This situation is very different to Lacey's Hightown Grammar School, where a significant minority of the pupils, around a third, were working class). In terms of intake, Central's constituency was culturally homogeneous 'dominated by shopkeepers and master craftsmen, the petty entrepreneurs' in the economy (*ibid*, p. 48). This class of people were naturally attracted by an academic curriculum that stressed practical orientation.

From the beginning then there was fierce competition for Central's credentials. Labaree judges there were three reasons: the ostensibly meritocratic admission and graduation procedures, the unique position of the high school in the local market and, perhaps most important of all, the special structural needs of the school's middle-class constituency. The position of selective preeminence is shown in that only one out of every fifty male first graders were eventually accepted by Central High School, and only one out of every 200 ever graduated. The demand of the middle class constituency was heightened by their accelerating sense of economic insecurity. They were challenged on two sides: firstly by increased competition from other entrepreneurs and on the other by the rapid growth in numbers and influence of wage labour thereby threatening proletarianization (*ibid*, p. 50).

In understanding the unique appeal of Central we need to fully comprehend the relationship between curriculum and class. To begin with Labaree judges that three of the guiding principles of Central's curriculum were resonant with middle class ideology — self-control, practicality and merit.

> The strong predilection for business over intellectualism and for practical education over classical education; like the emphasis on self-discipline, emanated from the daily experience and developing thought patterns of the proprietary middle class. (*ibid*, p. 48)

For the middle classes the curriculum taught at Central constituted 'cultural property' at a time when, as we have seen, their economic property was under threat.

> By acquiring that unique form of cultural property, the proprietors' sons could ease into a very different kind of middle class existence (to their shopkeeping and entrepreneurial parents) — one based on business employment rather than business ownership. The practical curriculum Central offered was relevant to such employment . . . students could learn a few

useful skills such as bookkeeping and drafting. But more important than the vocational training was the symbolic wealth that students accumulated at the high school. Such wealth had limited ability for those with substantial economic property, but for white-collar employees, this cultural property was what marked them off from the wage earners of the working-class. (*ibid*, p. 51)

But by 1880 the Philadelphia propriety middle class were coming under great pressure. Between 1880 and 1900 the proportion of proprietors had decreased whilst the proportion of business employees increased rapidly. In the face of these declining prospects the proprietary middle class began to shift its investment in the future from economic to cultural property. But what kind of cultural property in the form of curriculum was most valuable to a class in the middle of structural crisis? The proprietary middle class began to perceive schooling as a gateway to the professions (an avenue that was pursued by the local middle classes at a later date in Northern England at Hightown Grammar).

At this time, however, Central and the proprietary middle class encountered further challenges. The unique position and prestige of Central led ultimately to demands for more schools of this sort. The enrolments at Central represented one percent of total enrolments in city schools during the 1850s, by 1880 this had dropped to 0.5 per cent. Many middle class families therefore were failing to get their sons into Central:

Finally, in 1883, the school board yielded to middle-class demands and established a manual-training school as an alternative secondary institution (other such schools followed quickly, and by 1915 there were fifteen public high schools in the city) . . . To make matters worse, the new school's curriculum was similar to Central's. It offered a terminal, practical education with a manual training component that was a more systematic and more intensive form of Central's hands-on approach. (*ibid*, p. 53)

Central then faced a dual problem: its curriculum was inadequate for the changing structural needs of its middle class constituency, in particular it provided an inadequate curricular gateway for the professions; and secondly, it had surrendered both its monopoly position in the school marketplace and with it, the impressiveness and distinctiveness of the cultural property embodied in its curriculum.

In such a situation Central had to revise the curriculum it offered which suffered from 'oversupply' and 'underdistinction'. The continuing rise of American universities provided a focus for this task of reconceptualization, for between 1865 and 1890 related to the professionalization of the middle classes 'the university developed into the dominant force in American education'. Central High School was thus offered a choice — essentially a choice between precipitous down-grading or political subordination to the university:

The cultural property the university offered, which at the highest level was certification for admission to the professions, was much more attractive than anything the high school could offer. Central, like other high schools, had to make a choice: It could preserve its practical/terminal curriculum and become useless to those in quest of professional credentials, or it could adopt an academic/college preparatory curriculum and thus become subordinate to the university in the new hierarchy of the American education. (*ibid*, p. 54)

The broadening of public access to high schools — fifteen high schools in Philadelphia by 1915 — made the choice of curriculum at Central High a perilous decision. The common high school was in sight again and its curriculum and credentials thereby threatened to become common too. Central High School 'had a large and influential group of alumni and of prospective clients who wanted to acquire its selective benefits. Widening access to the high school could hurt the interests of this group in the zero sum game of educational credentialling.' Essentially the problem was how to respond to public pressure for broadly-based high school access without destroying the exclusiveness that was based on small numbers and the link between class, credentials and curriculum. The solution which Central High School chose in 1889 was one that, as we saw in the previous chapter, was a common American response: stratification and differentiation.

They established an academic track (which was college preparatory) and a commercial track (originally called 'scientific'). Students in the academic track had a credential whose value was unaffected by the increasing numbers of diplomas issued by non-preparatory programs at Central or in other schools. (Labaree, 1987, p. 10)

In this manner the common school pattern was combined with market and class exclusiveness: a historic compromise of sorts (and one which arguably had plagued American schooling ever since).

Central managed to preserve much of its distinctiveness and autonomy in the era of the comprehensive high school. It isolated the newly introduced mechanical and industrial courses in separate buildings and elevated the mechanical and commercial tracks into college preparatory programs (engineering and business respectively). Thus, by the 1920s, Central was, on the surface, a large comprehensive high school with a diverse student body; but within its main building, it was a college preparatory school in liberal arts and business, with a student body still dominated by the middle class as it had been for eighty years. (*ibid*)

Sydney Girls' High School (Australia)

Sydney Girls' High School was the first State girls' high school established in New South Wales in 1893 but not the first established in Australia as the Advanced

School for Girls, a State high school in Adelaide, was established four years earlier in 1889.

Norman (1983) contends that times were changing in the 1870s in New South Wales — 'the inhabitants of the colony, like so many amoeba at the mercy of the wind and tide, were floating towards a new education horizon' (p. 12). In particular, the Public Instruction act of 1880 brought together two concerns which had been largely ignored previously, high school education and education for girls. With regard to the latter, the opening of Sydney Girls' High School enabled women to take a big step forward and according to Norman

> one has a sense of girls, hundreds of them, held back like a dam by a wall of superficiality and lack of education. With the opening of Sydney High the dam broke, and the first small enrolment spilled out, followed by a flood of others. (*ibid*, p. 21)

The school, under the headship of Miss Lucy Walker, allowed girls to enrol if they passed the entrance examination. The subjects available over a period of three years which culminated in matriculation standard included:

Latin
Elementary mathematics
Modern languages — French, German
English language and literature, elocution
History
Physical science
Drawing — freehand and perspective
Music
Cookery
Needlework (*ibid*, p. 15)

In keeping with earlier priorities that a girl's education should be fitting her for decorative wifehood, Norman asserts that 'cooking, music and drawing were on the curriculum partly as a sop to those who feared that higher education would make a girl unfeminine and unfit for her basic role of wife and mother' (*ibid*, p. 16).

The new school was a special appeal to the middle classes as it provided an educational system for about half the going rate of private day schools. Many parents saw the chief value of the school as providing a direct link between the primary school and the university while others saw it chiefly as a finishing establishment. However, when family misfortunes occurred such as a mother's illness, the education of girls was readily suspended as a girl's first duty was to go where she was needed.

By the first decade of the twentieth century the secondary system had been regularized into two channels, the vocational schools and the academic high schools. Sydney Girls' High School became recognized as serving the latter as revealed by the subjects offered for the Leaving Certificate:

English
Latin
French
German
Mathematics I and II
Mechanics
Modern and ancient history
Botany
Geology
Art
Music
Greek

Up until the end of the First World War there was an excitement for girls attending Sydney Girls' High School — 'an excitement that girls were able to learn proper subjects, boy's subjects, useful subjects, real subjects. The teachers too were just as excited about being able to let girls share in this wonderful, fascinating world of the mind, which had been denied to them for so long' (*ibid*, p. 98).

In subsequent decades, according to Norman, it was no longer exciting to be allowed to learn proper subjects. But it was still a privilege to attend the school and the girls were expected to go out into the world and use their talents for the good of society. This they did, especially during the Second World War, when women were directed into various jobs by the Department of Manpower.

In the 1950s, and especially as a result of the Wyndham Report of 1957, schools were encouraged to become freer and more progressive, although there are contrasting accounts of the effects (see for example, Connell *et al* 1982). Comprehensive schools were established and many selective high schools were discontinued, although six remained in Sydney including Sydney Girls' High School. A range of core subjects were introduced in the 1960s including:

English
Mathematics
Science
Social studies
Guidance
Library
Art
Craft
Music
Physical education

and girls could choose two subjects from:

Art
Music

Needlework
French
German
Latin
Greek
History
Geography (Norman, 1983, p. 23)

This broadening of the curriculum continued into the 1970s and 80s as an ever-widening range of subjects was studied and more and more subjects became interdisciplinary. Yet there was also a narrowing as girls with their sights set upon university entrance began specializing in the prestigious subjects of mathematics and science, and which gave them a better chance of maximising their aggregate tertiary score.

London Technical and Commercial High School (Canada)

This case study, recently published by Goodson and Anstead (1993), is of interest because the focus is on school curricula set in a particular institution and not an institutional case history as such. The case history examines school curricula at London Technical and Commercial High School (LTCHS) over the period 1900–40 in terms of course streams, the overall focus on vocational education and the interactive patterns between teachers and students during this period. Thus the study focusses more on the details of curriculum than Lacey, Labaree or Norman, while dealing in a less sustained way with issues examined in those works.

The case study is also of interest because of the reflexive accounts by the researchers and the extent to which they subject their own activities to intensive analysis. They reflect upon various methodological issues such as the need to understand the local and wider context of Canadian education in the early twentieth century; sources of biases, sub-texts and mistakes that can occur in historical inquiry, the historian's own subjective understanding of the past; how to use oral testimony to explore and reconstruct the complexities of school life but to be aware of biases such as faulty memory and incorrect recall, personal values and ethical issues.

The range of primary material discovered is also substantial including a range of documents (Advisory Vocational Committee minutes, annual reports, student record cards, the local newspaper *London Free Press*, mementoes from LTCH's 75th anniversary) and oral testimony (interviews of surviving teachers and students).

The case study authors portray a curriculum at LTCHS which was shaped as a result of a struggle between various social groups and ideological forces. Educators acted both to mediate the struggle, and as an interest group themselves. Students too had a role in establishing curriculum forms and content, but in the end, they were primarily victims of an increasingly segregated school experience.

For example, the introduction of technical education at LTCHS did little to eliminate the stigma of inferiority attached to nonacademic knowledge. Vocational proponents recommended that subjects such as English, history and geography should be 'taught in accordance with the life activities of students and the principles of industrial and commercial experience' (*ibid*, p. 66) — yet the province's industrialists and businessmen did not consider that these efforts at practical schooling were as important as the traditional, academic curriculum.

The authors describe how Beal, the first school Principal, used various compromises to sustain the viability of his school — a mix of socially efficient curriculum and rhetoric, resting on a traditional framework of schooling. This was illustrated especially in the establishing of a matriculation course, a five-year program which Beal mentioned frequently as important yet he ensured that it did not become too popular (Goodson with Anstead, 1997).

Several subjects are given detailed attention by Goodson and Anstead. In particular, an in-depth examination is made of the commercial department at LTCHS. New courses added in the mid-1920s broadened the curriculum choice but were established to help raise teacher's professional status and brought about increased lines of segregation within the student population (one course for male students exclusively; another course enrolled only students with previous high school experience).

Reflecting Upon the Case Studies

These four case studies, derived largely from accounts by Lacey (1970), Labaree (1984 and 1986), Norman (1983) and Goodson and Anstead (1993) provide interesting pictures of four schools. It is important to note, however, that such case study accounts rely upon researchers collecting a wide range of primary source documents (for example, minutes of meetings, student record cards, local newspapers); having access to oral testimony; and being able to evaluate the data in context, especially in terms of place and time.

Case studies located in different national and cultural milieu make comparisons especially complicated. Nevertheless, some initial surface similarities can be noted in the evolution of Hightown Grammar, London School, Central High School and Sydney Girls' High School. Most significant for our subsequent analysis of school subjects is the establishment of an academic link between schools and universities for the selective 20 per cent of pupils at Hightown Grammar, for the selective 'academic track' at London School and Central High and for the majority of girls at Sydney Girls' High School and a college preparatory track at Central High School. The acceptance by these schools of an academic track was partly in deference to university demands, but also an aspect of the subordination of schooling to the demands of a predominantly middle class constituency. The dominance of universities in both cultures can be clearly evidenced. Randall Collins (1979), for instance, has noted that by the 1890s:

> The leading universities were now in a position to set standards throughout the educational world and began to rise to a position from which they

dominated all other forms of education: secondary, professional, and teacher training. In the 1890s, the leading universities organized in the American Association of Universities, began to exercise accrediting power over secondary schools by setting up standards of admissions. (p. 126)

The results of the embrace of the 'academic curriculum' were remarkably similar in three of the four case study schools. In the next chapter we shall go beyond the differentiation of the 'academic' and 'practical' curriculum and examine how the contest over differentiation becomes internalized within subjects.

Reflections and Issues

1 In terms of the subject(s) you currently teach (or are most familiar with), do you consider that a hierarchy exists? What examples can you offer to support or refute the claim that a hierarchy of subjects operates in most schools?

2 To what extent did the establishing of comprehensive schools in England and in the USA effect differentiation? What factors led to new structures being developed internal to schools, to perpetuate differentiation?

3 How did selective high schools, such as the Australian case study included in this chapter, withstand pressures from powerful lobby groups? To what extent were girls at Sydney Girl's High School given access to high status, academic subjects?

4 The four case studies highlight various pressure groups who were able to influence the scope and range of the curriculum over a number of decades in England, the USA, Australia and Canada. In terms of your teaching experience give details of groups who have been able to influence the school curriculum. In particular, indicate which strategies were successful and those that were not.

Suggested Reading

There are several useful articles including:

Connell, R.W., Ashenden, D.J., Kessler, S. and Dowsett, G.W. (1982) *Making The Difference*, Sydney: Allen and Unwin.

Goodson, I.F. and Dowbiggin, I. (1991) 'Vocational education and school reform', *History of Education Review*, **20**, 1, pp. 36–60.

Goodson, I.F. with Anstead, C.J. (1997) 'On Explaining Curriculum Change: H.B. Beal, Organizational Categories and the Rhetoric of Justification', in Goodson, I.F. with Anstead, C.J. and Mangan, J.M. *Subject Knowledge: Readings for the Study of School Subjects*. London and Washington, DC: Falmer Press.

Labaree, D. (1984) 'Academic excellence in an early U.S. high school', *Social Problems*, **31**, 5.

Labaree, D. (1986) 'Curriculum, credentials, and the middle class: A case study of a nineteenth century high school', *Sociology of Education*, **59**.

Useful books include:
Collins, R. (1979) *The Credential Society: An Historical Sociology of Education and Stratification*, London and New York: Academic Press.
Goodson, I.F., with Anstead, C. and Mangan, J.M. (1997a) *Subject Knowledge: Readings for the Study of School Subjects*, London and Washington, DC: Falmer Press. Chapter 5, 6 and 7 for a more detailed account of the London Technical and Commercial High School, Canada.
Labaree, D. (1988) *The Making of an American High School: The Credentials Market and the Central High School of Philadelphia, 1838–1939*, New Haven: Yale University Press.
Lacey, C. (1970) *Hightown Grammar: The School as a Social System*, Manchester: University Press.
Norman, L. (1983) *The Brown and Yellow: Sydney Girls' High School 1883–1983*, Melbourne: Oxford University Press.

Chapter 4

Subject 'Traditions' and Interest Groups

The Nature of Traditions

In their study of professions Bucher and Strauss (1976) developed a number of valuable guidelines which are of use in studying school subjects. Within a profession they discerned varied identities, values and interests and they characterized professions as: 'loose amalgamations of segments pursuing different objectives in different manners and more or less delicately held together under a common name at particular periods in history (p. 19). Most frequently professional conflicts arose, they noted, over the acquisition of institutional footholds, over recruitment and over external relations with clients and institutions. At times when conflicts such as these became intense professional associations were created, or if already in existence, became more strongly institutionalized.

In the study of school subjects, developing the analogy with the Bucher and Strauss model means that we view curriculum groups or subject communities as essentially 'arenas of conflict'. We do not then, view subjects as continuing homogeneous groups whose members share monolithic and similar values and definitions of role, common interests and identity. Rather subjects should be viewed as comprising a range of conflicting sub-groups, segments or factions. The importance of such factions will fluctuate considerably over time.

Curriculum groups or, within subjects, sub-groups or factions, may organize around different schools of thought about knowledge, pedagogy or social purpose. These competing schools of thought often exhibit sufficient continuity over time for them to be characterized as 'traditions'. In studying school subjects it is important to discern these underpinning traditions for they often exist in the intersection between schooling and the social and economic context. These 'traditions' within subject and curriculum groups are not, of course, timeless entities. However, in focussing upon them, as one aspect in the study of school subjects, we are alerted to the fundamental nature of some of the conflicts and struggles which take place around the school curriculum. 'Traditions' then are perhaps best viewed as 'centres of gravity' in the continuing contest over that which comprises the curriculum. What will be presented is not a complete list of these traditions but some traditions which represent clear constellations of curriculum styles. These traditions recur in the history of curriculum in certain cases that have been studied and reported. In this sense, the traditions illustrated in this chapter should be seen as kinds of strategic clusters employed to help our scrutiny of curriculum changes and conflicts.

Traditions and the Primary Curriculum in England

Blyth (1965) discerns three separate traditions in English primary education: the elementary tradition, the preparatory tradition and the developmental tradition (p. 20).

The *elementary tradition* originated in the changes in English education underway in the sixteenth and seventeenth centuries. During this time there was a separation of function between the established grammar schools and 'what could now be generically termed elementary schools, the vital successors of the song schools and their equivalents (*ibid*, p. 21).[1] These early elementary schools soon merged into a range of dame schools, parochial schools and rudimentary private schools which covered England in an uncoordinated patchwork by the end of the eighteenth century.

The elementary tradition as we know it, however, developed most clearly in another type of school which began to appear from the seventeenth century. The particular function of these schools was the education of social unfortunates: orphans and pauper children. The schools were known as 'schools of industry' or 'charity schools'. Elementary education developed then for the poor and unfortunate; it was viewed from the first as a regrettable necessity or a preventive measure to help in alleviating crime, disease and disorder.

As a national education system was initiated after the Act of Parliament of 1870, the elementary school became part of an emerging national framework. In the last decade of the nineteenth century the school leaving age was raised to 11 and then to 12. Elementary schools now became the main institution for the education of the working class. Blyth argues that the teachers were themselves major carriers of the elementary tradition 'because it was an education of the ordinary people by the ordinary people for the ordinary people; but under the aegis of administrators who were not ordinary people'. He judges that in this manner:

> the elementary tradition proved self-perpetuating. Most of its teachers were themselves too limited in ability and in education and too insecure both financially and socially to be able to conceive of their task in terms other than those of meticulous and conscientious compliance with the routines that they knew. Nor were they encouraged to do anything else. (*ibid*, p. 27)

In response to this tradition of teaching, the pupils developed their own traditions of resistance. Highfield and Pinsent (1952) note that:

> The puritanical moral mode characteristic of many of these teachers would make it appear to them a duty to check the habits of many of their pupils at any cost . . . the lower-class were prone to regard the teachers with contempt as kill-joys, sexless, tee-total prigs. In addition they identified the teachers with the law, the police and the 'boss-class' generally, against whom, they carried on a guerilla warfare. (p. 32)

A second tradition developed from different roots, unlike the elementary tradition the *preparatory tradition* has been historically related almost exclusively to grammar school education. The main developments of the preparatory tradition came in the nineteenth century and arose from two initiatives underway at that time. Firstly the reform and expansion of 'public' (in the United Kingdom this means private) boarding schools for boys and secondly the revival and expansion of day grammar schools for boys and girls.[2] The development of these two kinds of school were influenced by the revival at the time of universities, their general expansion and increasingly improved standards of teaching and scholarship.

By the twentieth century middle-class and upper-class England had a network of preparatory schools working to prepare pupils for secondary, public and grammar schools and for post secondary education normally in the universities. Hence, in the preparatory tradition, real education was beginning 'at just the same age as, in the elementary tradition, full-time education was assumed to be ending' (Blyth, 1965, pp. 34–5). So exclusive did this relationship become and so close to the link between 'prep' schools and public schools that by the early twentieth century some day grammar schools were beginning to look beyond the 'prep' schools to elementary school pupils for part of their recruitment. This development was the only chink in an elaborately defended system for the education of two distinct 'nations'.

A third tradition, the *developmental*, 'has worked its way into the matrix of English social life from the periphery as is customary in many instances of social change' (*ibid*, p. 35). The emphasis of the developmental traditions was on the child's development (as initially explored in the work of Rousseau, Pestalozzi and Fellanberg). There was, however, one part of the developmental tradition which was of indigenous origin, the infant school. Robert Owen in pioneering new styles of schooling at New Lanark had from the beginning insisted on separate infant schools. The wider establishment of infant schools for children from 5 to 7 provided a continuing power base for the developmental tradition. The work of Froebel and Dewey also promoted the developmental tradition, hence projects, cooperative activities and the elimination of subject divisions began to develop more widely, even in some elementary schools. In 1931 the Board of Education's own report, *The Primary School*[3], was published 'it firmly annexed the education of children throughout the Midlands years to the developmental rather than the elementary or preparatory tradition . . . From this point onwards, the basis of a separate developmental tradition in primary education had been incontrovertibly laid' (Blyth, 1965, p. 42).

Traditions and the Primary Curriculum in Australia

Over a much shorter timeframe, elementary, preparatory and developmental traditions can also be noted as traditions in Australian primary education.

In the early years of settlement in Australia, the Government turned to the established church, the Church of England, to provide a basic elementary education for the lower orders of society, in order to upgrade 'the moral fibre' of the children and their parents. The Church of England was able to obtain a monopoly on church schools initially, through the authority of the UK charter for a *Church and Schools Corporation* in 1824. However, subsequent governors in New South Wales equivocated on this and both Governors Bourke and Fitzroy permitted other religious groups to establish their own schools and provided financial grants to support their efforts. The established church was not successful either in promoting the Bell monitorial system based upon the Catechism because free settlers recruited as teachers in the early years were in favour of the Lancastrian monitorial system (prayers each morning, then monitors instructed small groups of children in reading, spelling, writing and arithmetic).

The period between the 1820s and the 1850s saw the growth of different church schools — the private grammar schools. These early versions of today's exclusive independent schools were established to satisfy the needs of a growing number of landholders and commercial traders who wanted a combination of 'classical' and 'modern' curricula for their children. These developments coincided with the establishing of the first universities, the University of Sydney in 1852 and the University of Melbourne, thus providing a total education for the select few who completed a grammar school education.

Developmental or child-centred orientations occurred in cyclical fashion, as revealed by peaks in the 1890s, 1920s, 1930s and 1960s. Child-centred orientations were first evident in the activities of some directors of education who espoused 'new education' ideals, such as Jackson (1896–1903) in Western Australia, Board (1905–1922) in New South Wales and Tate (1902–1928) in Victoria. Jackson pursued a 'practical' orientation to child-centred curricula and introduced for the first time in Australian schools practical courses of instruction in gardening, botany, woodwork, metalwork and cooking. Both Board and Tate introduced new subjects such as nature study and manual training during the first few years of the twentieth century.

Serious attention was also given to new ideas about teaching methods. The methods of Montessori with infant school children were eagerly studied in New South Wales, to the extent that a teacher, Miss M Simpson, was sent to Rome to study the methods at first hand and then to return and set up experimental classes at her Blackfriars School. This school became in time the training centre for teachers from many states who wanted to be trained in the Montessori principles of freedom for the child and auto-education.

In the meantime educators in the US were creating new directions for child-centred approaches. Dewey advocated a form of child-centred education whereby children's practical activities could be directed toward social needs. His writing was influential both in the US and overseas, and he was the inspiration behind several Australian publications (for example, Browne, 1932) and conferences (for example, the New Education Fellowship Conference undertaken by the ACER in 1937).

Advocates of individualized learning approaches in the US produced successful schemes such as the Gary Plan (1918, activity-oriented, social needs); the Dalton Plan (1925, use of student worksheets and subject laboratories); and the Winnetka Plan (1927, curriculum divided into 'tool subjects' and 'activities subjects', independent self-instruction in tool subjects). Australian educators were eager to try out these approaches in Australian schools, especially in the states of Victoria, New South Wales and Western Australia, but it proved difficult to provide individual progress patterns within highly centralized and standardized state education system. Few of the trials lasted more than one or two years.

Other attempts to introduce child-centred curricula gave rise to the establishment of experimental schools. Dewey had commenced a laboratory school at the University of Chicago in 1896 and many other educators followed suit at other universities. In Australia, Board established an experimental school at Brighton-le-Sands, New South Wales, in 1917. The amenities at this school included four ordinary classrooms, special rooms for Montessori and kindergarten activities, rooms for a range of manual training pursuits, rooms for various aspects of domestic science, a large gymnasium, a library, and such outside facilities as a poultry run, beehives and gardens (Hyams and Bessunt, 1972).

Another peak for child-centred curricula was to reappear again as a result of the *Plowden Report* (DES, 1967). This major report into primary education recommended informal learning for children as revealed in such statements as:

the school is a community in which children learn to live first and foremost as children and then as future adults, and

we should encourage the development of the whole personality of children, to satisfy their curiosity and develop their confidence, perseverance and alertness.

Many educators in Australia and the US were stimulated by the Plowden Report and by the accounts of 'lighthouse' schools in various English counties (especially Leicestershire), and they rallied to the slogans of 'open education' and 'open plan' classrooms. Various books promoted this approach. Prominent among these writers were romantic critics such as Holt (1981) and Silberman (1970).

Educationalists in South Australia started the movement towards open-plan primary schools, with the first such school built near Burnside in 1969. Other states quickly followed this pattern with open plan schools in Western Australia and Tasmania in 1970, multiple-area schools in Queensland in 1970, and 'flexipod' and two-teacher learning area schools in New South Wales and Victoria in 1972.

The swing of the pendulum began to turn in the late 1970s as empirical studies revealed that basic mastery in literacy and numeracy was not achieved as well in open classrooms as in conventional classrooms (Bennett, 1976; Angus *et al*, 1979). A new era of public opinion favouring mastery of basic skills became apparent in the 1970s and it was maintained in the 1980s and 90s.

Traditions and the Secondary Curriculum in England and America

We have noted in passing that a distinction between grammar schools and song schools had developed in the middle ages in England. This growing distinction is vital in understanding the development of traditions with regard to the English secondary curriculum. By the early nineteenth century, Williams (1975) has argued the class-determined nature of schooling was well established.

> The process of change from a system of social orders, based on localities, to a national system of social classes — a change extending from the fifteenth to the late eighteenth centuries — was now virtually complete, and its result was a new kind of class-determined education. Higher education became a virtual monopoly, excluding the new working class, the idea of universal education, except within the narrow limits of 'moral rescue' was widely opposed as a matter of principle. (pp. 156–7)

In the development of traditions within the secondary curriculum, as we shall see later, the establishment of an examination system denoted an important watershed. The university sector began to provide examinations initially called, as a factual description as well as a statement of intent, 'middle-class examinations' (University of Cambridge, 1958, p. 1). The University of Cambridge launched their senior and junior local examinations in December 1858, six months after the corresponding examinations were organized by the University of Oxford.

The significance of the examination system was to prove pervasive and enduring. By the 1880s the examination system established between the public and grammar schools and the universities was well developed, and this 'while raising educational standards within the institutions, had the effect of reinforcing the now marked limitation of the university to entrants from a narrow social class. In the curriculum, classics were 'business' and other subjects were extras, but the establishment of the Civil Service Commission and the Board of Military Education, from mid-century, had the effect of promoting mathematics and modern languages, and of further organizing the schools in terms of examinations' (Williams, 1975, p. 158).

Yet although the class-based nature of English education was built on firm foundations the nineteenth century was a period of struggle and contestation. The rapidly expanding population of the country was moving into work in the flourishing new industries of the 'workshop of the world'. This working-class became increasing vocal and organized. How to train, or indeed educate, these people (or rather whether to train *or* educate) became the contested terrain on which a number of interest groups emerged to articulate different traditions of education and curriculum.

The first interest group were those Williams styled the '*industrial trainers*'. Their arguments, initially highly influential, led to the definition of education 'in terms of future adult work, with the parallel clause of teaching the required social character — habits of regularity, 'self-discipline', obedience and trained effort' (*ibid*, p. 162). Williams argues that the industrial training tradition was challenged by an often paradoxical alliance of two groups: groups arguing for the workers' democratic right to education and those, often deeply opposed to such democratic fulfilment, who nonetheless argued that people's spiritual health depended on more than a specific training for work and required a liberal or humanist education. These groups Williams calls in turn the '*public educators*' and the '*old humanists*'.

In analyzing the struggle between these interest groups and traditions Williams views the resulting curriculum as essentially a political settlement, a compromise. Hence in this manner:

> An educational curriculum, as we have seen again and again in past pe-
> riods, expresses a compromise between an inherited selection of interests
> and the emphasis of new interests. At varying points in history, even this
> compromise may be long delayed, and it will often be muddled. The fact
> about our present curriculum is that it was essentially created by the nine-
> teenth century, following some eighteenth-century models, and retaining
> elements of the medieval curriculum near its centre. (*ibid*, p. 172)

In summarizing the role of the three interests in the political compromise which takes its form in the curriculum Williams judges that in general 'the curriculum which the nineteenth century evolved can be seen as a compromise between all three groups, but with the industrial trainers predominant' (*ibid*, p. 163).

The diagnosis of the curriculum compromise in England is in some limited ways echoed by work carried out by American scholars on curriculum history in the United States. Kliebard has defined four paramount interest groups. In the contest for control of the definition of the school curriculum Kliebard (1986) points to the changing orientation of the schooling process. He notes that by the late nineteenth century the school was becoming distant from its immediate community milieu in certain important ways. By this time, he argues, the typical school had become 'a mediating institution between the family and an increasingly distant and impartial social order'. Most significantly, he notes that:

> With the change in the social role of the school came a change in the
> educational centre of gravity; it shifted from the tangible presence of the
> teacher to the remote knowledge and values incarnate in the curriculum.
> By the 1890s, the forces that were to struggle for control of the American
> curriculum were in place, and the early part of the twentieth century be-
> came the battleground for that struggle. (pp. 1–2)

By the time this battleground had been defined, four interest groups had emerged who were to contest the American curriculum. The first tradition was represented by the group known as the *humanists* (similar in some ways to Williams 'old humanists'). The humanists were 'guardians of an ancient tradition tied to the power of reason and what they regarded as the finest in the Western cultural heritage' (Kliebard, 1982, p. 23).

Three other interest groups sought to reform the American curriculum along lines that moved away from the humanist tradition. There were *the developmentalists* who wished for a curriculum defined along the lines of the 'natural order of develop-ment' of the child.

> Although frequently infused with romantic ideas about childhood, the devel-
> opmentalists pursued with great dedication their sense that the curriculum

riddle could be solved with ever more accurate scientific data, not only on the different stages of child and adolescent development, but on the nature of learning. (Kliebard, 1986, p. 28)

From this kind of knowledge they argued a curriculum in harmony with the child's real interests, needs and learning patterns could be developed and defined.

Alongside the developmentalist reformers were the *social efficiency educators* (similar in some ways to the industrial trainers). They argued for analogies between schooling and industry, analogies that could be pursued at a number of levels.

By applying the standardized techniques of industry to the business of schooling, waste could be eliminated and the curriculum . . . could be made more directly functional to the adult life-roles that America's future citizens would occupy. People had to be controlled for their own good, but especially for the good of society as a whole . . .

This was combined with

a sense that the new technological society needed a far greater specialization of skills and, therefore, a far greater differentiation in the curriculum than had heretofore prevailed. (*ibid*, pp. 28–29)

Finally there were the *social meliorists*, who saw the schools as a major force for social justice and change.

The corruption and vice in the cities, the inequalities of race and gender, and the abuse of privilege and power could all be addressed by a curriculum that focused directly on those very issues, thereby raising a new generation equipped to deal effectively with those abuses. (*ibid*, p. 29)

In reviewing the struggle between these interest groups for control of the American curriculum Kliebard's conclusions bear a certain resemblance to Williams with regard to the English curriculum. Again we are left with a somewhat messy, inconclusive compromise which might in a sense, satisfy nobody.

No single interest group ever gained absolute supremacy, although general social and economic trends, periodic and fragile alliances between groups, the national mood, and local conditions and personalities affected the ability of these groups to influence school practice as the twentieth century progressed. In the end, what became the American curriculum was not the result of any decisive victory by any of the contending parties, but a loose, largely unarticulated, and not very tidy compromise. (*ibid*)

The work of Williams and Kliebard is of great importance in establishing some of the major tendencies and tensions within the curriculum. But such broad-brush modes of analysis do have their shortcomings. Above all the approach is too broad to allow much in the way of insight into questions of power. Williams notes that industrial trainers were predominant on balance and provides us with some general clues as to why; Kliebard hints that the social efficiency promoters of curriculum differentiation were also on balance paramount but leaves little in the way of analysis as to how or why this was the case.

Modes of analysis are required which provide ways of investigating *and* interpreting why these interest groups — the industrial trainers and social efficiency educators so strikingly similar in their beliefs and proposals — achieved prominence. What were the structural, financial and ideological bases of support — in a word, what was the contest over curriculum really concerned with? To investigate this issue we would need a more grounded conception of power, a more detailed account of the constituencies of support and constraint. Only then might we know the nature of the historic compromise which is curriculum as it impinges on different national, social and economic structures.

Traditions within School Subjects

As the broad territory of secondary schooling became progressively colonized and occupied by a range of subjects so part of the general contest between interest groups and traditions was played out within the confines of each school subject. One strategy for developing a more finely-grained sense of the struggle over the curriculum then is to focus in detail on particular subjects, for each school subject portrays in microcosm the kinds of tensions and tendencies outlined above. In this way the traditions and interest groups can perhaps be more closely identified and analysed than is the case with broader forms of analysis.

The school subject is a seriously under-investigated form. On examination we find that just as 'there are important differences within subject boundaries of the same order as the differences between subjects' (Ball and Lacey, 1980), so also there are major 'traditions', which exist with varying degrees of articulation and allegiance, *within* most school subjects.

The general traditions of schooling discerned above partially impinge upon each secondary school subject. Just as the general traditions express different priorities and purposes with regard to schooling, so too with the varying traditions which contest the definition of each school subject. The school subject then, beneath its common name, is most likely to comprise a series of factions holding very different views with regard to priorities and purposes. The ebb and flow in the patterns of influence and dominance for each faction are well captured in Kliebard's (1982) characterization of curriculum fashions:

Curriculum fashions, it has long been noted, are subject to wide pendulum swings. While this metaphor conveys something of the shifting positions that are constantly occurring in the educational world, the phenomenon might best be seen as a stream with several currents, one stronger than

others. None ever completely dries up. When the weather and other conditions are right, a weak or insignificant current assumes more force and
prominence only to decline when conditions particularly conducive to its
new-found strength no longer prevail. (p. 17)

Of course the analogy with the natural world is a little deceptive. In the world
of human contestation we enter a more complex political terrain: we are now viewing the school subject as a microcosm of political conflict at particular moments in
the history of schooling. In many Western countries, we have briefly reviewed the
situation in England and the USA, there are common state secondary schools. But,
as we have seen, this does not mean that a consensus about schooling has been
established, nor indeed that differentiation has ceased. Rather, we have argued some
of the conflict over schooling has fragmented and internalized within the school and
within the subject. In scrutinizing school subjects, the general conflict over schooling
is found in the competing traditions or factions which comprise the subject.

Having briefly examined the changing functions of schools in the English,
Australian and USA milieu, the next section reviews some of the work that has
been undertaken recently with regard to school subjects in these countries. This
work seeks to establish certain salient traditions at work within school subjects. The
continuity of these traditions with the more general traditions and conflicts over
schooling is clear and provides testimony as to internalization and fragmentation of
the conflicts which surround schooling.

School Subject Traditions in England

As was noted earlier in writing of the 'traditions' in English primary education,
Blyth (1965) discerned three: the preparatory, the elementary and the developmental. The preparatory tradition was 'almost exclusively related to what we now call
grammar school education, which developed in its turn mainly as an upper middle
class phenomenon', the elementary tradition 'with its characteristic emphasis on
the basic skills' was aimed at the lower classes. 'For those who were unfortunate,
indolent or culpable enough to be poor, the minimum of education was proper and
sufficient.' The third tradition, the developmental, bases its principles on concern
with each child along the lines recommended by education such as Rousseau or
Pestalozzi. Broadly speaking, Blyth's three primary traditions can be equated with
the three primary traditions discerned within secondary education: the *academic*,
utilitarian and *pedagogic* traditions.

In England we have seen how at Hightown Grammar the school developed an
academic curriculum which in due course linked up with university education and
the professional career destination of the student. An academic curriculum for
subsequent academic training in preparation for a professional life — the establishment of these links, in particular between the school and the university denote the
academic tradition. The origins of this tradition are to be found in the second half
of the nineteenth century.

The definition of public and grammar school subjects in the nineteenth century, established in the 1904 Regulations and confirmed in the School Certificate Examinations of 1917, proclaimed the objectives of education as primarily a preparation for professional and academic life. Eggleston (1977), commenting on the early nineteenth century, states:

> A new and important feature of the time that was to prevail, was the redefinition of high-status knowledge as that which was not immediately useful in a vocation or occupation. The study of the classics now came to be seen as essentially a training of the mind and the fact that a boy could be spared from work long enough to experience this in full measure was, in itself, seen as a demonstration not only of the high status of the knowledge itself but also of the recipient — the mark of a 'gentleman' rather than a worker. (p. 25)

Eggleston's last sentence points up the contradiction: it was not so much that classical liberal education was non-vocational but that the vocations were only those fit for upper-class gentlemen. 'As the educational history shows', Williams (1975) reminds us, 'the classical linguistic disciplines were primarily vocational, but these particular vocations had acquired a separate traditional dignity, which was refused to vocations now of equal human relevance' (p. 163).

We have avoided therefore the use of the terms 'vocational education' or 'vocational knowledge'. Instead, we refer to low-status practical knowledge as the *utilitarian tradition*. Utilitarian knowledge thus becomes that which is related to those non-professional vocations in which most people work for most of their adult life. In addition to the basic skills of numeracy and literacy, this includes commercial and technical education. Neither commercial nor technical education was ever seriously considered as a new dimension which could be added to the existing classical curriculum. It was specialized training for a particular class of man, and its confinement to low-status areas of the curriculum has remained a constant feature of English curriculum conflict. That the alternative view of a narrowly utilitarian curriculum is still powerful, is shown by the constant pressure for utilitarian subjects in spite of their recurrent failure to earn high status. The manpower needs of a changing industrial economy demand that utilitarian training will be consistently advocated by many industrialists, the latter-day successors to William's industrial trainers. When widespread industrial failure is endemic the continuing ambivalence of educational status systems causes serious concern and pressure for change.

Whilst different in character and social purpose, the low status of utilitarian knowledge is shared by the personal, social and common sense knowledge stressed by those pursuing a child-centred approach to education, the secondary school advocates of the developmental tradition. Here the emphasis is on 'how the child learns' and can be characterized as the *pedagogic tradition* within the English curriculum. The pedagogic tradition does not see the task of education as preparation for the 'ladder' to the professions and academic or as an apprenticeship to vocational work but as a way of aiding the child's own 'inquiries' or 'discoveries', and considers that this is best facilitated by 'activity' methods.

The pedagogic tradition normally challenges the existing professional identity of teachers at two levels, as a 'specialist' in a school subject, for which the teacher had normally been specifically trained and as an all-pervading authority figure within the classroom.

This tradition has been closely allied to the so-called 'progressive' movement in education. As Shipman (1971) has noted, the more progressive curricula have in past periods come to be concentrated on those sections of the pupil clientele not considered suitable for 'O' and 'A' level examinations. In this way the pedagogic tradition has suffered from the comparatively low status also accorded to the utilitarian tradition.

School Subjects and Interest Groups

In England and Wales the connection between certain subjects taught in school and external examinations was established on the present footing with the birth of the School Certificate in 1917. From this point on, the conflict over the curriculum began to resemble the contemporary situation in focussing on the definition and evaluation of examinable knowledge: knowledge, that is, with close links to the universities and hence to professional careers.

The academic subject-centred curriculum was strengthened in the period following the 1944 Education Act. The introduction of the GCE in 1951 allowed subjects to be taken separately at 'O' level (whereas the School Certificate was a 'block' exam in which the main subjects all had to be passed), and the introduction of 'A' level increased subject specialization in a manner guaranteed to preserve, if not enhance, the largely 'academic' nature of the 'O' level examination. There was little chance that a lower-status examination, such as the CSE, which was introduced in 1965, would endanger the academic subject-centredness of the higher-status 'O' and 'A' levels.

The major move to unite the 'O' level examinations (taken around age 16) and the CSE was the development of common examinations in the 1980s. Paradoxically this move to unite the different traditions from different school sectors was heralded as a major 'break with the past'. Whilst it is too early to judge the pedagogic or content base of the new initiatives their culmination in the 1987 National Curriculum makes one thing abundantly clear: the 'traditional' academic subject-centred curriculum has been massively reestablished and reconstituted. New studies of the National Curriculum and the development of 'criteria' for National Curriculum subjects afford a major opportunity for scholars to explore the force of the historical circumstances reported herein. It is not sufficient to argue as some scholars have done, 'Ah but that was before the National Curriculum.' If there is a message in curriculum history it is that the 'vestiges of the past' have great power. Studies of the development of the national curriculum must focus on historical continuities as well as the publicly avowed 'revolution in curriculum' with its implication of a new beginning.

Whilst the 'high ground' of the National Curriculum therefore appears to reinforce curriculum subject-centredness, it is important to note that there is further 'high ground' that remains untouched. 'A' level examinations, the route to universities, have so far been left untouched. Although the situation is currently under review, it is as if the 'O' varied routes to the sixth form and 'A' level examinations have been narrowed down to specific subject-centred channels — many of the newer subjects, social studies, sociology, environmental studies and so on have therefore been marginalised.

Moreover utilitarian traditions have been reinvoked in the guise of the Technical and Vocational Initiative. As a number of scholars, notably Shilling (1989), have noted, this provides a reinvigorated modality for the old intentions of the 'industrial trainers'.

The subject is the major reference point in the work of the contemporary secondary school: the information and knowledge transmitted in schools is formally selected and organized through subjects. The teacher is identified by the pupils and related to them mainly through his subject specialist. Given the size of most comprehensive schools a number of teachers are required for each subject and these are normally grouped into subject 'departments'. The departments have a range of 'graded posts' for special responsibilities and for the 'head of department'. In this way the teacher's subject provides the means whereby his salary is decided and his career structure defined.

Within school subjects there is a clear hierarchy of status. This is based upon assumptions that certain subjects, the so-called 'academic' subjects, are suitable for the 'able' students, whilst other subjects are not. In her study of resource allocation in schools, Eileen Byrne (1974) has shown how more resources are given to these able students and hence to the academic subjects:

> Two assumptions which might be questioned have been seen consistently to underlie educational planning and the consequent resource allocation for the more able children. First, that these necessarily need longer in school than non-grammar pupils, and secondly, that they necessarily need more staff, more highly paid staff and more money for equipment and books. (p. 29)

Byrne's research ended in 1965 before widespread comprehensivization, and therefore refers to the tripartite system. However, referring to the new comprehensive system, she wrote:

> There is . . . little indication that a majority of councils or chief officers accept in principle the need for review and reassessment of the entire process of the allocation of resources in relation to the planned application, over a period of years, of an approved and progressive policy, or coherent educational development. (*ibid*)

Byrne's judgment implies that the discrimination in favour of academic subjects for the able pupils would continue within the comprehensive school. Hence by scrutinizing the fate of the academic tradition in school subjects in the comprehensive school we have a valuable litmus test. If the academic tradition established supremacy then the change in the common school was clearly doomed to be largely cosmetic. The old grammar school tradition would inherit the high ground in the new school thereby ensuring the older patterns of differentiation were reconstituted or reestablished.

That comprehensive schools have placed overwhelming emphasis on academic examinations, in spite of the growth of 'pastoral systems', has been confirmed by Ball's (1981) study of Beachside Comprehensive. He notes that 'once reorganized as a comprehensive, academic excellence was quickly established as a central tenet of the value system of the school' (p. 18). He provides a range of qualitative and statistical indicators to confirm this contention and concludes that 'while the division is less clear-cut and stark than in the grammar school' nonetheless it is evident that 'the teacher-resources within the comprehensive school are allocated differently according to the pupil's ability'. Thus, the most experienced teachers spend most of their time teaching the most able pupils. This is a reflection of the fact that the social and psychological rewards offered by the school to its pupils accrue to those who are academically successful and that academic achievement tended to be the single criterion of 'success in the school' (*ibid*). The pattern discovered by Ball has been strengthened and confirmed by a range of new initiatives since the Tory Government took over in 1979: from the publication of examination results through to the confirmation of academic subject supremacy enshrined as the National Curriculum.

Three major subject traditions have been identified: the academic, utilitarian and pedagogic. The link between external subject examinations for the able student and the flow of status and resources has been clearly illustrated. Conflicts between separate subject traditions have to be viewed within this context of status and resource allocation.

The aspirational imperative to become an academic subject is fundamental and very powerful and can be summarized as follows: school subjects comprise groups of people with differing interests and intentions. Certain common factors impinge on all these sub-groups, most notably that the material self-interest of each subject teacher is closely connected with the status of the subject in terms of its examinable knowledge. Associations set up to represent school subjects often place this fact at the centre of their campaigns on behalf of the subject. Academic subjects provide the teacher with a career structure characterized by better promotion prospects and pay than less academic subjects. Most resources are given to academic subjects which are taught to 'able' students. The conflict over the status of examinable knowledge is, above all, a battle over the material resources and career prospects available to each subject community or subject teacher. Even subjects with clear pedagogic or utilitarian origins and intentions such as art, craft (in aspiration design and technology) and rural studies (in aspiration environmental studies/science) have had to present themselves as theoretical academic subjects if 'A' level status, alongside acceptance as a university discipline, ensures 'establishment'.

The attempts of interests groups to promote new subjects have focussed since 1917 on the pursuit of high-status examinations and qualifications. Subjects like art, woodwork and metalwork, technical studies, bookkeeping, typewriting and needle-work, domestic science and physical education have consistently pursued status improvement by arguing for enhanced examinations and qualifications.

Dodd (1978) has reviewed the history of design and technology in the school curriculum following earlier work on design by Eggleston. A major theme in the work is the desire among teachers of the subject for higher status:

> Heavy craft activities have been referred to by a number of different titles as their nature and contribution has changed. Concealed in this ongoing discussion is the matter of 'status' and 'responsibility', and although the most recent change from handicraft to design and technology reflects a change of emphasis, there is something of the former argument. 'Practical' describes quite adequately an essential part of the subject, but it is an adjective which is little used because in the terms of the Crowther Report, it is an 'emotionally charged word'. As the subject has developed there have been efforts made to encourage its acceptability by participation in certain kinds of external examinations (which have not always been the best instruments of assessment), the use of syllabuses (often malformed to make them acceptable to other institutions), and by euphemisms like the 'alternative road', but these have failed to hide the underlying low status which practical subjects have by tradition.

But, as we have seen, few subjects have been able to challenge the hegemony of the academic subjects incorporated in the 1904 Regulations and 1917 School Certificate and now reconstituted in the National Curriculum of 1987. This aca-demic tradition has successfully withstood waves of comprehensive reorganization and associated curriculum reform but is now coming under new pressure from the Dearing Report to be issued in March 1996.

School Subject Traditions in Australia

Traditional patterns of subjects, with their emphasis upon factual learning and skill development typically comprised the Australian secondary school curriculum and this was largely confined to private schools until the early decades of the twentieth century. The textbooks, the majority of which were written by overseas authors, empha-sized an academic discipline approach, as did the external examination structures.

Historical accounts of senior secondary curriculum in the state of Victoria have been undertaken by Musgrave (1992), and in mathematics in particular by Horwood (1992).

Musgrave describes the centres of power in Victoria in the 1850s–1900s. Pro-perty owners and professionals were the powerful figures initially but with the growth of industrialization new groups associated with commerce, public administration and technology emerged as the power brokers. The school curriculum which was largely based in the 1850s upon the British aristocratic curriculum (classics and mathematics) expanded by the 1880s into an array of utilitarian subjects including commerce, modern languages, and scientific subjects, with a hierarchy of schools and examinations to match.

> As these new groups emerged they desired power and status for themselves and their children through formal education. A hierarchy of schools came into being, matching the levels of the labour force — at the top the exclusive private schools followed by lesser private secondary schools, the high schools and commercial coaching colleges, particularly after the ending of that odd form of quasi-secondary schooling, the state provision of 'extras'. This hierarchy was matched by a hierarchy of examinations which by the 1950s ran from matriculation (honours) down to intermediate single subjects. (Musgrave, 1992, p. 313)

Horwood (1992) notes that the private schools, many of whom were registered as class A schools by the University of Melbourne (based upon a Scottish practice), had a major influence upon the mathematics syllabuses and the related examinations via their membership of the Schools Board which commenced in 1913. The Schools Board with strong membership from registered schools and the university ensured that the interests of student continuing on to university were served. Each school subject was administered by a subject standing committee and in the case of mathematics, a traditional curriculum, largely determined by the expectations of university mathematicians and registered school teachers, was assured during the 1930s and 40s.

But evidence of discontent began to appear in the 1950s when the advent of Commonwealth University Scholarships revealed the low pass rates in mathematics subjects and the far higher pass rates in the humanities. The Schools Board was required to review the difficulty level of mathematics subjects and to look for alternatives. A new suite of mathematics syllabuses was prepared by the Mathematical Association of Victoria in 1964 but inadequate implementation provisions led to chaotic situations which were not addressed until the Education Department and the Mathematical Association of Victoria stepped in and offered a range of in-service courses and conferences to secondary teachers.

> The wider educational milieu had changed. The era of mass secondary education had arrived, and as large numbers of secondary students proceeded to the higher levels it became increasingly evident to teachers in the classroom that the courses in place, dominated as they were by a desire to select students for tertiary entrance, were inappropriate. (*ibid*, p. 13)

Further experimentation occurred during the 1970s as teachers responded to a newly-found freedom to devise a plethora of courses such as business mathematics and applied mathematics. The Education Department established a strong Curriculum and Research Branch to initiate projects and to provide materials to teachers. As noted by Horwood (*ibid*, pp. 15–16), major changes had occurred by the 1970s and 80s whereby the professional mathematician had been largely excluded from input into the content of mathematics curriculum, and the emphasis in the mathematics curriculum had switched from selection for university entrance to personal development.

School Subject Traditions in the USA

The conflicts and compromises surrounding the US high school curriculum have been briefly dealt with in foregoing sections — in particular the assault of the social efficiency educators on the academic style school curriculum has been noted. The effect of these different traditions on school subject categories can be analyzed since the more general conflicts were partially played out behind the school subject label. Hence, as vocationalism promoted by social efficiency educators began its long march through the American high school this tradition could be discerned within the microcosm of the school subject. Thus as many school subjects now began to internally restructure or differentiate they became infused with elements drawn from vocational education. Kliebard (1986) judged that in the three decades after the Committee of Ten's Report in 1893 and since it recommended its four model 'programmes' each with different but distinctly academic emphases:

> direct training for one's future occupational role had emerged as a major, if not the predominant, element in the high school curriculum for that segment of the school population whose 'probable destiny' did not include attendance in college. (p. 150)

Hence:

> The academic subjects that the Committee saw as appropriate for the general education of all students were seen by many later reformers as appropriate only for that segment of the high school population that was destined to go on to college. In fact, subjects like French and algebra came to be called college-entrance subjects, a term practically unknown in the nineteenth century. Even subjects like English became differentiated with standard literary works prescribed for those destined for college, while popular works and 'practical' English were provided for the majority. (*ibid*, pp. 15–16)

This resulted in 'the increasing popularity of such courses as business mathematics and business English as legitimate substitutes for traditional forms of those subjects'. In short, as the American high school became differentiated, so we can discern precisely the same internalized tendencies within the school subject. The subject, in short, provides a valuable microcosm for our study of the general tendencies at work within American secondary schooling.

George Stanic has recently studied one of the mainstays of the high school curriculum, mathematics. He found that the subject was vitiated by precisely the same traditions which Kliebard discerned at the general level. This study looks at mathematics education from the turn of the century to the late 1930s. This was the period when the American high school came under the influence of the social efficiency educators and where differentiation grew from the changing circumstances of the US high school, and, as Labaree has noted, the changing prospects and position of the proprietary middle class.

For students in 1890, secondary education may have been almost a rite of passage to an esteemed place in society. When a relatively small percentage of high-school-age students was attending and graduating from high school there was little need to be concerned about individual differences in intellectual capacity. Society was in a position to reward anyone who completed high school. However, the rite-of-passage idea became less viable as more and more people were attending and graduating from high school. Just completing high school was no longer a necessary and sufficient condition for achieving an esteemed position in society because the number of high school graduates outstripped the number of esteemed positions available. In such a milieu, questions about individual differences became more important, at least in part because pointing to individual differences in capability helped to justify and explain the changing purpose and function of high school attendance and graduation (Stanic, 1987, pp. 150–1).

The implication of such changes on mathematics education were differently perceived by each of the interest groups which Kliebard discerned. Hence, for the humanists, in general, it was argued that pupils should take as much mathematics as possible. This was because it was considered, until mental discipline theory began to be called into question, that mathematics developed reasoning power but also because mathematics was considered a vital element of the cultural heritage. The developmentalists considered that criteria related to individual interest and native capacity should be used in judging how much mathematics pupils should study. The social efficiency educators took a differential view. Hence, for the mass of the people, Snedden argued they needed to study no more than sixth-grade arithmetic to meet the needs of their daily lives and occupational destinations. The social meliorists were ambivalent about mathematics; on occasion they argued for mathematics as a central aspect of schooling but they also wanted to deemphasize the role of mathematics in knowledge acquisition.

This uncertainty about the desirability of mathematics for all children was most clearly seized upon in the period 1900–1930 by the social efficiency educators but also in lesser degree by the developmentalists. Snedden was on one of the committees for the American report of the International Commission of the Teaching of Mathematics. These committees provided an important arena for the discussion of school policy with regard to mathematics in the years 1911 and 1912. The social efficiency thrust towards differentiation can be clearly evidenced in some of the sub-committees. The members of the sub-committee on 'Mathematics in Grades

One to Six' complained that 'teachers still tend to teach future workmen in the lower schools as they themselves were taught by scientific scholars in the universities' (Snedden, 1911, p. 159).

In the final *Report of the American Commissioners of the International Commission on the Teaching of Mathematics* a humanist position seems dominant. We learn that the 'utilitarian possibilities' of mathematics should not cause us to forget that the main purpose of its teaching are to acquaint the pupil with the content of a portion of a domain of thought that is fundamentally characteristic of the human mind as such. Stanic (1987) summarizes the balance of interest groups as reflected in the report:

> The American commissioners — Smith, Osgood and Young — expressed their humanist position; but in the writings of some of the committees and subcommittees and even in the somewhat defensive tone of the humanist American commissioners, one can see that the humanist position in the mathematics education was being challenged. The committees and subcommittees espoused ideas representative of the humanist, the developmentalists and the social efficiency educators. And, in its lack of social meliorist ideas, the American report reflects a condition which has characterized the field of mathematics education throughout the twentieth century. (p. 162)

The growing challenge from the social efficiency educators which was a general feature of the second and third decades of the twentieth century in American education led to a preoccupation of 'crisis' among mathematics education by the 1930s. In fact the humanist position in mathematics seems to have largely withstood the assaults of the social efficiency and developmentalist traditions with a number of individual defections. Stanic judges that from 1900 through to the 1930s the humanist tradition retained its saliency:

> The continuity during these years is evident in the persistent attempts on the part of humanists educators to justify the teaching of mathematics based on its uniqueness as a vehicle for developing reasoning power and on its place in our western cultural heritage: in fact the mental disciplinarians never really faded away in the field of mathematics education. (*ibid*, p. 171)

Mathematics, therefore, was able to largely withstand the critique of the social efficiency educators — to avoid the charge that the version of mathematics that was taught was only suitable for college preparation and therefore that a 'vocational' and 'socially efficient' version of mathematics must be provided for 'the majority'. To the end, Snedden insisted that mathematics beyond sixth grade arithmetic be elective. But the mathematics educators provided an elegant humanist response which clearly took issue with the challenge of social efficiency educators which we know achieved far more success in other subjects. The National Committee on

Mathematics Requirements provide a firm defense of the status quo which defused the social efficiency critique at its most central point:

> The separation of prospective college students from the others in the early years of the secondary school is neither feasible or desirable. It is therefore obvious . . . that secondary school courses in mathematics cannot be planned with specific reference to college entrance requirements. Fortunately there appears no real conflict of interest between those students who ultimately go to college and those who do not, so far as mathematics is concerned. (*ibid*, p. 170)

With this eloquent style of defense the humanist tradition continued to maintain supremacy in the struggle over the mathematics curriculum. The distinctiveness of this defense and its success shows that it is vital to understand the struggle within each subject. Otherwise we face the danger of merely 'reading off' for each subject, similar tendencies to those discerned in such general studies as that of Kliebard. The subject in short, provides a microcosm for curriculum struggle where the more general battles have to be fought again — sometimes general tendencies prevail, other times, as in the case of mathematics, not. Each subject must therefore be studied in its own right.

Reflections and Issues

1   To what extent is it useful to portray 'traditions' as 'centres of gravity' in a continuing contest over the knowledge domain, pedagogy used or social purpose of the school curriculum? With reference to the curriculum you teach at a primary school or a secondary school, describe the main 'traditions' and the 'centres of gravity'. How have they changed over the last decade, or several decades, and why?

2   Explain why industrial trainers appeared to gain dominance as the major centre of gravity of the secondary school curriculum over the decades. What factors were responsible in the early decades of this century? Are they similar to the factors operating in the 1980s and 90s?

3   With reference to subjects you teach currently or for which you have a specialized knowledge, do you agree that the 'traditional' academic subject-centred curriculum has been massively reestablished and reconstituted? Give reasons why you accept or reject this statement.

4   How is it that mathematics as a school subject in the USA did not change in the directions required by industrial trainers and social efficiency educators? Did the limited incentives and/or limited access for girls to study mathematics affect the pattern? Is it still a significant factor? Has this been a similar pattern in other countries? Can the factors and issues for mathematics be generalised to other school subjects?

Suggested Reading

There are several useful articles including:

Ball, S.J. and Lacey, S.C. (1980) 'Subject Disciplines as the Opportunity for Group Action: A Measured Critique of Subject Sub-Cultures', in Woods, P. (Ed) *Teacher Strategies*, London: Croom Helm.

Bucher, R. and Strauss, A. (1976) 'Professions in Process', in Hammersley, M. and Woods, P. (Eds) *The Process of Schooling: A Sociological Reader*, London: Routledge and Kegan Paul.

Goodson, I.F. (1997) 'The Micro Politics of Curriculum Change: European Studies', in Goodson, I.F. with Anstead, C.J. and Mangan, J.M. *Subject Knowledge: Readings for the Study of School Subjects*. London and Washington, DC: Falmer Press.

Goodson, I.F. with Anstead, C.J. (1997) 'Subject Status and Curriculum Change: Local Commercial Education, 1920–1940', in Goodson, I.F. with Anstead, C.J. and Mangan, J.M. *Subject Knowledge: Readings for the Study of School Subjects*. London and Washington, DC: Falmer Press.

Goodson, I.F. with Anstead, C.J. (1997) 'Subjects and the Everyday Life of Schooling', in Goodson, I.F. with Anstead, C.J. and Mangan, J.M. *Subject Knowledge: Readings for the Study of School Subjects*. London and Washington, DC: Falmer Press.

Kliebard, H.M. (1982) 'Education at the Turn of the Century: A Crucible for Curriculum Change', *Educational Researcher*, **11**, 1.

Stanic, G. (1987) 'Mathematics Education in the United States at the Beginning of the Twentieth Century', in Popkewitz, T. (Ed), *The Formation of School Subjects*, London and Washington, DC: Falmer Press.

Useful books include:

Ball, S.J. (1994) *Education Reform. A critical and post-structural approach*. Buckingham: Open University Press.

Goodson, I.F. (1995). *The Making of Curriculum: Collected Essays. 2nd Edition*. London and Washington, DC: Falmer Press.

Goodson, I.F. (1993). *School Subjects and Curriculum Change. 3rd Edition*. London and Washington, DC: Falmer Press.

Goodson, I.F. with Anstead, C. and Mangan, J.M. (1997) *Subject Knowledge: Readings for the Study of School Subjects*, London and Washington, DC: Falmer Press.

Kliebard, H.M. (1986) *The Struggle for the American Curriculum 1983–1958*, Boston, London and Henley: Routledge and Kegan Paul.

Williams, R. (1975) *The Long Revolution*, London: Penguin Books.

Notes

1 Sometimes the adjective 'elementary' was formally used, for example, Mulcaster, R. (1582) *The First Parts of the Elementary*.
2 In England 'public schools' are in fact private fee paying schools' grammar schools would be partially fee paying until the mid-twentieth century.
3 Normally the primary school catered for the years from 5 to 11.

Chapter 5

Subject Departments

The subject department provides the most common organizational vehicle for school subject knowledge, certainly in secondary schools, but unlike 'the curriculum' it has not been widely researched or much noted in our studies of schools. In many ways subject departments play the same role in schools as compartments in an oil tanker. 'A well designed oil-tanker is a honeycomb of many small internal compartments so that, as the ship rolls, it's cargo does not all swill over in the direction of each roll, exacerbating the aberrations.' Parish (1993) goes on to say that 'stability depends on these 'sealed internal compartments' which ensure checks and balances against too much movement' (p. 7). The same could be said for subject departments.

Of course, as with subjects themselves, subject departments have different resonances in different educational systems and countries. But also as with subjects, there are considerable similarities and common features.

According to Siskin's work on American schools, the term 'department' was first mentioned in 1751 with reference to Benjamin Franklin's Academy in Philadelphia which had Latin, English and Mathematics 'departments' (Siskin, 1994, p. 38). Other writers of histories of schools (for example, Sizer (1964), Cuban (1984)) have referred to departments but have not given them detailed attention. Perhaps, the first educator to produce a detailed analysis of the potential role of subject departments, was Kilpatrick in 1905. Kilpatrick asserted that the use of departments within primary and secondary schools would enable a teacher to teach the same pupils over a number of years. He maintained that this would be of immense benefit to pupils as it would provide them with individual education by teachers who would get to know them very well over a period of years. Kilpatrick also argued that there would be financial benefits for a school to be organized into departments because these specialists would be constantly seeking out equipment to use in their classrooms, often paying for these items themselves! (This feature may recur given the tone of the contemporary Republican Congress under Newt Gingrich.)

It is interesting to note that the plan for the use of subject departments, as exhorted by Kilpatrick, had minimal impact upon primary schools (because the former were newly evolving and it was unclear what organizational form they would take) but was adopted quickly in secondary schools. Subject departments spread rapidly in secondary schools because they appeared to be able to provide the solution for those 'education reformers who were concerned with efficiency, rational management, and differentiation' (Siskin, 1994, p. 44). (N.B. This links to the arguments addressed in chapter 2.) As a result, some of the patterns of status hierarchy in schools were essentially derived from subject status 'pecking orders' in universities.

In the USA early divisions of departments were not based upon subjects but upon other criteria. For example, Tyack (1974) refers to a 'Girls Department' and a 'Boys Department' in some nineteenth century secondary schools (p. 51). In some schools departments were based upon the career prospects of students as revealed by such titles as a 'Classical Department' (traditional college — preparatory program) and a 'Department of Commerce' (those not headed for college but for trades) (Labaree, 1988, p. 155). Cuban (1984) refers to four departments of Classical, Scientific, English and Commercial in his study of an Ohio secondary school in the nineteenth century. Siskin (1994) notes that these department labels should not be confused with current terms for departmental divisions, and so any purported similarity is deceptive (p. 48). For example, the curriculum of English departments in an 1892 survey indicated 'various sciences, fragments of philosophy, history and political economy, some English literature, and perhaps a modern foreign language', as well as 'subjects representing such fields as astronomy, geology, and logic' (Krug, 1964).

Tyack (1974) argues that 'academic departments' as we currently know them, emerged a little later as a result of departmentalized universities. That is, the organization of knowledge along disciplinary lines became the major factor responsible for subject departments rather than early factors such as school size and internal functional differentiation.

In the USA during the early decades of the twentieth century, vigorous educational debates occurred between proponents of the 'classics' and the 'modern' subjects (Krug, 1964). Some classics subjects such as Greek and Latin did have difficulty in justifying their continued inclusion in the school curriculum and lost their departmental status, sometimes retreating to the territory of foreign language departments (Siskin, 1994, p. 55). Other subjects such as history were modified to include more contemporary knowledge and citizenship orientation. Newly-emerging subjects such as industrial arts, home economics, agriculture, and business became far more popular and in some cases attained department status in schools. Some subjects such as algebra were able to withstand onslaughts from progressive education proponents and maintained their high status in the school curriculum.

By the 1930s in the USA, the pattern of secondary school subjects located in departmental homes were the traditional mathematics, modern science and English and the newly-created social studies. The arguments over previous decades had subsided and the patterns linking schools and universities became dominant from thenceforth — 'a developed, established, and legitimated system of matching the organizational divisions of departments to the knowledge divisions of subjects' (*ibid*, p. 56). Teachers, although greatly affected by the departmental structures, were not involved directly in the battles over subjects. When the training of secondary school teachers started to occur in universities in the 1920s in the USA, this enabled even closer links to be developed between school departments and faculties at universities.

A Contemporary Analysis of Subject Departments

To a teacher, it is frequently the subject department, rather than the school, which is seen as the central and immediate unit of organization (Little, 1995, p. 2). Moreover, 'subject' is not merely the stuff of curriculum, texts and tests; it is fundamentally a part of being a teacher (*ibid*, p. 11). Subject departments, in terms of how they currently function in schools, can be characterized according to *administrative* and *social relations* functions.

Administratively, subject departments are responsible for time and space in terms of students and staff. For example, Hord and Diaz-Ortiz (1987) contend that subject departments tend to be a major communication link between staff, coordinate timetables, prepare budgets, manage equipment and materials and participate in textbook selection.

> In form, if not always in fact, departments constitute a central feature of the structure of authority in high schools — a structure of authority in which teachers' claims to resources and to collective autonomy are closely linked to subject specialization. (Little, 1995, p. 16)

Judith Warren Little has investigated several schools where subject department organization has been challenged (for example, Little, 1995 and forthcoming). She has found that subject allegiance remains high among teachers in these institutions, who use claims of subject expertise to justify their status.

> The importance that teachers attach to *subject* expertise as an element of professional competence strongly shapes their view of how one properly accedes to leadership. (Little, forthcoming)

In fact, the supervisory powers of administrators above the level of the department may be illusory. Bruckerhoff (1991) cites one proof of this:

> On a number of occasions I observed teachers discussing with one another the quality of their lectures or other methods they were using or thinking of using. When I asked about the role of the building principal and his assistants in relation to the formal routines of teaching, teachers remarked that they did not have discussions about content or methods with their principals. (p. 26)

School architecture, as revealed in faculty structures and detached buildings, enable subject department heads to administer groups of teachers effectively. Yet, the patterns of organization can vary enormously from one subject department to another, even within the one school.

The power relationships between the head of a subject department and its members can vary from autocratic to non-directive and democratic. Siskin (1994) refers to some departments as 'fiefdoms, vying to acquire for their members scarce 'material endowments', such as classrooms, schedule priority, or money' (p. 203). Accumulation is a key administrative role for each subject department and in terms of seeking budget, equipment, staff time and high calibre students; these resources are pursued relentlessly by departmental heads. But there is also the allocation of resources internally to subject department members and heads which often demand support and cooperation in return for allocating resources to staff. Woods states that 'the rewards of cohesion are tangible and immediate in such fields as the timetable, teaching of desirable or undesirable pupils, accommodation, per capita allowances for books, etc. and secure academic status' (Woods, 1980, p. 151).

Ball and Lacey (1980) contend that the subject department is in itself an arena of contestation in which social strategies are organized on the basis of biography, latent culture and situational constraints. The relative status of a staff member in terms of experience and length of teaching (biography) can be a factor in determining the room allocated or the students they will teach. Latent culture, as revealed through department norms such as cooperation and team work or competition and isolationism, can complicate the daily routine of department members. Situational constraints can take many forms including external budget constraints and edicts as well as building constraints.

Bruckerhoff (1991) points out how far some subject departments may depart from their monolithic image.

> The social studies teachers at Truman High behaved in petty or defensive ways in reference to particular areas and aspects of their work. Each clique had worked out strategies for keeping what it had and laid plans for taking valued 'possessions' away from the other informal group, the most highly valued territory being required senior-level courses. With the backing of their respective clique, teachers bickered for exclusive rights to it. (p. 120)

In the same department, Bruckerhoff found teachers carving out individual niches, both as a way of creating a distinct professional identity, and as protection against job loss or undesirable transfer (*ibid*, p. 106).

Subject departments also provide administrative links with distant colleagues working in the same subject area. These external contacts can contribute to the strength and bargaining power of department heads in their claims for increased resources. Subject departments therefore play an important mediating role between what we might call the 'knowledge demands' of the wider epistemic subject community and the 'institutional demands' of the organizational community of the school. This position of mediation between arenas might be stated another way: the subject department provides a physical territory which the subject, as a mental creation or social construction can inhabit; the subject department then mediates between notions of physical and mental territory.

Subject departments also exhibit a very powerful *social relations* function. Friendships and interests will develop in an atmosphere where teachers spend time together, share materials, and generally co-exist in a common 'comfort zone'. Subject departments constitute the primary point of reference, or professional home for most teachers (Siskin and Little, 1995, p. 6). Perhaps the social cohesion occurs because 'people have concrete things to tell one another and concrete instructional help to provide one another' (Siskin, 1994, p. 158).

The amount of cohesiveness within a subject department can vary over time but studies by Little (1982) and Siskin (1994) indicate that interconnectedness between department members occurs frequently.

> What appear in these teachers' stories, with remarkable persistence, are accounts of interconnectedness among colleagues: formal teaming arrangements at Oak Valley allow math teachers to collectively plan courses; informal mentoring partnerships at Ranch bring new teachers, or experienced teachers with new assignments, into the classrooms of their more experienced colleagues; Science teachers at Highlander bring classroom problems into the lounge for collaborative analysis and practical suggestions. (p. 159)

The formal and informal relationships between teachers can create disparate working cultures between and within schools (Bruckerhoff, 1991, pp. 2–4; de Brabander, 1993).

> Teachers who work in a particular place, at a particular time, hold in common a generalized idea about the practice of teaching. [. . .] Teachers will construct their idea of work within small groups over time through contributions from different individuals, each of whom has in mind a personal idea of work that more or less complements the more abstract, generalized idea. (Bruckerhoff, 1991, p. 9)

It is the result of interactions between department team members that lead to special routines, norms and values being developed. These routines are distinctive, strong and meaningful to the department and they can greatly influence the wider school culture. A striking example of this identification, as noted by Siskin (1994) in her research is that secondary teachers she interviewed commonly talked about their department as 'we' (p. 170).

Yet, as noted by Ball (1987), Goodson (1993 and 1994) and Little (1982) there can be a bewildering number of reference groups for teachers in addition to the subject department, such as teacher unions, various political factions and groups of friends. Notwithstanding, it can be argued that the subject department is the primary social world for many secondary teachers. The department is the vehicle for much of the routine communication between teachers and it provides the membership where deep bonds of loyalty are developed.

As might be expected, subject departments do vary considerably in terms of influence and cohesiveness because of the personalities of chairpersons/deans and the dispositions of members. Writers such as Huberman (1990), Cusick (1953) and Bruckerhoff (1991) have used various terms to produce typologies of subject departments such as 'socially cohesive community', 'administrative convenience' and 'split'. The four categories developed by Siskin (1994) provide a comprehensive

Table 1

BUNDLED	BONDED
Low Commitment High Inclusion	High Commitment High Inclusion
FRAGMENTED	SPLIT
Low Commitment Low Inclusion	High Commitment Low Inclusion

set and include 'bundled', 'bonded', 'fragmented' and 'split', as depicted in table 1 (p. 176).

'Bonded' subject departments are the ideal in that all members have a high degree of commitment towards department goals and they work collaboratively to achieve these ends.

Slightly lower on the ideal continuum are the 'bundled' subject departments, but they are found more commonly in schools. Members work collaboratively when needed and coordinate their efforts to obtain maximum impact, but their individual concerns often predominate over collective concerns. Sharing does occur in these departments but in a limited form, as teachers are wary of foregoing their autonomy.

'Split' subject departments are lower on the continuum. Members have strong commitments to common goals but there are conflicting factions within the department due to differing loyalties. Sometimes a department can enjoy a period of being 'bundled' or even 'bonded' but disagreements in priorities emerge to such an extent that factional interests limit any cooperation between members.

The lowest point on the continuum is when a subject department is 'fragmented' in that members can be characterized as being low on commitment and on inclusion. That is, members of these subject departments tend to work in isolation, and they interact minimally on matters of teaching and organization. If friendships do occur within these departments they happen sporadically and incidentally. There is minimal effort by the subject department in fostering a sense of commitment. Yet, for a number of teachers, they may prefer a 'fragmented' atmosphere and achieve independence even though they may lose out collectively in terms of resource allocation and overall influence at their respective schools.

Leadership factors are also important in shaping the direction and cohesiveness of subject departments. Drawing upon Olsen's (1979) leadership categories evident in university departments, Siskin maintains that 'collaborative', 'administrative', 'dictatorial' and 'non-leader' categories can be related to the four-fold typology described above (see table 2) (Siskin, 1994, p. 240).

Thus, 'bonded' subject departments with a 'collaborative' head will provide tremendous momentum with all members striving for consensus and taking responsibility for decisions made to achieve particular ends.

At the other extreme, a 'fragmented' subject department with a 'non-leader' provide the epitomy of isolation and self-interest and as a consequence, their influence overall in the school is usually quite minimal.

Table 2

Bonded departments High Commitment High Inclusion Leadership Consensus-based Shared Decision-making **Collaborative leader**	Bundled departments Low Commitment High Inclusion Leadership Competence-based Chair Decision-making **Administrative leader**
Split departments High Commitment Low Inclusion Leadership in power struggle Chair decision-making **Dictatorial leader**	**Fragmented departments** Low Commitment Low Inclusion Leadership by default, burden Unclear decision-making **Non-leader**

The status of the school subjects associated with subject departments, is an element which has been studied in a number of countries and detailed examples are available in the education literature. For example, in a study of English secondary schools, Ball (1987) noted that

> In the English education system certain subjects start out in such a contest with in-built advantages. The strongly entrenched status hierarchy among subjects, which is based upon a combination of exchange-values and academic orientation, handicaps those departments which represent practical or enactive subjects. The most powerful and most influential departments are commonly, but not invariably, the 'big four': maths, English, languages and science. The traditional status of these subjects is certainly a necessary condition for the influence that they wield in the school but not always a sufficient one. To make the most of their advantage these departments must ensure, both in terms of objective measures like examination results and through impression-management strategies, that they retain the confidence and goodwill of the headteacher and their colleagues. (pp. 41–2)

Siskin (1994) also refers to the clout and status of the big four subjects and notes that status is evident in the physical placement of a subject department within a school.

> Most visibly, physical placement can reflect political differences among subjects: which department has its own wing or building, good classrooms, or convenient location depends on its position in the subject hierarchy. At Highlander, for example, which is 'a math-science speciality school', science and math hold high status positions quite literally. They have the third floor of the building, up 'on top' where the noise of the hectic schedule is reduced and the security problems are lessened. While on the lower floors teachers complain about the noise and lock their doors against

wandering students, up on the third floor one science teacher commented that 'in fact this is one of the quietest schools I've been in'. (p. 213)

The big four subjects have a secure, well-institutionalized status in many countries. According to Siskin the big four, both symbolically and in concrete ways, in terms of staff size, needs for space, their priority in schedules and in their budgets, dominate over other subject departments (*ibid*, p. 216). Hargreaves' (1990) study of Canadian schools noted that the higher-status, academic subjects were granted more generous time allocation per subject, more favourable slots on the timetable and more likely to be compulsory for students than the lower-status, practical subjects (pp. 303–20).

The status associated with a particular subject department can be traced in part to the students associated with it (Little, 1993, p. 139; Anstead and Goodson, 1993, pp. 459–81), but also to several other factors.

Subject status arises not only from the perceived rigor of one's under-graduate education and professional preparation, but also from the perceived intellectual demand of course content in the secondary curriculum. (Little, 1993, p. 140)

According to Little, this means that:

Vocational teachers respond to subject hierarchies in part by campaigning for academic legitimacy. (*ibid*, p. 139)

In schools where academic achievement and preparation for college attract the greatest concentration of symbolic and material resources, vocational departments are seen as backwaters. Vocational teachers are more vulnerable to split assignments and are more likely to travel between schools than are teachers in academic departments. Vocational teachers' motivation and opportunity for intensive participation in a department are diminished as their vocational departments are less able to act as guarantors of preferred teaching assignments, breadth and depth of course offerings, and full-time department membership. (*ibid*, p. 157)

Recent developments with the National Curriculum in the United Kingdom indicate an emphasis on the 'big three' (core subjects of English, mathematics and science) and ten foundation subjects. The emphasis upon standard assessment task (SATs) at ages 7, 11 and 14, together with the publishing of results per school for the three core subjects, has reinforced their status and integrity within the school curriculum (Siskin and Little, 1995, p. 11). The proposed compulsory nature of the foundation subjects has been gradually whittled away by subsequent decisions by the Secretary of State so that only technology and foreign languages now remain as compulsory subjects.

The implementation of the National Curriculum in the United Kingdom has also revealed some interesting variations which Ball and Bowe (1992) refer to as schools 'recreating' and 'producing' rather than 'implementing' and 'reproducing' (p. 114). Based upon recent case study research of subject departments in four schools, they contend that the extent to which schools implement the National Curriculum depends upon leadership styles of heads of departments, contingency factors (staffing, student recruitment, inherited plant and facilities) and powerful contextual factors such as commitment and history.

> We do have evidence that low capacity, low commitment and no history of innovation results in a high degree of reliance on policy texts, external direction and advice, which in some circumstances verges on panic or leads to high uncertainty and confusion and a sense of threat. Equally we have evidence that high capacity, high commitment and a history of innovation may provide a basis for a greater sense of autonomy and *writerliness* with regard to policy texts, and a greater willingness to *interpret* texts in the light of previous practice, and a greater likelihood therefore of 'reconciliation' and 'mutation'. (*ibid*, p. 112)

Furthermore, Ball and Bowe argue that subject departments have been reinforced by the way in which the National Curriculum has been introduced. Cross-curricular concerns, for example, personal and social education, have not been widely supported although they have been promoted by the National Curriculum Council.

> After all, departmental structure and subject-based curricular have a long and powerful history that seems far more likely to feed off the National Curriculum structure rather than be weakened by it in any move into a Whole Curriculum. (*ibid*, p. 103)

The reinforcement of the concept that teachers are subject specialists has also occurred in a number of countries. For example, the impact of the Council for the Accreditation of Teacher Education (CATE) in the UK has been to reemphasize subject study for trainee teachers and thereby to reduce the time allotted to educational studies such as philosophy of education and sociology of education (Marsh, 1990; Howey, 1990). Grossman and Stodolsky (1995) studied subject sub-cultures in high schools in the USA. Hewitson *et al* (1991) noted similar trends in Australia.

Conclusion

The emerging work on subject departments elucidates the power of subject knowledge and subject sub-cultures (Siskin and Little, 1995, p. 14). In particular, the 'subject characteristics' of departments organize a range of assumptions, needs and demands. This has the effect of creating 'microworlds' within the school. Often these subject microworlds share characteristics which are common across regions and even countries. Hence to understand the distinctive microworlds inside the secondary school (and indeed middle schools and elementary schools as subject specialism begins to re-emerge at these levels), we must study the assumptions and features embedded in school subjects.

The importance of school subjects become clearer as we are reacquainted with the resilience and continuity of school subject knowledge. The subject department draws many of its characteristics from the history and social organization of the wider epistemic subject community. These characteristics are effected by the range of social and political factors which impinge upon a subject community. But these influences are distinct and divorced from the organizational and micropolitical imperatives within, particularly, schools and school districts.

Little (1993) argues:

> Departments exude a certain spirit, one that varies widely both within and between schools. They also confront quite different conditions of teaching. The conditions supportive of departmental collegiality include a full complement of subject specialists; a subsidized and meaningful department head position; a budget adequate to encompass both program development and professional development; a coherent stance toward curriculum policy; and norms supportive of collective problem solving, innovation, and intellectual growth. (p. 157)

As we have discussed earlier, each subject community comprises a range of distinct 'traditions'. These traditions will be represented within subject departments. Hence a department might be dominated by a particular subject tradition or might provide a 'contested terrain' where several traditions compete (Goodson with Anstead and Mangan, 1997, chapter 4). Each department will provide a unique configuration caught as it is between the separate traditions and tendencies of the subject community and the institutional forces of the school. In this sense subject departments have points of reference and influence which, in some sense, transcend many of the forces which seek to organize and structure the school. It could be that one of the recurrent factors in the failure and partial take-up of reform initiatives is the autonomy of the subject department. But it could be that the subject department (as with the oiltanker analogy we began with) provides a set of checks and balances against precipitous and over-politicized change initiatives. Given the mean-spirited tenor of some recent restructuring initiatives this may be no bad thing. Certainly the subject department seems to be a distinctive microworld sufficient to warrant major study in the future.

Reflections and Issues

1 Describe the departmental structures that operate at the school at which you teach or with which you are very familiar. If they are subject-based are there differences in power and status between them? Have these degrees of differentiation varied over the years? To what extent are these differences and differentiations gender-based? Explain.

2 What social and educational ends are served or thwarted by the model of the subject department? To what extent is an investment in subject and commitment to students difficult to reconcile? Discuss.

3 With reference to a secondary school with which you are familiar, explain how the physical buildings and layout facilitate interactions between teachers teaching in the same curriculum area.

4 Examine a specific subject department in a secondary school and examine the special routines, norms and values that appear to be in operation. How relevant are the four typologies outlined by Siskin (1994)?

5 To what extent are power relationships within a subject department affected by gender? Are gender contestations mainly covert or overt? Do they vary across subject departments? Use examples from secondary schools you have visited or currently employed as a teacher.

Suggested Reading

Useful articles include:

Ball, S.J. and Bowe, R. (1992) 'Subject departments and the 'implementation' of the National Curriculum', *Journal of Curriculum Studies*, **24**, 2, pp. 97–116.

Goodson, I.F. with Mangan, J.M. (1997) 'Subject Cultures and the Introduction of Classroom Computers', in Goodson, I.F. with Anstead, C.J. and Mangan, J.M. *Subject Knowledge: Readings for the Study of School Subjects*. London and Washington, DC: Falmer Press.

Useful books include:

Cuban, L. (1984) *How Teachers Taught*, New York: Longman.

Krug, E. (1964) *The Shaping of the American High School*, New York: Harper and Row.

Little, J.W. and McLaughlin, M.W. (Eds) (1993) *Teachers' Work*. New York: Teachers College Press.

Siskin, L. (1994) *Realms of Knowledge: Academic Departments in Secondary Schools*, London and Washington, DC: Falmer Press.

Siskin, L. and Little, J.W. (Eds) (1995) *The Subjects in Question: The Department Organization of the High School*. New York: Teachers College Press.

An Introduction to Subject Histories

The field of curriculum history and the study of the emergence of school subjects has grown rapidly in recent years. In the early chapters we have looked at some of the reasons for the growth of this field of study and we hope captured some of the excitement and potential of the work being undertaken. But the rapid development of the field does pose problems for a text seeking to summarize and introduce work on the historical emergence of school subjects. For new scholars approaching the study of specific subjects there is no adequate bibliography or summary of the wide range of work that has been completed and is currently underway.

In providing an introduction to the field there are two main approaches that could be adopted at this point in time. The first would be to provide a broad, bibliographic survey of all the work on curriculum history. This would offer a summary of the work on all school subjects being conducted in a wide range of countries. A second approach would be more modest. It would focus on a number of school subjects and would examine their histories in a limited number of countries.

In this book we have chosen the second approach. At root this is because wide-ranging bibliographic surveys, whilst much needed, can miss in depth what they provide so well in breadth. Our concern here is to look in some depth at work in science, in mathematics and in English. The focus within these subjects, as in the book generally, is mainly on English, Australian and North American studies. Hence the focus leaves out a good deal of the curriculum and even more of the world. The bias towards 'mainstream' subjects and the ethnocentric bias are both regrettable. Yet the intention in this book is to interrogate the more substantial and wide-ranging work on school subjects. For the moment this tends to be anglocentric work on mainstream subjects; this is not a situation which is likely to prevail for long as this field of study expands. However, choosing this focus with all its limitations offers the possibility to scrutinize historical work on school subjects in depth in national milieux which we have already sought to portray in some detail in foregoing sections. Hopefully, by focussing on the limitations and dilemmas in this work, new studies of other subjects and other countries will benefit and hopefully will proceed apace. The lacuna in this respect needs to be rapidly addressed if our studies are to review the global dimension of the 'new world order'.

So, in the following chapters, we shall try to highlight some of the most generative studies of school subjects that have been undertaken to date. Generative, that is, not only in the substantive sense but also methodologically. The earlier studies of school subjects, up until the 1960s in general, tended to be largely narrative and were preoccupied with changes in content. Even in this early period, however, there were some significant exceptions to these narrative, content-based studies. Foster Watson (1909), in his study of the origins of the teaching of modern subjects in England, was concerned as early as 1904 that the history of these subjects be 'known in connection with the history of the social forces which brought them into the educational curriculum' (p. viii). Our concern then is to select certain studies of school subjects which are substantively and methodologically generative and which point us towards promising new paths in the rapidly emerging field of curriculum history. The intention is not to provide comprehensive studies of the particular subjects of mathematics, science and English: for this readers are directed to the specialist secondary and indeed primary texts. Rather the intention is to 'shop window' some of the most generative sources and provide some guidance to the literature on the histories of the selected school subjects.

Chapter 6

Subject Histories: Science

Studies of School Science

One of the most developed areas in the study of school subjects is science education. The history of the subject may well explain this flourishing scholarly activity: science was a subject that achieved an established place in the secondary school curriculum only after an extensive and highly visible political struggle. This chapter provides a brief historical background but readers are directed to more comprehensive works by science specialists, most notably the summaries by Brock (1975), Jenkins (1980, pp. 27–86) and McCulloch (1993, pp. 200–46). In Britain, a substantial conflict over the *form* which science education would take took place in the mid-nineteenth century: this struggle, as we shall see, affords substantial insights into the social construction of the science curriculum. This dominant form would prevail not only in British state schools, but also in the curriculum of many other countries, perhaps not surprisingly given Britain's role in the nineteenth and twentieth century as an 'imperial centre'.

Yet, as is the pattern for curriculum history generally, most early histories of science education adopt a somewhat uncritical narrative tone and follow an essentially evolutionary and chronological pattern. Whilst following this narrative form a pioneering work is D.M. Turner's *The History of Science Teaching in England*. Following an even tighter 'acts and facts' format with little analysis or social history is G.D. Bishop's *Physics Teaching in England from Early Times up to 1850*. Nonetheless, the volumes provide valuable data which might be employed in a more analytical analysis of the history of physics as a school subject.

The period of more analytic studies of school science began seriously in the 1960s, a period of more sustained social analysis generally. Some interesting work looked at the relationship between scientific and technical education. This began with Cane's study of scientific and technical subjects in the English curriculum around the turn of the century (Cane, 1959/60, pp. 52–64). M. Argles' *South Kensington to Robbins* provided for the century or so following the Great Exhibition of 1851. Roderick and Stephens (1972) later produced *Scientific and Technical Education in Nineteenth Century England*; this is a valuable source of data but to some extent regresses back to less analytical and more narrative form.

The most hopeful and prophetic scholarship in the sixties turned back to examination of the work of the early pioneers of science education. This work on developments before the existing dominant paradigm of 'science' was established allowed insights into the early struggles over 'what counted as school science'.

Price's excellent study of George Combe was a case in point (Price, 1959/60, pp. 219–29). Perhaps most important of all was Ball's work on 'Richard Dawes and the teaching of common things' (Ball, 1964, pp. 59–68). This study showed that early initiatives in science teaching in elementary schools had progressively sought to engage the interest of ordinary pupils by focussing on the 'Science of Common Things'. Somewhere along the way it would seem this version of school science had been driven out by 'pure laboratory science'. A number of scholars began to seriously pursue investigations of this kind.

The origins of science in the British elementary schools can be found in certain initiatives in the early nineteenth century. Hodson has judged that the earliest attempt to include science in the curriculum of elementary schools seems to have taken place at a school in Cheam founded by Charles and Elizabeth Mayo (1849), whose 'Object lessons' were designed to promote 'habits of accurate observation, correct description and right judgment upon the things of nature and art'. Textbooks written as aids to infant teachers wishing to adopt object lessons, including *Lessons on Objects/(1831)* and *Lessons on Shells/(1832)*, proved highly successful and object lessons quickly became established as the basis of science education in the early years of a child's elementary schooling. It is noteworthy that the principal aim of this science education was not scientific understanding but 'religious understanding and moral improvement' (Hodson, 1988, p. 142).

Moves towards a more secular science education followed soon after these initiatives and are closely associated with the work of Richard Dawes, first studied by Ball in 1964. Dawes' initiatives have been much more fully documented in David Layton's germinal study *Science for the People*, a book which illustrates the rich potential of detailed study of school subjects. In 1842, Dawes established the National Society Schools at King's Somborne and began to define plans for teaching the 'Science of Common Things' (Layton, 1973, pp. 41–2; also detailed in Layton, 1972a, pp. 38–57).

In 1847 the schools had been in existence for five years and Dawes set to work at spreading the news about the curriculum initiatives he had launched. He wrote *Hints on an Improved . . . System of National Education* and *Suggestive Hints Towards Improved Secular Instruction Making it bear upon Practical Life*.

The success of Dawes' schemes was consistently attested to in reports by Her Majesty's Inspectorate beginning in 1845. In 1848 the Committee of Council on Education contained a detailed account of the organization and teaching of the Science of Common Things.[1] The Report was compiled by the Rev. Henry Moseley who became a close ally of Richard Dawes' work in science education and vigorously advocated the Science of Common Things.

To promote the Science of Common Things, Layton (1973) estimated that three resources were necessary; 'appropriately designed and inexpensive scientific apparatus; secular reading lesson books containing interesting scientific information; and most importantly, suitably trained teachers . . .' (p. 45). With the support offered within Her Majesty's Inspectorate these resources were not long in coming. Firstly, in 1851 a Government grant for the purchase of school apparatus was established. Standard sets of apparatus for teaching the Science of Common Things were produced by a leading scientific instrument manufacturer in London and two-thirds of the purchase costs of this equipment could be recovered from the Government grants. Secondly, the provision of books was made possible by a government scheme but most existing books were of little use for teaching the Science of Common Things. To remedy this situation James Kaye Shuttleworth, the Secretary to the Committee of Council on Education, began to commission the writing of appropriate school lesson books. Thirdly, Moseley was given instructions to devise an appropriate scheme for the training colleges to instruct new teachers. At this point, the Science of Common Things seem poised to establish itself as the most important version of science education within the elementary school curriculum. As Hodson (1988) has judged with regard to the three prerequisite conditions cited above:

> With these three essential conditions necessary for the development of Dawes' scheme reasonably satisfied, and those schools already using the scheme reporting considerable success, the movement seemed poised for rapid growth. (p. 144)

At this point the Science of Common Things was being supported at the highest level and new resources were becoming available. In particular there was accumulating evidence that this form of science teaching was indeed solving some of the problems of how to teach the subject to the masses. In short, the mass clientele in the elementary schools were increasingly receiving a viable, successful and engaging science education.

Very rapidly at this point, however, matters seemed to go into reverse. Richard Dawes was moved to a new post at the Deanery of Hereford and therefore had to change his focus from education to his new duties. At almost the same time Henry Moseley was moved to become Canon at Bristol Cathedral. Hence the two prime movers of the Science of Common Things were removed at a stroke.

Henry Moseley's successor as Inspector reversed his actions and changed the status of physical science from that of a compulsory subject to that of an optional one. By the end of the decade the supply of trained science teachers, the prerequisite for any broad-based implementation of the Science of Common Things had more or less ceased. In 1859 grants for science teaching were slashed and in 1862 with the initiation of the Revised Code and 'payment by results' all specially targeted financial resources for science were withdrawn.

The major question remains for curriculum historians: why was this successful early initiative in mass science education so systematically aborted? Layton's (1973) study provides a number of tantalizing clues. In summarising the movement for the Science of Common Things he noted:

> Here was no crumb of upper-class education charitably dispensed to the children of the labouring poor. Instruction was related to a culture which was familiar to them and proved opportunities for the use of reason and speculation by drawing upon observations which pertained to everyday

life. Understanding and the exercise of thought were not prerogatives of the middle and upper classes. (p. 53)

Elsewhere Layton judges that as the scheme operated: 'Here was knowledge at work in a manner which engaged the intelligence of children of the labouring poor, of whom it had been taken for granted that they should have 'no business with anything where the mind is concerned' (*ibid*, p. 43). In its operation in fact the Science of Common Things had begun to expose the very basis of the hegemonic structuration of traditional academic knowledge. Hence Moseley wrote, anticipating Bernstein *et al.* by more than a century:

> Words familiar to the ears of our children, and recognised by them in their true meaning when they are first taught to read them, are strange to the children of a labourer, and unintelligible; and those more complicated modes of expression which are proper to elaborate forms of thought and which exercise the reasoning faculties of our children from an early period, conceal effectively from the apprehension of the idea in the construction.[2]

Moseley saw early then that the promotion of middle and upper class grammar and a 'literary' modality for schooling was partially an expression of class domination and a likely guarantor of class reproduction. In challenging the very modality of schooling the Science of Common Things was challenging the means by which the social order was produced, reproduced and legitimized. A curriculum initiative which educates the poor is a curriculum which the more it succeeds the more it challenges the social order. The proclamation of the success of the Science of Common Things by Moseley and others was in this sense strategically inept for it awakened the fears of the middle and upper classes and led in this sense directly to the destruction of the very scheme it was seeking to promote.

Another interpretation provided by Hodson and Prophet (1983) questions Layton's defence of Dawes, and argues that Dawes was just as concerned as were his opponents to control and regulate the working class in the interests of the established social hierarchy. Initially the reaction which led to the dismantling of the Science of Common Things had been mounted in the newspapers of the middle and upper class. In the late 1850s a campaign was launched in *The Times* which coincided with the moves described above to move the main promoters of the scheme and withdraw support for teacher training and for the provision of financial resources. *The Times* indicated a strategy for both aborting the Science of Common Things and replacing it with a more 'acceptable' version of science. Firstly, *The Times* advocated an end to scientific education in elementary school for the 'lower orders'. Essentially the fears that were expressed were that the 'lower orders' were becoming better educated than their superiors — a dangerous inversion which would challenge the whole mythology on which governance was based. A Parliamentary Committee of the British Association for the Advancement of Science was set up to examine the form of science education which the upper classes might now require. The Chairman of the Committee, Lord Wrottesley (1860), later voiced his concerns when confronted by the products of the 'Science of Common Things' initiative:

> ... a poor boy hobbled forth to give a reply; he was lame and hump-backed, and his wan emaciated face told only too clearly the tale of poverty and its consequences ... but he gave forthwith so lucid and intelligent a reply to the question put to him that there arose a feeling of admiration for the child's talents combined with a sense of shame that more information should be found in some of the lowest of our lower classes on matters of general interest than in those far above them in the world by station. (quoted in Hodson, 1988, p. 167)

He added:

> It would be an unwholesome and vicious state of society in which those who are comparatively unblessed with nature's gifts should be generally superior in intellectual attainments to those above them in station. (*ibid*)

Wrottesley then states the problem clearly; the solution, however, took more time to identify and negotiate.

In *The Times* the second line of argument had been that science was required which was 'pure' and 'abstract'. The conception of pure science practised in 'laboratories' had first surfaced according to W.H. Brock in 1839. In his valuable bibliographic essay Brock (1979) notes: 'My starting date, 1839, is arbitrary. It is the year in which the German chemist Liebig moved into an enlarged laboratory at Giessen, enabling him to expand the output of students. We may take this as a symbolic starting point for the development of modern science education' (p. 68). Immaculate as Brock's scholarship is, we see how history is written in the 'image of the victors'; how the history of a subject is retrospectively reconstructed to suit that version of events which celebrates the ultimately dominant tendency within the subject.

Brock is of course correct that the research laboratory at Giessen was a model for 'pure laboratory science' and indeed attracted many British students in the mid-nineteenth century.

At the same time Liebig was pioneering his research laboratory in Giessen, new developments were underway in America. Whilst these initiatives did not directly or immediately affect developments elsewhere there are important studies of the moves there towards a pure laboratory science which provide us with insights about the process of establishment. In fact Yale had pioneered the teaching of chemistry at the higher education level with the appointment of Benjamin Silliman as Professor of Chemistry as early as 1802. This appointment led in due course to moves to develop a 'School of Philosophy for the higher reaches of literature and science' (Kuslan, 1969, p. 631), this became the Department of Philosophy and Arts. The pressures on the scientists to earn status and prestige in particular ways were, however, noted in the inaugural address of the Rev. Theodore Dwight Woolsey as President in 1846. He spoke of the sciences 'being built on observation and experiment, rather than on primary truths discerned by reason, and assuming the form of systems chiefly according to the principle of resemblance and not through the exercise of logical powers'. As a result he judged the sciences 'do not tend to discipline our most important faculties' (*ibid*, pp. 431–2).

To further his own research initiatives and also to generate the rational and reflective aspects of the scientific endeavour, the new chair of 'Chemistry Applied to the Arts', Benjamin Silliman had set up a private laboratory for chemical and mineralogical research. He fitted up a small analytic laboratory '. . . in the old College laboratory and the business of daily instruction in experimental and analytical chemistry was commenced' (Fisher, 1866, quoted in Kuslan, 1969, p. 433). But many organizational and status problems remained: 'His students were not members of the college nor were they officially recognized.' However 'by 1846 the laboratory had been in operation for four years, and young Silliman had demonstrated not only that he could teach chemistry and mineralogy, but that he could obtain from his students, . . . creditable research in a small laboratory' (*ibid*, p. 433).

In Silliman's laboratory a new pattern of learning and scholarship emerged which anticipated future graduate school science: 'The program previously pursued in Silliman's small laboratory seems to have been similar in some ways to modern graduate school programs. They had attended lectures in the sciences and worked at research problems he suggested. Their results were published in the *American Journal of Science*, . . .' (*ibid*, p. 447). The problem that arose however was one of establishing a degree of uniformity and regularity. Originally no formal curriculum existed and no degree was awarded on completion of study; 'with only one professor this was a complicated state of affairs; each student arriving at a different time, and without a common background of knowledge must somehow be taught the fundamental techniques. The obvious solution was a formal program of regularly scheduled classes and laboratory hours, and this is what now came into existence' (*ibid*).

Hence in different places, in Giessen and Yale, but also in a variety of other locales a new pattern of scientific learning and teaching began to emerge in the mid-nineteenth century. The Giessen model was certainly adapted by the many British scholars who visited the laboratory there. Liebig's work was a seminal influence on the new versions of school science that were developed in Britain in the period following the dismantling of the Science of Common Things.

> The ideal of the research school he founded there, (i.e.: in Giessen) which later was to attract large numbers of young British scientists, was research and inquiry for its own sake. This provided a concept of 'pure laboratory science' which was to dominate school science curricula especially for the more able children, throughout modern times. (Hodson, 1988, p. 141)

But the vital point to grasp is that initially this version of science was defined in universities. The needs of the university science community for status and resources pushed them steadily in the direction hinted at in Woolsey's inaugural address. The result was a transformation both of the mode of scientific inquiry and of the discourse in which that inquiry and the results thereof were communicated or not communicated to wider publics:

A necessary, although by no means sufficient, requirement for this re-markable surge of intellectual activity was the introduction into scientific thought of conceptions of which there were no directly observable in-stances. The idea of linear inertial motion is a classic example from the seventeenth century. The doctrine of atoms, explaining — in Perrin's phrase — 'the complications of the visible in terms of invisible simplicity' is an illustration from a later period. By the use of theoretical entities or con-structs which were not obviously derived from an everyday view of the world, but which were creative products of the scientific imagination, the explanatory and predictive powers of science were progressively increased. If at times the ideas might appear to confound common sense, as was the case with the heliocentric theory of Copernicus, nevertheless, for initiates, as Galileo recorded, 'reason was able . . . to commit such a rape upon their senses, as in despite thereof to make herself mistress of their credulity'. Such conviction was aroused especially when, in addition to their quali-tative value, the conceptions of science lent themselves to quantitative statement. The application of mathematics to the description of nature was a further vital step in the growth of modern science. (Layton, 1973, p. 168)

The consequence of accepting that science would henceforth be essentially defined in universities was potentially devastating for a school science developed for mass education. The handover of control and the narrowing and abstraction of the discourse often put science beyond the realm and language of understanding of ordinary children and indeed ordinary people.

But the passing of control to the universities and the definition of science in their image as 'pure laboratory science' dealing in abstracted and disembodied study solved the problem posed by the kinds of science represented by the Science of Common Things. A science had now emerged which was linked to the univer-sity elite, a largely upper class, masculine elite, rendered in the image and language of that elite and perfect for sponsoring the interests of that elite. The converse of this version of school science, now generally accepted as real, *bona fide* school science was that the subject became substantially disconnected from the ordinary working class learner in particular female working class learners. In short, a form of science had been achieved that resonated with the social order. From this point on science rapidly attained state support and a broad-based take up within the secondary school curriculum. The promotion of pure laboratory science in the schools got underway in the late 1850s and rapidly gained momentum through vigorous government support.

Edgar Jenkins (1979) has provided us with some most valuable insights into the promotion of laboratory sciences. The initiatives largely began in the mid-1850s and he notes two in particular:

At the Bristol Trade School, opened in 1856, boys of 12 years and upwards conducted chemical analyses in a laboratory attached to the school
and the pupils were encouraged to make some of the apparatus needed for
laboratory work in physics.

Whilst science teaching began:

at Rugby 'in the cloakroom on the ground floor in the Town Hall', although
a small chemical laboratory was completed at the school by 1860 and
more generous accommodation was provided shortly afterwards. (p. 252)

The Government's active promotion of this model began in earnest in the late
1860s.

The general pattern discerned in Britain has been found by scholars developing histories of the school curriculum in other parts of the world. Kuslan (1982) has
carried out a pioneering study of the place of chemistry in the normal schools set
up to train teachers for the elementary schools in New England in the nineteenth
century. Up until the 1860s he found that laboratory instruction seldom existed:
'Although student demonstrations in chemistry were a daily occurrence in the
normal schools, there were no individual laboratory experiments because of inadequate facilities' (p. 214).

The first Normal School chemistry laboratory was constructed at Salem in
1874. This was several years after the first high school laboratories: Dorchester
High School of Boston in 1870 and the Gives High and Normal School at Boston
in 1871. The first teacher of chemistry at the latter school was a woman specifically
chosen because of her laboratory instruction skills.

In 1874 the Bridgewater Normal School requested a laboratory similar to that
at Salem arguing that 'pupils cannot be properly prepared to teach Chemistry
without this laboratory. It is indispensible to the advanced course of teaching.'[3] Of
the other normal schools Trainingham acquired its laboratory in 1874, Westfield in
1876, Providence in 1879 and New Britain in 1885. 'Within a few years after the
inauguration of individual work in chemistry and long before most educational
institutions were provided with laboratories for this purpose, the normal schools
required all students to spend many hours in their well-equipped chemistry laboratories' (*ibid*, pp. 214–5).

Tomkins study in Canada found that early science covered natural history 'the
simplest elements of botany and zoology, including human physiology taught by
means of object lesson' and natural philosophy which 'chiefly meant the rudiments
of physics and chemistry'. Tomkins judged that by the 1880s the teaching of
chemistry in a somewhat basic factual and rudimentary form was 'well established'
in most of the provinces of Canada; however, little laboratory work was done in
the period before 1890. He claims that it was the move towards laboratory science
and a scientific method based upon this that helped the status passage of the subject. He also notes the growing influence of the universities in defining the subject.
Hence:

By 1890 science had gained acceptance at Toronto as both a pass and honours matriculation subject. Ontario high schools were now required to have laboratories in order to gain collegiate status. The 'pure' science of the university disciplines meant, as it would continue to, that applied aspects received short shift in the curriculum. (Tomkins, 1986, p. 87)

The collegiate status that Tomkins refers to was the status given to the high status secondary schools (the British equivalent would be the grammar schools) normally known in Canada as 'collegiate institutes'. For secondary schools to be accepted as a high status collegiate school science had to be taught in laboratories — the link between status and pure laboratory science was therefore tightly enforced. Tomkins summarized the evolution of secondary school science in this manner in Canada: 'The subject gradually moved from object teaching and nature study, with their pedagogical and utilitarian objectives, towards academic pure science that had high status by 1900' (*ibid*, pp. 82–3).

The transition to laboratory science was an allied development in the universities as has been instanced earlier. The triumph of pure science, however, depended on 'laboratory science' being finally transformed into a priority for 'laboratory research'. Looking at physics, Yves Gingras (1986) has conducted some pioneering work on this period in the development of science. Gingras argues that 'the emergence of research in physics in Canadian universities was the result of the importation of a practice from Europe during the last quarter of the nineteenth century'. As a result 'a new generation of university professors, trained in British and German physical laboratories, was more inclined towards research than teaching' (pp. 182–3).

More recent British work on the emergence and development of physics as a school subject in the post-war period has added considerably to our knowledge of the social history of science subjects. This helps us understand the vital constituents of 'grammar school science' — physics and chemistry. Brian Woolnough's *Physics Teaching In Schools 1960–85* is accurately sub-titled '*Of People, Policy and Power*'. By developing a detailed biographical profile of some of the key advocates of science education in British schools he adds considerably to our understanding of how school subject change is initiated. Particularly valuable are his insights over the continuing struggle between physics as separate subject and movements towards general science (the would-be successor of the Science of Common Things in certain important aspects) (Woolnough, 1988, p. 11).

In early nineteenth century Britain, physics and chemistry were the leading science subjects; botany and zoology followed some way behind in popularity; and biology hardly existed as an identifiable discipline. Advocates of science stressed not only the intrinsic value of their subject as a disciplinary training, but also the utilitarian potential. To progress, the branches of science had therefore to exhibit these dual characteristics, and as a result we learn botany and zoology could find support 'only in so far as they contributed to useful ends, such as the extermination of insects destructive to timber in the dockyards' (Layton, 1973, p. 21). The teaching of these areas of science was limited throughout the nineteenth century but, significantly, whilst botany declined as a school subject, biology began to emerge in the curricula of some schools (Tracey, 1962, p. 429).

The consequent chronological priority of the physical sciences was probably of considerable import for the history of biology in schools and it has been claimed that because physics and chemistry were 'first in the field' the task of establishing biology in school curricula was rendered immeasurably more difficult. Changing the 'image' of biology was primarily facilitated by the work of scientists in a number of emerging specialist fields. Their work both developed the utilitarian potential of the subject and its claim to 'disciplinary rigour'.

The slow growth of biology is eloquently attested to by the activities of examination boards. The Oxford and Cambridge Examining Board introduced biology into its examinations in 1885. Initially it attracted few candidates, but as Waring (1980) has noted, by 1904 'a new biology paper was attracting more candidates than chemistry'. She notes that 'as pressures mounted for recognition of the schools as institutions for the pre-clinical scientific training (in chemistry, physics and biology) of intending medical students going on to study for the Diploma of the Conjoint Board of the Royal College of Physicians and of Surgeons, the numbers rose'. At first only a limited number of schools were allowed to train candidates but in 1911 all public schools were granted such recognition (p. 7).

Considerable evidence is available that biology was neglected in the decade or so following the First World War. In 1918, Jenkins (1979) states, 'biology in boys' secondary schools was represented almost exclusively by nature study, taught to the lower forms, and by botany and zoology taught to the few senior pupils intending to study medicine' (p. 119). Contemporary evidence judged that biology was 'disgracefully neglected' throughout the 1920s and a report of the Imperial Agricultural Research Conference in 1927 noted 'inadequate provision for biological teaching' in every level and type of school (*ibid*, p. 121). But rapid change was on the way and Jenkins has argued that 'it was the decade after 1930 which, more than any other, saw biology gain an established place in the secondary school curriculum' (*ibid*, p. 123). By 1931 all eight examination boards had adopted biology as a school certificate examination.

The contested and belated development of biology is related to the gendered character of grammar school science. As McCulloch (1993) has argued 'the Science Masters Association continued to act as the 'guardian' of theoretical and experimental science' (p. 217). Hence, to gain fully parity of esteem biology had to make a subsequent transition to a 'hard science'.

A solution to the lack of structure and disunity of biology came with the development of molecular biology. Here, at last, was the rationale for claiming parity of esteem with the physical sciences. Molecular biology provided both high prestige and an overarching theory which unified many aspects of the subject. Moreover, since plants and animals look very similar at the cellular level, the division between botany and zoology appeared far less justifiable. Jenkins summarized the development in this way: 'The enormous success of crystallographic and cytochemical studies in the field of molecular biology of which the elucidation of the structures of DNA is the best-known example led to pressure to reform the teaching of the life sciences so as to incorporate both the relevant biochemistry and the reductionist/experimental approach which had brought such triumphs'. At last the 'arrangements for greater coordination' which Bernal in 1939 had argued could come from advances in research were at hand and for a period biology could be presented as a unitary science (Jenkins, 1979, p. 153).

Other work on the gendering of science is Jenkins' important section on girls scientific education (*ibid*, chapter 5). Also, Carol Dyhouse's past and ongoing work develops historical insights into the structured gender differentiation of the school curriculum (Dyhouse, 1976 and 1981). Mary Waring's book on the Nuffield Science Projects of the 1960s provide valuable clues about the gendered nature of school science (Waring, 1979).

Woolnough provides a detailed account of the battle to replace the 'grammar school sciences' of physics, chemistry and biology by the integrated science which many judged more suitable to the comprehensive schools which rapidly emerged after 1965.

Woolnough provides a most insightful historical commentary on the struggles between single subject science and general science. He states that 'history reflects the tendency to favour general science on educational grounds when the social climate is easy, but to revert to the separate sciences on vocational grounds when the economic times get hard' (Woolnough, 1988, p. 246). The choice is then between a scientifically liberated public and the manpower needs of a technological society. 'It appears that while a more liberal peoples science may satisfy the former, physics is maintained to fulfil this latter demand' (*ibid*).

There may, however, be other complications than the social climate causality noted by Woolnough. For example, several recent publications in the 1990s have argued for a reduced emphasis upon single disciplines and scientific purism. For example Jenkins (1992) and Bybee (1977) argue that science to be taught in schools should be relocated within contemporary technologies 'rather than, as at present, be concerned with the grammar and syntax of the scientific disciplines, or in the language of the National Curriculum in England and Wales, with "The exploration of science"' (Jenkins, 1992, p. 231).

In a similar vein, Wenham (1992) asserts that scientific purism severely limits the range of scientific methodology available to students. Student's investigative activities are typically singular problems whereas traditional science teaching concentrates upon general hypotheses and theories (pp. 549–62).

Fensham (1988) argues that innovative endeavours are strongly resisted by academic scientists and teachers who have become soundly socialised by their own scientific studies in higher education.

He provides details of strenuous efforts made to introduce an integrated science course, 'Physical science, society and technology' but which foundered under powerful lobbies by prestigious universities and especially physics and chemistry professors. Fensham (1993) concluded that such efforts to provide a substantial reform of the knowledge content of school science education to make science and technology more relevant and more accessible to all students, will inevitably unleash strong forces of resistance from academic scientists.

Boyle (1990; pp. 25–38) contends that science in the National Curriculum is far from radical. It is subject-based and confined by predetermined outcomes to such an extent that students have little opportunity to 'think creatively in order to solve problems and develop intellectual skills that enable them to acquire their own knowledge' (*ibid*, p. 36).

Cheung and Taylor (1991), Smith (1994) and Jenkins (1994) also support a constructivist approach to learning whereby there is an emphasis upon science process component skills and integrative investigative skills. Bentley and Drobinski (1995) asserts that problem solving investigations in particular are giving female students a greater ownership of ideas, planning and procedures.

Conclusion

The chapter has portrayed some of the developments in school science which witnessed remarkable changes of emphasis in these scientific subjects over the decades as individuals and groups struggled for control. For instance, the Science of Common Things was challenged and aborted by the middle and upper classes partially because it was too successful with the lower orders in elementary school. Subsequently, the establishment of science laboratories became the symbol for elite science, and university controlled.

The emergence of biology is a special interest because of the numerous pressures and demands which occurred. Utilitarian pressures, issues related to gendering, associated issues of parity of esteem with physics and chemistry, interdisciplinary constraints, the rise in status due to the emergency of molecular biology, were just some of the elements that produced the emerging tapestry of school biology.

In the following chapter we study developments in school mathematics. It is useful to keep in mind the developments in school science and begin to investigate common patterns and issues as we interrogate another mainstream subject.

Reflections and Issues

1 In the light of your knowledge and experience of secondary schools, what examples would you use to support the contention that science has only achieved an established place in the secondary school curriculum 'after an extensive and highly visible political struggle'?

2 Have there been initiatives at your school, or a school with which you are familiar, in promoting general science in addition to, or to replace some of the individual science disciplines? What have been the outcomes?

3 Do you consider that the school subject of biology has changed markedly over the decades? If so, why do you think that this has occurred? How do non-science teachers, parents and students perceive biology in terms of practical, academic and personal aims?

4 To what extent does the study of the historical evolution of science provide evidence of the gendering of science?

Suggested Reading

There are several useful articles including:

Ball, N. (1964) 'Richard Dawes and the Teaching of Common Things', *Educational Review*, **17**.

Bentley, D. and Drobinski, S. (1995) 'Girls, learning and science in the framework of The National Curriculum', *The Curriculum Journal*, **6**, 1, pp. 79–100.

Cane, B.S. (1959–60) 'Scientific and Technical Subjects in the Curriculum of English Schools at the Turn of the Century', *British Journal of Educational Studies*, **8**.

Dyer, K.G. (1976) 'Crisis in Biology: An Examination of the Deficiencies in the Current Expansion of Biological Education', *Journal of Biological Education*, **1**, No. 2.

Jenkins, E. (1992) 'School science education: Towards a reconstruction', *Journal of Curriculum Studies*, **24**, 3, pp. 229–246.

Useful books include:

Jenkins, E.W. (Ed) (1993) *School Science and Technology: Some issues and perspectives*. Leeds: Centre for Studies in Science and Mathematics Education.

Layton, D. (1973) *Science for the People: The Origins of the School Science Curriculum in England*, London: George Allen and Unwin.

Tomkins, G.S. (1986) *A Common Countenance: Stability and Change in the Canadian Curriculum*, Scarborough, Ontario: Prentice Hall.

Waring, M. (1979) *Social Pressures and Curriculum Innovation: A Study of the Nuffield Foundation Science Teaching Project*, London: Methuen.

Woolnough, B. (1988) *Physics Teaching In Schools 1960–85*, London, New York and Philadelphia: Falmer Press.

Notes

1 Committee of Council on Education, *Minutes 1847–8*, pp. 7–27.
2 H. Moseley in the Committee of Council on Education (1847) *Minutes 1844*, London, 2, pp. 508, quoted in Layton (1973) p. 85.
3 Kuslan (1982) quoting *Annual Report of the Massachusetts Board of Education* (1875), p. 24.

Chapter 7

Subjects Histories: Mathematics

The early origins of mathematics have recently become the subject of a good deal of scholarly study and as a result we know about some of the early episodes in the definition of the subject. Frank Swetz's seminal study *Capitalism and Arithmetic: The New Math of the 15th Century* not only provides us with vital information but provides a timely historical reminder of the recurrent waves of innovation within areas of knowledge. Likewise, Geoffrey Howson has provided a valuable *History of Mathematics Education in England* pursued through the study of nine biographies of key mathematics educators. Howson (1982) comments on the recent nature of curriculum history work in this subject area:

> To my knowledge this is the first book to be published which attempts to tell the story of the development of mathematics education in England. That this should be so is rather surprising; for one can turn to histories of the teaching of science and to a history of mathematics teaching in Scotland. Any attempt to fill such a gap is, therefore, fraught with difficulties, for the 'only book' is likely to be invested with an authority it may not deserve. (p. ix)

He adds a note on the decision to concentrate on nine biographical studies.

> Extra problems may also arise as a result of my having chosen to present the material through the medium of biographies. Emerson's claim that 'there is properly no history; only biography' could be used to justify this decision. The truth is, however, more mundane; for I abandoned a 'chronological' account thinking it would have little appeal for the general reader as apposed to the serious student. I believe also that a biographical account, even though it requires frequent scene-settings and 'flashbacks', better demonstrates the great part which individuals have always played in the advancement of mathematics education in England. (*ibid*)

Howson's own explanation is worth quoting at length for it fairly sets out the basis for his biographical approach and begins to think through the limitations of such an approach. Given the underdeveloped state of the history of mathematics education in England the decision is no doubt justifiable. But it still leaves us (with one exception) with a history of the great men of mathematics education. Moreover the 'scene setting' and flashbacks is too partial, perhaps inevitably given the focus, to grasp the major economic and political movements which provide the context for the biographies. Yet it remains a most valuable source.

In common with Swetz, Howson points to the fifteenth century as a period when 'the seeds were being sown for a period of great growth (*ibid*, p. 5),' and like Foster Watson before him he stresses the importance of the Spaniard Vives in defining and promoting the subject. Vives was engaged as a tutor by Henry VIII for his daughter Mary and was a protegé of Wolsey and More, Fascinatingly. Vives from the beginning focussed on the recurrent historical tension between the abstract and the practical. Mathematics he said provided mental discipline 'for flighty and restless intellects which are inclined to slackness and shrink from or will not support the toil of continued effort'; here was a subject he argued 'to display the sharpness of mind'. On the other hand Vives saw the perils of abstract, decontextualized knowledge for it 'leads away from the things of life, and estranges men from perception of what conduces to the common weal' (*ibid*, p. 5). Howson comments perceptively:

> The dual aspects of mathematics, the practical and the contemplative were clearly distinguished then by Vives, and recognised the need healthily to reconcile the two. The subsequent history of mathematics education in England is largely a chronicle, on the one hand, of how this problem was ignored — with the result that a bipartite system of mathematics education was effectively created — and, on the other hand, of how individual educators have constantly sought to effect a reconciliation. (*ibid*)

Taylor has provided an important history of *The Mathematical Practitioners of Tudor and Stuart England*, one of a number of valuable volumes on the history of mathematics to be provided by Cambridge University Press. Whilst certain individuals promoted the study of mathematics in the universities, notably Sir John Cheke, the first Reguis Professor of Greek at Cambridge, who encouraged the study of the subject and in particular of Euclid's geometry, little work was undertaken in the universities. Taylor judges that of the times he was studying, 'the universities at large appeared indifferent or even hostile to any mathematics that went beyond the meager medieval curriculum upon which a single lecture course was provided at Cambridge' (*ibid*, p. 12).

In the event Oxford was first to move in establishing a professorship of geometry in 1619 (although not without some opposition from the gentry who sent their sons to Oxford). Cambridge did not establish a professorship until 1662 when Sir Henry Lucas's will provided for the establishment of the Lucasian Chair. The first Professor, Isaac Barrow, significantly had produced a translation — into Latin not English since this was the language of communication in the universities — of Euclid's *Elements*. Barrow moved on, and presumably upwards, from the Lucasian Chair to the more influential Chair in Divinity.

Mathematics then was formally established at Cambridge through the Lucasian Chair but progress was slow. A century and a half later when Augustus De Morgan entered Trinity College there were at last signs of change and development:

It was a time of transition in the university's mathematics life. In purely mathematical terms the isolation of English mathematicians from their Continental contemporaries was coming to an end: gradually analytical methods and the notation of the differential calculus were finding their way into the course. Educationally, the days of the incompetent professor were numbered, although the Lucasian Chair was held in De Morgan's student days by Thomas Turton, a mathematical nonentity (later Dean of Westminster and Bishop of Ely), who is reputed never to have lectured. (*ibid*, pp. 76–7)

As we saw the first translation of Euclid was undertaken by the first Professor of Mathematics at Cambridge. The dominance of Euclid at Cambridge was therefore established early and sustained long into the twentieth century in fact. The dominance of Euclid was in crucial part a reflection of the dominance of Cambridge in defining mathematical education. Howson noted that 'the extent to which Cambridge, Cambridge-trained men, and Cambridge-aimed pupils dominated mathematical thought in the secondary schools and the universities must be stressed' (*ibid*, p. 135). He quotes the opinion of *The Times* of 1906.

The study of higher mathematics in the British Empire is now practically concentrated at Cambridge. Thither come graduates from the Scottish universities and all the best men trained in the provincial universities of England and Wales. Practically all the professorial chairs of mathematics and mathematical physics in London and the provincial universities of England, in the universities of Scotland, the Colonies and India are filled by Cambridge men. (*ibid*, p. 144)

The manner in which the teaching of Euclid in fact developed can be seen in the number of new editions: fifty-two in the first two decades in the 1830s and seventy-three in the 1840s (*ibid*, p. 131). By this time Euclid was becoming a major part of the mathematics curriculum in the great public schools as mathematics itself finally became a secure part of the curriculum of those schools. The public schools were, of course, dominated by classics and the teaching of mathematics as Euclid reflected this classical bias. In 1864 the Clarendon Report noted at a leading public school, Harrow, amongst sixth-form leavers, about half had studied six books of Euclid (Cooper, 1985, p. 37).

The dominance of Euclid was reflected in both the examinations set for schools by the 'Cambridge Syndicate' and by the Oxford Delegacy. These examinations were set from 1858 and 1857 respectively and came to be a major influence on the school sixth form curriculum. Howson (1982) writes:

That Euclid should have become the accepted textbook for school geometry is perhaps surprising. There was, of course, no long tradition of teaching mathematics let alone Euclid, in English public schools; neither was it the case that our Continental rivals used Euclid in theirs. From Recorde's time (re the sixteenth century) onwards there were English geometries which departed from Euclid in their order and method of presentation. Yet such geometries came to be associated with those who practised mathematics for a living. Those who learned it as part of an 'education', at university, did not use such utilitarian works, but read Euclid. (p. 130)

So the division between the academic tradition and the utilitarian tradition first noted by Vives was maintained. As a leading Cambridge don Whewell asserted, 'not as an instrument (for the solution of today's mathematical problems) but as an exercise of the intellectual powers; that is, not for their results, but for the intellectual habits which they generate' (*ibid*, quoting Whewall, p. 130).

Opposition to the dominance of Euclid in mathematics education was developing and in 1868 surfaced in both the Taunton Commission and a book by J.M. Wilson, *Elementary Geometry* (cited in Howson, 1982, p. 131). Wilson's book brought forth a response which is summarized by Howson and asserted that 'those who wished to retain Euclid were more competent to form an opinion on the subject than the reformers, that is, the majority of Cambridge mathematicians opposed change' (Howson, 1982, p. 133). He also noted that whilst united in opposing Euclid the reformers had not agreed on a replacement and that a change in the examination system, which would be required to achieve reform, was unlikely.

In 1871 a new Association for the improvement of Geometrical Teaching was formed by the anti-Euclid reformers. The first aim of the Association was to draw up an alternative syllabus to Euclid. But in fact their efforts produced a very modest reformist approach — the need for practical relevance was nowhere fully embraced or embodied:

> The AIGT, then, made no attempt to reunite the two streams of mathematics education in Britain, the academic and the vocational. It persevered with an élitist, non-utilitarian syllabus which bore little relation to the more practically-oriented geometry syllabus examined by the Department of Science and Art. (*ibid*, p. 135)

Howson adds 'Yet, what chance would these have been of gaining Cambridge's agreement to a technically-based syllabus?' In short the Association's loss of nerve was really a pragmatic response to the hegemony of Cambridge in the contemporary world of mathematical education.

The emergence of a genuinely alternative paradigm for mathematics was delayed therefore and did not emerge until later in the work associated with John Perry (1850–1920). The work of Michael Price (1986) on the 'Perry Movement' is an invaluable aid in reconstructing its significance. Perry came from a very different milieu to that of Cambridge and the public schools. He took up a founding apprenticeship and attended engineering classes at Queens College, Belfast, where he graduated with a Bachelor of Engineering in 1870 (p. 104). From the beginning therefore Perry was immersed on the practical world of work and this focus always remained important in his approach. This approach was developed further when he moved to become a mathematics and physics teacher at Clifton College, one of the new proprietary schools. In 1875, however, he moved to Japan and became involved in the education of engineering. In 1879 he returned to England and started teaching at what became Finsbury Technical College, an institution which helped pioneer technical education; in 1882 he became Professor of Mechanical Engineering at the College. Price has judged that Perry's work, and that of his associated colleagues at Finsbury, notably Ayrtor and Armstrong, led to the development of a new paradigm of 'practical mathematics'. 'The emergence of an alternative paradigm for mathematics in relation to the developing needs of engineering and technical education is of great significance.' What was required Price notes

> was a much wider and more applicable mathematics curriculum than the conventional 'academic' routine, and one which fully exploited experimental, numerical and graphical methods. This entailed swift progress to provide a working knowledge of a wide range of useful topics in mathematics, as opposed to the laborious academic treatment of the various branches of arithmetic, algebra, etc., following rigorous pure mathematical lines, with utility neglected. The Department of Science and Art offered an alternative to Euclid from 1859, namely practical plane and solid geometry, which was essentially geometrical drawing, but the Department's pure mathematics, from 1864, followed conventional academic lines in arithmetic, algebra and Euclid. (*ibid*, p. 105)

Perry began to produce textbooks which spelt out his alternative views, *Practical Mechanics*, *Applied Mechanics* and *The Calculus for Engineers*. Introductory lectures on practical mathematics were given when Perry moved from Finsbury in 1896 to become Professor of Mathematics and Mechanics at the Royal College of Science in London. These lectures were subsequently published by the Department of Science and Art in 1899 (*ibid*, p. 106). From this time Perry began to take aim at the Cambridge version of pure mathematics. His subject, practical mathematics, was he said 'exceedingly different from what used to be the study of the mere mathematician on the same subjects'. In code the mere mathematicians were the purists of Cambridge. His vision of practical mathematics was a radical new departure.

> In detail, the elementary stage of practical mathematics as an examination subject was innovatory in a number of respects when compared with the traditional treatment of the elementary branches of mathematics. In arithmetic, emphasis was placed on decimals rather than fractions, including approximations, and the use of both logarithmic tables and slide rules. In algebra, the use of formulae featured prominently, as well as the study of functions and graphs, using squared paper, and leading to some early ideas in the calculus. The deductive ideals in the calculus. The deductive ideals of liberal geometry, based on Euclid, were largely ignored and replaced by a treatment based on measurement and drawing mixed with arithmetic and algebraic methods. Furthermore, the scheme encroached on some of the

traditionally advanced branches of mathematics by including some work in simple trigonometry, three-dimensional geometry and vector methods, as well as calculus. Overall, the scheme was notable for its *breadth* of subject-matter and its *mixing* of hitherto separately treated branches of the subject, as well as for its distinctive methodology. (*ibid*)

Perry's alternative paradigm came at a time of considerable vulnerability for the conventional Cambridge model of mathematics as represented in the major examination syllabuses. As we have noted there was already rumbling within the ranks of mathematicians as seen by the founding of the AIGT. But in other ways the academic and classical tradition of schooling found itself surrounded by different visions and sectors of education. Not least this was because of new developments in the early years of schooling and in technical and scientific education. Wormell, a headmaster at the time wrote:

> although the educational methods which are associated with the name of Froebel have been brought very near to perfection in the kindergarten, they are to a great extent suspended when the pupils passes from the infant school. They reappear, however, in the schools and colleges devoted to technical and experimental science . . . (*ibid*, p. 109)

He adds 'it is very desirable that we should bridge over the gap'.

The changes within the secondary sector themselves put further pressure on traditional mathematics. A member of the College of Preceptors wrote in 1903:

> The change was inevitable . . . when teachers began to teach science — as well as other subjects — scientifically and with more due regard to the pupils' share in education, when the demands of the laboratory and the workshop, of technical schools and colleges, made themselves felt, reform was bound to come in the *teaching* of mathematics . . . It is part of a general movement. (*ibid*, p. 113)

In fact the very pattern of cultural domination came under scrutiny. Charles Godfrey, a Cambridge man, taught by a Cambridge mathematician at school could nonetheless write:

> In England we have a ruling class whose interests are sporting, athletic and literary. They do not know, or if they know do not realize, that this Western civilization on which they are parasitic is based on applied mathematics. This defect will lead to difficulties, it is curable and the place for curing it is school. (Howson, 1982, p. 158)

Godfrey, as a result became heavily involved in the reform movement.

The general sense of crisis over school mathematics was captured by an article published in 1902 about the Perry Movement and Perry's gallant crusade:

In England almost alone has there been solid refusal to budge with the times on the part of university mathematical examiners and public school headmasters. They have stuck to the literal inspiration of their Euclid, and by their influential stolidity have retarded for more than a full generation the intellectual development of the British race. (Price, 1986, p. 113)

Perry's 'crusade' therefore seemed well-timed for concern about mathematics was being voiced by various dissenters. Price has summarized the major aspects in Perry's alternative paradigm:

1   Take account of the pupil's motivation and interests.
2   Base abstract ideas on concrete experience to promote understanding.
3   Employ activities involving the hand and eye, and not just the ear, in conjunction with the brain, and 'graphic(al)' methods in particular.
4   Adopt experimental and heuristic methods: 'Experiment, estimation, approximation, observation, induction, intuition, common sense are to have honoured places in every mathematical classroom in which the laboratory method has sway.'
5   Postpone logical rigour and any early concern for the foundations, and generally restrict the formal deductive elements, admitting various forms of 'proof'.
6   Simplify, broaden and unify the subject-matter of mathematics, ignoring traditional artificial divisions.
7   Correlate mathematics with science and laboratory work, and generally relate mathematics to life and its applications (*ibid*, p. 114).

The social and political values which Perry held were clear in a number of his pronouncements and here his challenge to England's ossified class structure was precise:

I hold a brief in the interests of average boys and men; any strong language and possible excess of zeal are due to the fact that nearly all the clever men have briefs on the other side. (*ibid*, p. 117)

Practical mathematics here saw as 'a system for teaching mathematics to all persons, of all kinds and all ages' (*ibid*, p. 115).

These kinds of values and Perry's social class background were anathema to the elite of Cambridge and the public schools. But the pressure to reform was now intense and this elite, as we have seen, found itself surrounded on all sides by reformists — even within its own ranks reformists were appearing. In 1899 the Department of Science and Art had adopted Perry's practical mathematics. More significantly in 1901 the Civil Service Commission which controlled examinations for army entrance took the decisive step to dispense with Euclid.

Reform therefore became inevitable for change was underway within the elite. Forsyth, who held the Sadleirian Chair of Mathematics at Cambridge, approached Charles Godfrey, the reformist mentioned earlier a mathematics master at Winchester

College, a leading public school. The catalyst was an invitation to Perry from the Education Section of the British Association to address their members on 'The teaching of mathematics' in September 1901.

It was clear to Forsyth that Perry's denunciation of school mathematics as it existed would receive widespread support ... Perry's syllabus would clearly have to be given serious consideration, but the syllabus and, one suspects, Perry himself were anathema to many pure mathematicians. Might not an alternative to Perry's proposals be found? (Howson, 1982, p. 148)

Forsyth, along with Godfrey, now played a major role in defining the reform of mathematics which Perry's crusade had made inevitable. Both the British Association and the Mathematical Association (formerly the Association for the Improvement of Geometrical Teaching, founded in 1894) played a role in this reform. But to the end the Mathematical Association remained reluctant to fully embrace change, even though it was undergoing a change of focus. Godfrey wrote:

On the eve of our liberation the Mathematical Association published a report on Geometry teaching, a very conservative report as it was considered impracticable to secure the abolition of the sequence (i.e. Euclid's). (Price, 1986, p. 120)

In the event the British Association's Committee on mathematical education chaired by Forsyth made much clearer recommendations for reform. Forsyth therefore retained a degree of control and privately sought to leave Godfrey a prime role in defining the reformed subject: 'he told Godfrey and Siddous that they were to be invited by Cambridge University Press to write a textbook on elementary geometry for use in schools'. In syllabus reform Oxford locals changed first, then London Matriculation and finally Cambridge. The exam changes at Cambridge were summarized as follows:

1   In demonstrative geometry, Euclid's Elements shall be optional as a textbook, and the sequence of Euclid shall not be enforced. The examiners will accept any proof of a proposition which they are satisfied forms part of a systematic treatment of the subject.
2   Practical geometry is to be introduced, along with deductive geometry, and questions will be set requiring careful draughtsmanship and the use of efficient drawing instruments.
3   In arithmetic, the use of algebraical symbols and processes will be permitted.
4   In algebra, graphs and squared paper work will be introduced; and a knowledge will be required of fractional indices and the use of four figure tables of logarithms. (*ibid*, p. 123)

Howson (1982) provides an elegant summary to this period in the reform of mathematical education. He concedes that Perry's views 'were to be translated into action in some quarters of the secondary school system'. However, he notes

Perry's methods made special demands on the intelligence of the teacher and few really understood him. One suspects that, taking into account the switch in bias of the higher grade schools as they were absorbed into the new state secondary system, it was the reforms acceptable to the academic Forsyth rather than the technical Perry which gained more general acceptance. Concessions were made to the scientist and engineer, but these were limited. More importantly, few concessions were made to the boys and girls who would end their mathematical education at the age of 16. (p. 151)

Since the latter group were Perry's major target group we can see how at the last gasp his social and political priorities were redirected by Cambridge and public school interest groups.

The analogies with a later period of reform, the 1960s, are considerable. In the earlier period there was a period of substantial reorganization in the new state secondary system. The reorientation of the higher-grade schools that had begin to articulate an alternative vision of education for their primarily working class clientele was being actively pursued. The outcomes were in some ways comparable to the manner in which the new comprehensive schools of the 1960s came to embrace the academic curriculum of the grammar schools rather than alternative paradigms of education developed in the secondary moderns and in pioneer comprehensive schools.

Moreover, some of the school textbooks in the 1900s provided remarkably similar approaches to those embraced by reformers of mathematical education in the 1960s. David Maris (1907) *A School Course of Mathematics* employed approaches very similar to the later School Mathematics Project *Book 1* published in 1965. Similarly W.J. Dobb's *A School Course of Geometry* (1913) anticipated many methods later embodied in School Mathematics Project texts.

In his book, *Renegotiating Secondary School Mathematics*, Barry Cooper (1985) identifies two distinct curricular traditions during the long, stable period in mathematics education which preceded the reforms of the 1960s. Independent, direct grant and grammar schools featured a modified version of the old curriculum of 'mathematics' based on Euclid.

The curriculum content was now — in these schools — arithmetic plus pre-1800 algebra, geometry and trigonometry, these all being taught and examined separately. (p. 37)

In other secondary schools the curriculum had a much greater emphasis on 'practical' arithmetic. While those placed in the top stream by ability might be given a course more like that of grammar schools, for boys of lesser ability and almost every girl, it was applied arithmetic related to everyday life — family budgets, industrial applications, or agricultural problems (*ibid*, pp. 44–6). Neither had much to do with university courses of study, though, which explored other branches of 'pure mathematics', along with new topics in applied maths, such as mathematical modelling and other areas of study made possible by new computer technology (*ibid*, pp. 54–7).

In the late 1950s the need for national strength in science and technology, and the rising employment of mathematicians in industry, fed a concern over the state of Britain's mathematics education (*ibid*, pp. 92–3 and 128). Funding increased dramatically after Sputnik awoke public opinion, but the initiatives had come earlier.

As mathematics reform became an issue throughout the Western world — reflecting a change in the relationship of school, mathematics and industry — citizens of each country worried about being left behind (Moon, 1986, pp. 197–9). The Royaumont Seminar, held in France in late 1959, and others in a series of international conferences, sought to turn these concerns into concrete changes (*ibid*, p. 44).

> The conclusions (of Royaumont), as well as arguing for the inclusion of modern algebra in school courses, also included arguments for the unification of traditional branches of elementary mathematics, possibly through a vector approach or 'motion geometry' (introduced into most West German schools in 1957, according to the survey results), for increased use of 'modern symbolism', for removing much of traditional school geometry and algebra, for ending the separate study of trigonometry, for introducing probability and statistics, and for more attention to be paid to preparing pupils for axiomatic approaches. (Cooper, 1985, p. 161)

At the end of the 1950s, two British conferences involved school teachers, university mathematicians and industrial representatives, all of whom wanted more 'modern' maths in the curriculum. Cooper describes these conferences as major sources of delegitimation for the existing curriculum. In particular, the industrial representatives attacked the academic, theoretical teaching of mathematics, seeking more 'real-world' mathematics (*ibid*, p. 104). This contrasted with the suggestions of the Royaumont Seminar, which had increased interest in pure algebra and geometry. By the end of the 1950s, then,

> pressure groups external to the schools, in the form of an alliance of university mathematicians, representing mainly the applied segment of the subject, and employers of graduate labour invested some of their considerable resources of time, money and status into conveying to teachers from the selective sector (who prepared their students and employees) their 'requirements' of the school curriculum. They legitimized these by reference to the nation's 'needs' for scientific and technological manpower. (*ibid*, p. 150)

When this debate first appeared on the pages of *The Times* it opened the issue of mathematics reform to the public — and made politicians take more notice. Tales of a drastic shortage of teachers, though not necessarily linked to curriculum reform, increased the sense of urgency (*ibid*, p. 165; Moon, 1986, p. 126). At this point, mathematicians were able to define both the issues and solutions ('modern mathematics,' especially the work of the modern algebraists) for politicians who took up the cause (Cooper, 1985, pp. 200–1).

A point had been reached, therefore, where, as a result of the activities of various interested groups and individuals, and particularly because the debate had become articulated with that on science and the economy, 'mathematics' — at least at school level — was likely to be subjected to some major redefinition for the first time in many years. Potential redefiners (. . .) were now in a situation where resources might well be expected to become available and, furthermore, the climate of opinion was such that those supporting current definitions would inevitably find themselves on the defensive. (*ibid*, p. 221)

The struggle thus shifted to a battle over the nature of the inevitable reforms (*ibid*, pp. 223–31). This resulted in two multi-school projects on the American 'Research and Development' model — the new gospel spread since 1958 by the (American) School Mathematics Study Group (SMSG). Both the School Mathematics Project (SMP) and the Midlands Mathematical Experiment aimed to produce school texts and emphasized modern algebraic study, though the SMP proved much more successful (*ibid*, pp. 235–74). The Association of Teachers of Mathematics (ATM) also promoted new conceptions of pedagogy and of modern algebra.

As for primary school maths, Bob Moon (1986) explains:

Inevitably, the promotion of SMP was matched by an increasing interest in primary mathematics. Accepting the case for reform at the secondary level led inevitably to a review of primary practice. Almost parallel, therefore, with the SMP launch, in 1963, a number of people were proposing a similar project for the primary age range and this marks the point when the Nuffield story begins. (p. 127)

At this time the Nuffield foundation had already sponsored projects in science and French.

'Nuffield Maths' was formally launched in September 1964. This date could be seen as marking the beginning of the British response to the international movement for mathematics reform at the primary level. Nuffield, and offshoots of the project, were to dominate development for a decade or more. (*ibid*, p. 122)

As Nuffield project leaders took the work of Piaget and 'discovery learning' seriously, they resisted the production of textbooks or pupil material, and published teachers' guides only haphazardly — leading to problems with dissemination (*ibid*, pp. 135–40). By contrast, the popularity and status implications of SMP texts — aimed originally at only those students deemed most able — soon led them to move 'downwards'. This left them exposed when the conservative reaction started to blame school maths for a variety of ills in Britain's economy and society (Cooper, 1985, pp. 255–6).

When, as an unintended consequence of the employers' initial activities, the actual redefinition, which included as a result of intra-subject politics some modern algebraic emphases, became established 'lower down' the system, many employers of non-graduate labour reacted negatively. (*ibid*, p. 282)

As Moon (1986) points out, this backlash was symbolized in the public vocabulary by the use of more ambiguous term 'new maths' to describe what had been called 'modern mathematics' (p. 141).

By the end of the 1960s, the focus of curriculum change had turned to questions of implementation. Research replaced reform as the central concern (*ibid*, pp. 58–9).

> The thrust of debate had moved away from modern mathematics versus traditional mathematics or reform versus status quo towards a more diversified assembly of interests and problems. (. . .) The previously taken for granted relation between modern/new mathematics and reform was questioned by many. (*ibid*, p. 60)

> The cause of the 'new maths' which had dominated the first decade of reform became almost an historical issue and the noisy warfare of the protagonists became subdued by the expansion of mathematics education into a plethora of interrelated fields of enquiry. Mathematics educators as a group came to adopt a more neutral stance towards policy issues. (*ibid*, p. 68)

The great hope of the 1960s — the massive curriculum projects — started to founder.

> As the alliance of interests around reform, and, therefore, around the project, began to crumble so the institutional base for such professionalized activities had to move. A change from professional reformers to professional, academic researchers is noticeable in each of the case studies. . . . the decline of the project was in part a reflection of the movement away from the transitory form of such activities by those with most personal interest in them. The newly-emerging group of mathematics educators were to see reform type projects as too flimsy a base on which to establish a professional future. (*ibid*, pp. 209–10)

The 1970s saw the conservative backlash continue and grow, a loss of interest in reform, and a tightening of resources. A direct progression from the *Black Paper on Education* (1970), through Callaghan's 1976 Ruskin College speech, led to the Cockcroft Committee, appointed in 1978. Politicians and representatives of industry alike returned to old rallying cries, and raised the issue of standards (*ibid*, pp. 155–8). Meanwhile, as Nuffield wound down, the locus of curriculum innovation widened, but also became more diffuse. Then the Bullock Report of 1975 turned primary school teachers' attention away from mathematics to language (*ibid*, p. 145).

The Statutory National Curriculum introduced into England and Wales in 1988 produced traditional content-oriented subjects in the main, and mathematics was no exception. The attainment targets in mathematics present largely a content list with only one attainment target identified in process terms (Burton, 1992, p. 162). Suggestions in the guidance to teachers emphasise a questioning, student-driven curriculum but this is contradicted by the assessment instruments (*ibid*, p. 163). Cooper (1992) concurs with this stance and adds that when 'real' and 'practical' problems are included in some test items, they disadvantage working-class children because they are 'less likely to step outside of an 'everyday' frame of reference' (*ibid*, p. 241).

The struggle for mathematics continues but it is evident that proponents of interpretative/negotiation of meaning approaches (Burton, 1992, p. 163) are not in the ascendancy and this means to some commentators that 'school mathematics continues to serve the interests of a privileged minority' (Willis, 1988, p. 16). The Dearing Reports may pose further threats to mathematics teaching and to the validity of the assessment of mathematical achievement (Cooper, 1995).

Mathematics in the USA

Arithmetic was simply not taught in seventeenth-century American schools, and only taught to children over 10 or 12 in eighteenth-century public schools. This latter group represented a very small minority of the population, though other students also picked it up from private schools or tutors (Cohen, 1982, pp. 118–23). In addition, Patricia Cline Cohen tell us, 'arithmetic instruction remained inflexible and barren of innovation throughout the eighteenth century' (*ibid*, p. 125).

Widespread changes in attitudes to arithmetic occurred around 1800.

> Arithmetic had been thought of as a body of numerical rules and definitions that applied primarily to commercial life; arithmetic had no other uses, in the popular view, and only certain groups of people needed to know it. But at the end of the eighteenth century arithmetic began to lose its commercial taint because more applications were evident and because commerce itself was no longer restricted to a small segment of the American population. (*ibid*, p. 117)

The commercial revolution stimulated reckoning skills and pulled more people into the market economy at the same time as the political revolution created a state which used statistics as proof of its own effectiveness (*ibid*).

> These were the years when increasing numbers of people were drawn into a commercialized economy requiring a competence in the fundamentals of arithmetic. New economic, religious, and political ideas all stimulated the

spread of reckoning skills and contributed to the prestige of numbers and quantification, a prestige that had become very great by the antebellum decades. (*ibid*, p. 12)

Teachers taught an approach to problem solving based on memory, not understanding; students had to find the memorized rule which applied to a given situation. Partly this resulted from the subject's nature at the time.

Arithmetic was a commercial subject through and through and was therefore burdened with the denominations of commerce. Addition was not merely simple addition with abstract numbers, it was the art of summing up compound numbers in many denominations — pounds, shillings, pence; gallons, quarts, and pints (differing in volume depending on the substance being measured); acres and rods, pounds and ounces (both troy and avoirdupois), firkins and barrels, and so on. (*ibid*, p. 121)

The change to a decimal money system, after 1792, made arithmetic more accessible, while creating a demand for new, American, texts.

When 'the self-consciously utilitarian spirit of the new nation invaded education and elevated arithmetic to the status of a basic skill along with reading and writing' (*ibid*, p. 127), it was because arithmetic could teach students to think (*ibid*, pp. 130–3).

As widespread rational thinking came to be perceived as necessary to the workings of democracy, educators looked to mathematics as the ideal way to prepare a republican citizenry. (*ibid*, p. 149)

With all the new emphasis on arithmetic as a foundation for rational thinking, it became especially clear that eighteenth-century texts, based on memory work at the expense of logic, had to be completely revised. A revamped arithmetic that fostered rationality through mental discipline had to be simplified so that young children could not only learn it but understand it. (*ibid*, p. 133)

Instruction in arithmetic thus evolved from the memorization of rules, to drills in the four basic operations (*ibid*, p. 134). This was supplemented in the first decades of the nineteenth century by the manipulation of physical objects, such as counters — 'mental arithmetic'.

The conventional notion that arithmetic was a memory-based subject fit only for mature minds and chiefly a preparation for business was completely overturned. (*ibid*)

Over the course of the nineteenth century, topics in mathematics moved down the age ladder in schooling. As each level of education instituted new entrance requirements, the curriculum of the preceding level was altered. Thus algebra and geometry, as college entrance requirements, came to dominate the secondary school curriculum — especially at the 'academies' which taught a classical program comprising Latin, Greek and mathematics. Similarly, advanced arithmetic work flowed down into the elementary schools, after high school entrance exams came to emphasize complex problems (Jones and Coxford, 1970, p. 27; Krug, 1969, p. 94).

At the middle of the century, the dominant form of mathematics pedagogy — the use of inductive problem solving, based on Warren Colburn's books — faced a challenge from a more deductive approach. The 'science of numbers' started students with general rules, from which they solved specific problems (Jones and Coxford, 1970, pp. 25–6). Yet this approach was itself overturned when the 'Quincy system' (introduced in the 1870s) returned primary level arithmetic to an inductive, object-based, pedagogy (Cremin, 1968, pp. 129–30).

At the secondary level, the concept of 'mental training' or 'faculty discipline' triumphed as the central goal of schooling by the last decades of the century.

> Arithmetic instruction seemed particularly suited to the development of reasoning and the will, among other faculties. (DeVault and Weaver, 1970, p. 99)

The perceived value of the subject in strengthening students' ability to think resulted in a push for widespread mathematics training in high schools, with a particular concentration on complex work and mental arithmetic (*ibid*, p. 102; Stanic, 1986, pp. 210–3).

This phase ended in the early part of the twentieth century, when followers of the social efficiency movement argued that the point of school maths should be to teach those skills and items of knowledge which would be applicable to everyday, practical problems in life. The curriculum, then, should feature such issues as cooking problems, or the calculation of prices (Cremin, 1968, p. 195). Moreover, supporters of social efficiency felt that a sixth grade comprehension would suffice for the majority of students; subjects such as algebra were of no use except for that tiny minority heading for specialized careers (Krug, 1969, pp. 308–9). They were supported by a few concerned individuals who feared that the pressure and complexity of mathematics threatened to do harm to students (*ibid*, p. 347). As a result,

> both in terms of requirements for high school graduation and in terms of percentage enrollments in traditional mathematics courses, mathematics as a school subject was in a state of decline during the early years of the twentieth century. (Stanic, 1986, p. 214)

Between the wars, the focus on social utility slowly faded from mathematics teaching. At the same time, the sudden popularity of junior high schools meant

> the elementary school came to focus its attention on the K-6 program. In mathematics this program consisted, in the main, of arithmetic. The major

emphasis was on the computational aspects of that subject. As a result the critical issues in the elementary school did not develop around the question of what to teach, but rather about *when* and *how* to present the agreed-upon arithmetic concepts. The issues centered about (1) the *readiness* of youngsters to learn mathematical ideas and manipulative skills, (2) the *postponement* of instruction in arithmetic based on an assumed lack of readiness, (3) the dependence upon *incidental learning* of mathematics mainly via projects, (4) a new psychologically based stress on teaching for *meaning* and *understanding*, and (5) the role of *drill*. (Jones and Coxford, 1970, p. 48)

While senior high schools continued to emphasize divided approaches to mathematics, a new concept — general mathematics — did move into some grade 9 classrooms (*ibid*, p. 53).

The general mathematics concept was based on a reorganization of school mathematics that deemphasized compartmentalization. In essence it was to consist of a sound, gradual development of algebra, geometry, trigonometry, and introductory statistics throughout the six years of secondary school, a development that would stress interrelationships.

For grades 7 and 8 the general mathematics concept was extensively accepted, probably because it conformed to the philosophy that the junior high school was to be exploratory in nature and because text materials were available. For the grades above the eighth, general mathematics as defined here, although repeatedly urged, has never been generally accepted. (*ibid*, pp. 51–2)

Developments in pedagogical theories led to two new approaches to maths instruction in the 1930s and 1940s. One stressed 'meaning', and teaching students to think about problems, while the 'readiness theory' stressed the careful study of the student's ability to learn mathematical concepts. Implementation, though, lagged far behind rhetorical support (DeVault and Weaver, 1970, pp. 131–2).

Despite the impressive new theories of the progressive era, and the experimentation with new methods — such as the project-centred approach — the content of mathematics education had changed little. Mathematics, as practised in the universities, and in technological industries, moved further and further beyond the stuff of elementary and high school classrooms.

By 1955, partly as a result of the unrest growing out of World War II, the lay public throughout the country had been told in magazine articles and in books that the academic substance of the school curriculum was grossly inadequate. It was sad that the content not only of mathematics but of other subjects as well had for too long been determined by professional educators with little or no impact from the scholars of the various disciplines.

Aroused both by these reports in the mass media and by personal concern, academicians turned their attention to the school curriculum. (Jones and Coxford, 1970, p. 76)

Other cries of 'teacher shortage' linked to a fear that the Soviet Union was winning the important technology battles in the Cold War (Aichele, 1988, p. 4).

As a result, the 1950s saw many curricular projects — of different sizes and varying ambitions — set up to explore the reform of mathematics education. In 1958 professional mathematicians founded the most famous of these, the School Mathematics Study Group. SMSG brought an intensive, research and development approach to mathematics reform. Team members wrote experimental materials, which were tried out by selected classroom teachers (with support from the project team) and then revised on the basis of this experience before publication (Wooton, 1965).

A chief spur to this movement was the National Defence Education Act of 1958, itself primarily a result of public outcry over the Sputnik launch. NDEA provided generous funding for existing and new projects, most of them controlled by university mathematicians, with schools left as simply the final user of new curricular materials (Kliebard, 1986, pp. 266–8).

According to Osborne and Crosswhite (1970),

In the early years of the revolution, the hallmark of the new programs became their extensive use of the concepts, terminology, and symbolism of sets. This was a brand-new area in school mathematics. (p. 282)

A 'back to basics' reaction started in the late 1960s for several reasons, including the curriculum reform movement's narrow focus on college-bound students. The backlash took the form of a 'basic skills' campaign. Opponents used a common feature, the use of other number bases for calculations, as a focus for popular resistance to the 'new maths' (*ibid*, p. 283). Mathematics teachers and reformers soon recognized the power of this resistance, and the pace and range of curriculum change slowed dramatically in the 1970s.

Yet new initiatives emerged in the mid-1980s as part of a drive for national standards. The National Council of Teachers of Mathematics (NCTM) was the first subject area to develop a standards document in 1986 (O'Neil, 1993, p. 8). The 'Curriculum and Evaluation Standards for School Mathematics' advocates four basic standards relating to problem solving, reasoning, communication and linkages with the real world (Romberg, 1993, p. 37). Many states are revising their curriculum frameworks to reflect the standards and some new performance assessments are being used (O'Neil, 1993, p. 8). Yet, research studies indicate that to date, only small numbers of teachers are aware of the NCTM standards (NCTM, 1992) and are actively experimenting with teaching methods congruent with the standards (Sosniak, Ethington and Varclas, 1991, pp. 119–31).

As we have seen the early growth and development of school mathematics in the United Kingdom was to a large extent dominated by the teaching of Euclid.

Attempts at reform were short-lived until the emergence of John Perry and supporters developed a new paradigm of practical mathematics. In the USA a more practical, general mathematics, emerges in the 1940s. The 1950s saw the development of national curriculum projects as a result of public outcry over the Sputnik launch (School Mathematics Study Group), to be followed by Nuffield Mathematics in the UK in the 1960s. Public demands for 'back to the basics' and criticisms of 'new mathematics' waxed and waned in both countries prior to the establishing of a National Curriculum in the UK in 1988 and the emergence of National Standards in the USA in 1986.

Reflections and Issues

1 Do you consider that there is still a major gulf between those educators who support an academic tradition and those who support a utilitarian tradition in mathematics? Give examples from schools or areas with which you are familiar.

2 To what extent do modern mathematics subjects 'relate mathematics to life and its applications', as exhorted by Perry in the early 1890s? Describe any school mathematics topics that you are aware of and that appear to be focussed upon this goal.

3 What parallels are there between the genesis of 'Science of Common Things' and the Perry Movement for a more practical mathematics? Examine in particular the facilitating and inhibiting forces at work in both instances.

4 The NCTM standards contend that a new curriculum is needed to produce mathematical power, with a citizenry and society empowered by mathematics. What are some implications for teachers, students and parents and how achievable is the goal?

5. To what extent do you support the stance that school mathematics serves the interests of largely middle-class males? Can this assertion be substantiated empirically? If so, what initiatives should be taken to counteract it?

Suggested Reading

Useful articles include:

Burton, L. (1992) 'Evaluating an "entitlement curriculum". Mathematics for all', *The Curriculum Journal*, **3**, 2.

Cooper, B. (1992) 'Testing National Curriculum Mathematics: Some critical comments on the treatment of "real" contexts for mathematics', *The Curriculum Journal*, **3**, 3, pp. 231–243.

Horwood, J. (1994) 'Towards control of a mathematics curriculum', *Curriculum Perspectives*, **14**, 1, pp. 11–16.

Hunting, R.P. (1987) 'Issues shaping school mathematics curriculum development in Australia', *Curriculum Perspectives*, **7**, 1, pp. 29–38.

Useful books include:

Cohen, P.C. (1982) *A Calculating People: The Spread of Numeracy in Early America*. Chicago: University of Chicago Press.

Cooper, B. (1985) *Renegotiating Secondary School Mathematics A Study of Curriculum Change and Stability*, London and Washington, DC: Falmer Press.

Howson, A.G. (1982) *History of Mathematics Education in England*, Cambridge University Press.

Moon, B. (1986) *The 'New Maths' Curriculum Controversy*. London and Washington, DC: Falmer Press.

Price, M.H. (Ed) (1986) *The Development of the Secondary Curriculum*, London, Sydney and Dover: Croom Helm.

Chapter 8

Subject Histories: English

Early Developments

In recent years, the social history of English as a curriculum area and of English teaching has been the subject of a good deal of historical investigation. The reasons for this 'turn to history' are varied but a primary reason has been the recognition that literacy, what Bill Green (1993) calls 'the insistence of the letter', is implicated in the very symbolic structure of schooling and curriculum as well as of intrinsic interest in terms of the history of English itself. Tony Burgess (1993) has made this point in a recent article:

> There has been a gradual recognition in English teaching that these broader, social issues lurk within literacy . . . English teaching may be described as having shifted in its focus from a concentration on the processes of reading towards an understanding of wider literacy. In doing so, it has rediscovered history. (pp. 107–8)

The significance of the earlier absence of focus on history and sociology has been commented on by Allan Luke (1993):

> Unfortunately, literacy education in its practical syllabus forms — language arts, reading, children's literature, secondary composition, English as a second language, and so forth — typically fails to connect with critical histories and sociologies of curriculum. By default as much as by design, decisions about practice in curriculum planning agencies, editorial offices and staffrooms are more likely to be based upon, for example, student needs hierarchies, ability grouping and standardized tests, organic growth and process models, learning styles, cognitive hierarchies and skill taxonomies and other commonplace approaches to curriculum, than they are to be based upon articulated understandings of how languages and literacies work in communities and institutions. These are the political legacies of modernist literacy curriculum which continue to exert a powerful influence over schooling, even as it turns to address postmodern economic, social and political conditions. (p. viii)

English, then, provides an interesting subject area for viewing patterns of change but also of remarkable continuity both in terms of the development of this curriculum area but also in terms of the symbolic structures of state schooling. Ian Michael's work on the early origins of English teaching, points to continuities in many issues and concerns. Two central concerns are the place of 'talk' in the process of learning English and the place of grammar. Even in the early stages there were those who argued against the teaching of English as the teaching of grammatical classifications. Michael (1987) quotes Horne Tooke who lists in 1829 'thirty-eight "kinds" of conjunction in order to illustrate the farrago of useless distinctions . . . which explain nothing' (p. 322).

Michael's work discerns some patterns in the development of English but 'to talk of stages is to oversimplify what is a complex pattern of changes occurring at different times, at different speeds and with differing degrees of stability. To put dates to the stages or to the entry of particular components is to over-simplify still further.' Nonetheless he argues 'it may be helpful to make the attempt though the result is crude, and suggests a precision that it cannot offer'. Like other subjects, English is a compromise of different component parts.

> At first, besides reading and spelling, there were two main components, grammar and rhetoric, overlapping but separately designated. Minor components were logic, overlapping slightly with grammar, and pronunciation, treated usually as a part of both spelling and grammar but overlapping slightly with rhetoric.
>
> In a second stage the expressive and interpretative aspects of rhetoric tended to separate, so that there were three major components, closer together in that they often appeared in the same vernacular curriculum and sometimes, but not often, shared the name 'English'.
>
> In a third stage the alliance was still closer in that the name 'English' was more widely applied, but each component (literature, composition, grammar) could invoke its autonomy when desired. Pronunciation was linked with some of the performance aspects of expressive rhetoric and, as elocution, was at times a major component.
>
> In a fourth stage there were added two additional components: the historical study of both literature and language. (*ibid*, p. 379)

Michael therefore provide a tentative outline of the pre-history of the emergent subject from early times to the mid-19th century:

> From early times reading, spelling and pronunciation; some oral expression; perhaps some drama, for which there is no textbook evidence.
> By 1525   Some written expression.
> By 1550   Snatches of literature.
> By 1586   Grammar.
> By 1650   More substantial literature; more sustained written expression.

By 1720   Some explicit teaching of literature; linguistic exercises in, or derived from, grammar and rhetoric.
By 1730   Elocution.
By 1750   More substantial dramatic work.
By 1770   More sustained teaching of literature; more attention to language and written expression.
By 1820   History of the language.
By 1850   History of literature. (*ibid*, p. 381)

Whilst Michael's study takes us to the mid-nineteenth century, fortunately Shayer's British study of English teaching 1900–1970 provides a valuable chronological extension to Michael's work. In reviewing the state of English in 1900, he comments on 'the careful division of English into quite separate components — almost into separate subjects — and the fact that the overall term "English" is applied to the grammar work' (Shayer, 1972, p. 5). The Board of Education's 1900 English guidelines for elementary schools confirm these points:

Standard 1   (7 years)
Reading   To read a short passage from a book not confined to words of one syllable.
Writing   Copy in manuscript characters a line of print, commencing with a capital letter. Copy books to be shown.
'English'   Pointing out nouns.
Standard 2   (8 years)
Reading   To read a short passage from an elementary reading book.
Writing   A passage of not more than six lines, from the same book, slowly read once and then dictated.
'English'   Pointing out nouns and verbs.
Standard 3   (9 years)
Reading   To read from a reading book.
Writing   Six lines from one of the reading books of the standard, read once and then dictated.
'English'   Pointing out nouns, verbs, adjectives, adverbs, personal pronouns and forming simple sentences containing them.
Standard 4   (10 years)
Reading   To read a passage from a reading book or history of England.
Writing   Eight lines of poetry or prose, slowly read once, then dictated.
'English'   Parsing easy sentences, and showing by examples the use of each of the parts of speech.
Standard 5   (11 years)
Reading   To read a passage from some standard author, or reading book, or history of England.
Writing   Writing from memory the substance of a short story read out twice; spelling, handwriting and correct expression to be considered.

'English'	Parsing and analysis of simple sentences. The method of forming English nouns, adjectives, and verbs from each other.
Standard 6	**(12 years)**
Reading	To read a passage from one of Shakespeare's historical plays, or from some other standard author, or from a history of England.
Writing	A short theme or letter on an easy subject; spelling, handwriting and composition to be considered.
'English'	Parsing and analysis of a short complex sentence. The meaning and use of the most common Latin prefixes in the formation of English words.
Standard 7	**(13 years)**
Reading	To read a passage from Shakespeare or Milton, or from some other standard author, or from a history of England.
Writing	A theme or letter. Composition, spelling and handwriting to be considered.
'English'	Analysis of sentences. The most common prefixes and terminations generally. (*ibid*, pp. 4–5)

Whilst English was therefore taught in the elementary schools (predominantly for the working class), at secondary level the subject's position was weak and politically somewhat precarious. Some researchers have linked late nineteenth century moral panics to the teaching of literature, as morality would teach the new urban workers how to behave, and ensure that women (who had taken an increasing share of responsibility for the formal education of children) passed on the 'English spirit' to boys in their care (Ball, Kenny and Gardiner, 1990, pp. 48–50; Doyle, 1982, pp. 23–4). Court (1992) argues, 'the inherently class-conscious and racially ethnic character of British education produced a discipline far more explicitly concerned with social and ethnographical issues than its American counterpart' (p. 2).

This also applied to the Empire — that 'great classroom for the teaching of English' (Morgan, 1990, p. 210). English study, especially Shakespeare, would homogenize the Empire and then the world. By the turn of the century nation, Empire, race and language had become 'inextricably linked' (*ibid*, p. 218). In 1904 the Board of Education sought to strengthen the subject's position by including in the Secondary Regulations a directive that all State secondary schools should offer English language and literature. However, in the high status public and grammar schools, English remained outside the mainstream curriculum where 'classics' still predominated.

Likewise in the universities, the subject remained undeveloped. While Franklin Court's work locates the origins of English study in Scotland, where people felt that it would be crucial to their economic development after the accession of James VI of Scotland to England's throne, Brian Doyle traces it back further, to an emergent sense of cultural nationalism following the Tudor break with Rome (Court, 1992, pp. 17–18; Doyle, 1982, pp. 19–22).

In the middle of the eighteenth century Hugh Blair called for appreciation, and a fixed literary culture, while Adam Smith applied a novel moral argument to the study of literature.

> What he actually initiated was an attitude toward English literary study that taught that truly 'great' writers, by virtue of their sterling characters, reinforce the natural moral authority that claimed to be the theoretical base of free-market capitalism. The great challenge was to eliminate the spectre of self-serving corruption that threatened the dream of *laissez-faire*. The ideal economic order was attainable and English literature would have a place in the transmission of values and standards by which the dream would be realized.
>
> Smith secured the bond between literary study and the values of the middle class by imbuing each with a respectability that, thanks to the economic gains enjoyed by the mercantile class in the second half of the century, also carried with it the belief that reading 'literature' was a way to gain the cultivation that historically had been the province of the educated aristocracy. After the eighteenth century, 'literature' would serve to sustain the authority of the middle class, not just the authority of royalty and institutionalized religion. (Court, 1992, pp. 28–9)

> The teaching of 'Rhetoric and *Belles-Lettres*' was established at first at the margins of power and status in Scotland and the English Dissenting Academies, and eventually found a place in the curriculum of the first English utilitarian college (University College, London, founded in the 1820s) as 'English language and literature'. And when university colleges were founded in provincial cities later in the nineteenth century, some provision was usually made for instruction in 'English and history'. (Doyle, 1989, p. 11)

With the triumph of philology — the scientific study of literature — in the late 1830s, rhetoric and composition lost place, and literature studies became subservient at University College, however.

> In contrast to the English program at University College, which was optional, King's College made English part of the core curriculum and combined it with the study of history. In April, 1830, the college advertised for a professor to teach English literature and 'modern history and other subjects'.
>
> It was a key moment in the history of English studies, for combining English literature with history for the first time initiated a movement that, as the century progressed, aligned literary study even more closely with the representational value of literature. Literature came to be taken as a symbolic index to history. It served the need to find in the past traditional precedents that made current conceptions of progress and politics congruent with growing ideals of English nationalism. (Court, 1992, p. 87)

> By the 1850s, English literary study began to represent 'culture' as the heritage of an accumulated ineluctable racial memory upon which the ideological framework of western civilization was constructed. (*ibid*, p. 78)

London University's first professorship in English language and literature was designated in 1828 (Court, 1988, pp. 796–807) and the first English matriculation examination paper was set in 1839 but was primarily English as grammar. Not until twenty years later was English literature accepted for the Bachelor of Arts course. Whilst newer provincial universities began to teach the subject, the major universities of Oxford and Cambridge combined to stand aloof. 'Oxford resisted the subject until almost the end of the century, and then admitted it only grudgingly in the compromise form of philology and Old English studies, while Cambridge, although emphasizing the purely literary side much more from the very beginning, was equally cautious' (Shayer, 1972, p. 3).

English in Twentieth Century England

The 1904 directive from the Board of Education was a crucial historical watershed in establishing English as a secondary school subject. Before this directive Ball has judged that 'there were certainly very few teachers who could be called or would have called themselves teachers of English' (Ball, 1985a, p. 53). In scrutinizing the development of English as a school subject he describes the founding of the English Association as a second important milestone. He quotes the recollection of Boas that 'as classics, history, modern languages and other subjects had supporting associations one was needed to uphold the claims in education and otherwise of the mother tongue' (*ibid*, p. 55).

Doyle (1989) has argued that the foundation of the English Association in 1907 was both an indication of the declining power of classics and an assertion that English could play a key role in the generation of a national and imperial culture:

> One of the signs of the eclipse of classics by English was the foundation in 1907 of the English Association which was to propound very effectively the view that the new discipline had become 'our finest vehicle for a genuine humanistic education' and that 'its importance in this respect was growing with the disappearance of Latin and Greek from the curricula of our schools and universities'. However, the eventual transference from the classical curriculum to a modern alternative, and the enhancement of English and Englishness which was one of its major products, drew on the raw materials provided by the scholarly work of the middle decades of the nineteenth century. In the process of inventing the new English, these materials were substantially transformed to serve a national and imperial culture. (p. 21)

Doyle sees the English Association as a major pressure group for promoting English through the new Board of Education whose 1904 Secondary Regulations included English:

> The English Association was set up to promote the maintenance of 'correct use of English, spoken and written', the recognition of English as 'an essential element in the national education', and the discussion of teaching methods and advanced study as well as the correlation of school with university work. From the beginning, personnel attached to the new Board of Education seem to have been sympathetic to the view of English as the most natural candidate to lead a mission of cultural renewal: at any rate, from its inception the English Association set out to ensure that such was the case. (*ibid*, p. 31)

Central to the Associations' early development of its mission was the need to develop a 'university discipline' and a university power base. In this respect Ball (1985a) states the: 'intellectual battle to establish English as a discipline in schools was closely related to and allied with the very similar battle to establish English as a contemporary discipline in the universities' (p. 56). This was essentially because the problem that English faced was that 'in common with some other subjects which emerged in the school curriculum during this period, the advocates of English had no established academic 'plausibility structure' and no extant epistemic community available in the universities to further their cause' (*ibid*, p. 57).

The development of a university base for English had begun in the Dissenting Academies and in London but up until the late nineteenth century there was little substantial change. English was largely associated with its main existing clienteles; women and the working class. As Doyle (1989) notes:

> Before 1880 most teaching of languages and literature was either associated with women, or allied to the utilitarian pursuit of functional literacy, and therefore occupied a dramatically lower cultural status than the upper-class masculine studies of classics and mathematics. Furthermore, although by the nineteenth century the education of upper-class males was carried out largely through the medium of English, the most valued subject matter (intellectual and symbolic) was contained in, or based upon, works in the classical languages of Latin and Greek. During this period, therefore, the very notion of an academic discipline devoted to the study of English (as opposed to teaching that was incidental to familiarization with the classics), and especially English literature, would have made little sense within the universities. Looking at the subsequent history one's faced with an unlikely course of events: low status symbolic materials were transformed into a high status discipline which came to occupy a central place within the national curriculum. (pp. 2–3)

English then worked its passage from low to high status, from the periphery to the centre:

In fact, it was largely through the middle-class and scientific bias of the new provincial colleges that English language, literature and history came to serve as a so-called 'poor man's classics', and it was only at the very end of the century that Oxbridge became sufficiently concerned to begin to succumb to the then 'national demand' for such studies and introduce new 'schools' and 'tripos' regulations that would allow the ancient institutions to take a lead in these new areas. Oxbridge, then, was only lifted to the apex of the study of English language, literature, and history when it was subjected to the demands for national efficiency and leadership. (*ibid*, pp. 24–5)

Taking a different viewpoint, John Dixon (1991), in *A Schooling in English*, argues that the late nineteenth century university extension movement represented pressure not from a hegemonic elite, but from people at the bottom of the social scale (pp. 2–7). It was there that 'an alternative method of teaching literature was invented' (*ibid*, p. 7).

Central to the analysis of the 'passage' of English is the nature of the subject as a gendered discipline. Inglis (1995) has seen this in optimistic light 'since the making of English literature as a serious intellectual subject at Cambridge in the 1920s, the preponderance of its students have been women, and its great significance has also been as a strong, sweeping current of liberation in the great tide of the women's movement as it has begun to come in over the past thirty-odd years' (p. 119). But a far more negative case can be made about the nature of English as a gendered discipline and the passages for status and resources that were travelled. Dennis Baron (1986) has written about the ongoing, relations between grammar and gender.

The catalogue of opinions about women and language is both copious and negative, and much of what follows can be characterised as a history of shame. Although it cannot be stressed too strongly that such opinions are based on a combination of myth and misogyny rather than on linguistic fact and that many of them are so absurd as to be laughable, their compilation in this volume presents what can be viewed as a depressing litany of insults. (p. 9)[1]

This point has been more generally made by Bill Green (1993b).

If 'insistence of the letter' involves an assertion of the signifier over the signified (crudely, of 'form' over 'meaning' or 'content') and also refers to the 'significant materiality' of language and textuality, then there is also a need to recognize and stress the *gender* dimensions and implications of this position. The 'return of the repressed' in culture and schooling is to be conceived, as much as anything else, as a reference to the fluid and the 'irrational' the so-called 'promiscuous', the dynamics associated with the priority of becoming over being, and the assertion of the interpersonal over the ideational aspects of schooling, which can be mapped readily onto the ideological category 'woman' — thus evoking the general binary (man:woman) which has figured so prominently in Western thought as well as modern(ist) schooling. The first term is always effectively privileged over the second, in a similar fashion to the relations between signifiers and signifieds in hegemonic regimes of knowledge and signification. In this regard it is important to note that Lacan (1977) explicitly associates his formulation of the insistence and agency of the letter with 'Reason since Freud', thus evoking the crisis of those forms of Cartesian rationality and subjectivity that have for so long been foundational to the phallogocentric culture of modernism. This highlights the gender politics deeply inscribed in the current-traditional forms of curriculum and literacy, and the need accordingly to call into question the hegemonic regimes of gender and genre in the project of rational schooling, as well as those current research practices which effectively sustain them. (pp. 117–18)

Despite the ranges of diversity within English, conflict lines began to be drawn after 1906 in ways that effected the relationship between English as a school subject and English as an emergent university discipline. During the period after World War One English became firmly established as a school subject, distinct from the previous broad study of the national culture (Doyle, 1989, pp. 27–8; Ball, Kenny and Gardiner, 1990, p. 52).

Victory over Germany in the First World War heralded a restoration of national pride and an upsurge of patriotic feeling; a sense of national mission and identity, which had been lacking as the capitalist crises deepened in the build up to the Great War, was evident once again. The goal, as the new educators saw it, was to force home the advantage and promote English as the subject which could lock onto, and act as a focus for, this new national pride. (Ball, Kenny and Gardiner, 1990, p. 51)

During the 1910s and 1920s this 'battle for English' was fought on both external and internal fronts.

On the one hand it was a territorial dispute between English as a subject and classics. On the other hand there were the origins of an internecine dispute within English about the definition of the subject a dispute between the view of the subject as 'grammar' and other views of the subject. As we have seen a tension between English as a language and English as literacy study was there from early times. This was to gather force in the twentieth century. Shayer speaks of English as a substitute for classics and links this to the 'classical fallacy'. The origin of this fallacy

lies in the uneasy transition from the almost exclusive study of the classics as the one true literary discipline to the acceptance of English at the turn of the century, with the belief that despite its pale substitute nature, it

(English) could be respectable — providing (and only providing) it was treated 'classically'. (Shayer, 1972, p. 6)

Shayer examines textbooks such as L.C. Cornford's *English Composition, 1900*, where

> we find the business of writing English expanded into an incredibly com-
> plicated and tortuous process. Before even pen can be set to paper a score
> of difficult rules must be mastered and sundry models carefully studied.
> Here, in short, is English composition presented in the worst Latin man-
> ner, with all the spontaneity crushed and an air of deadly aridity hanging
> over the process. What is so false in such an approach is the assumption
> that writing in one's own language is purely a matter of externals, the
> confronting of a mental obstacle course that the writer will best get through
> if he keeps his personal feelings in abeyance. (*ibid*, p. 7)

In 1891 John Churton Collins in his *The Study of English Literature* had written:

> Since its recognition as a subject of teaching it (English literature) has
> been taught whenever it has been seriously taught on the same principle
> as the classics. It has been regarded not as the expression of art and
> genius, but as mere material for the study of words, as mere pabulum for
> philology. All that constitutes its value as a liberal study has been ignored.
> Its masterpieces have been resolved into exercises in grammar, syntax,
> and etymology. Its history has been resolved into a barren catalogue of
> names, works, and dates. No faculty but the faculty of memory has been
> called into play in studying it. (*ibid*)

In 1921, the Newbolt Report was produced by a committee appointed by the Board of Education and comprising mainly members of the English-associated. 'On the basis of its deliberations the Committee proposed a strategy for national cultural renewal by means of a system of education led by the universities, and with English as the central pedagogic instrument for the gaining of nationally valuable experience' (Doyle, 1989, p. 4). Doyle has argued that this Report sought to link English to 'state concerns' and to 'those of a wider movement within civil society' (*ibid*, p. 42). However, the universities developed substantial autonomy and from any state direction this had vital implications for English as an emergent subject.

> In consequence, the identity of English studies during the inter-war period
> was forged, not out of the discourses of the Newbolt Report, but rather in
> terms of the subject's consolidation as an autonomous academic discipline
> and learned profession. Furthermore, in becoming fully inserted into the
> structure of university education, the distance of the discipline from school-
> ing, state policy, continuing and adult education, and indeed lay literary
> culture, was progressively accentuated. By the time English had situated

itself as a centre of learning and teaching at all universities in the early 1930s, its ethos and evaluative criteria were those associated with a masculine profession, rather than with a programme of national cultural intervention. (*ibid*, p. 69)

The journey from low to high status, from periphery to centre was then also a journey in terms of gender politics and modes of domination:

> the academic discipline of English studies followed the familiar dynamics of a professionalizing process in which the conditions of being human were themselves masculinized. Masculinization of social institutions is of course not necessarily displayed as overt sexism or discrimination. For example, women were not excluded from the discipline, particularly as students. In fact they were allowed some professional space (albeit not specifically 'as women') to engage in scholarly work on the 'man to man' discourse with which the field was largely concerned. Although overt proclamations of the need to maintain English as a 'manly' educational pursuit by no means disappeared during the inter-war period, the pages of the *Review* reveal few of the defensive and often hysterical avowals of the discipline's 'manliness' that had been characteristic of the earlier period. As Hearn has remarked: 'Where masculinity is secure, it need not be strenuously affirmed.' In practice during the inter-war period English was (and largely remains) securely established as a stable and male-dominated professional field despite the presence of a majority of female students. (*ibid*, p. 71)

Doyle quotes Gross:

> By the 1920s a mood of sombre professionalism had set in, best exemplified by the founding of the *Review of English Studies* in 1925. The academic *apparatchicks* were in full command, and it was too late to change the pattern that had been laid down.

It is clear that his 'mood' could only have come to dominate the study of English by deflecting the major challenges to its status as a 'real discipline'. This had involved countering charges of the discipline's 'effeminacy' as well as its associations with the lay literary world. Indeed, the achievement of a disciplinary identity based upon academic research had by the late 1930s more or less excluded the amateur scholar-gentleman. However, the 'sombre professionalism' or intellectual self-sufficiency of inter-war English studies had not been achieved without some breakdown of mutual comprehension within the discipline itself. Despite many attempts to establish acceptable modes of mutually intelligible professional literary language, such efforts had been undercut by increasing specialization and an at times impenetrable scholarly discourse. (*ibid*, p. 91)

By the time of the Newbolt Report in 1921 English was making some progress but always in the shadows of, and therefore by analogy with, classics. The classical fallacy was therefore consolidated by patterns of prestige and power. Eleanor Wright (1986) has completed an elegant historical study of English at this time. She judges that:

> Also, English was not perceived as a real discipline in the traditional sense, particularly by universities and public schools, an attitude which had not entirely disappeared by as late as the 1960s. Clearly it was important that the study of English could demonstrate that it could make tough intellectual demands on pupils and was as worthy a language with as prestigious and complex a literature as the classics. A way of doing that was to imitate the pedagogy, displaying similar rigour, content and style. (p. 71)

The pattern of progress up until this time was clear as was the strategy for advancement:

> At the universities, particularly the ancient ones, the study of English was even more precariously situated. In the late nineteenth century, its value at Oxford was in providing suitable courses for weaker candidates such as women and 'the second- and third-rate men who were to become schoolmasters', and it was its development as a study of philology which ensured its respectability after the First World War. More progress had been made at Cambridge in establishing the critical study of English literature as an independent discipline (despite the mockery enshrined in its nickname 'the novel-reading tripos'), not least to provide a suitable background for prospective school teachers, which formed a basis for the crusading work of F.R. Leavis in the 1930s. Nonetheless, the Newbolt Committee felt constrained to take time to dispatch the view that English was a soft option at university level. Its recommendations show that, at university level also, English did not enjoy a status equivalent to the traditionally established disciplines such as classics, history, science and mathematics. It asked that English students should enjoy equal access to entrance scholarships, that postgraduate work in English should be endowed, that English should be compulsory for matriculation, that schools of english should be equal in status to other arts schools and 'that the endowment of an English chair should be at least equal to that of any other humanistic chair in the same university'. The evidence which it had received indicated that none of these provisions existed at that time. In effect, the Newbolt Committee was claiming that such advantages, which were also indicators of status and value, should now be granted to English. (*ibid*, pp. 53–4)

One of the reasons for the continuing eminence of the 'grammarian tradition' within English was this 'classical fallacy' and along with this the sustained importance of classics at both the high-status public school and university levels. But new tendencies were beginning to emerge as English began to consolidate its place as a university subject. Most notable was the Cambridge School of English, the first major challenge at university level to the classical grammarian tradition. Mathieson (1975) states that the Cambridge English school had, 'since the 1930s produced not only professors and senior lecturers in university English and education departments throughout the country, but authors of many influential journals, and many secondary school teachers passionately committed to Leavis' critical approaches to English' (p. 138).

F.R. Leavis and his followers, seeing literature as an answer to threats against social harmony, called for a reunification of traditional and literary culture, with morality at the centre (Bergonzi, 1990, p. 43; Ball, Kenny and Gardiner, 1990, pp. 53–4).

> As to appropriate pedagogic strategies, for Leavis teachers remained at the centre of the equation, instilling sensitivity and responsiveness into their students. He set an essentially individualistic, organic conservatism over and against the mechanical, utilitarian tradition. A vision of complete, humane, human development based on access to a culture lay at the core of Leavis' ethico-political system. (Ball, Kenny and Gardiner, 1990, p. 55)

A second tertiary level base for the opposition to the grammarian tradition came later at the London Day Training College (later to become the Institute of Education of the University of London). James Britton, a student at the College and later a Professor of Education at Goldsmiths College (now a College of the University of London) wrote, 'I began my teaching career in 1930 in a storm of controversy about the teaching of English grammar. It was not at that time a question of whether to teach it, but how. The mast my colours were nailed to was that of "the reform of grammar teaching". And certainly the enemy was a real one — the best-selling English textbooks were mines of unproductive busywork' (Britton, 1973, p. 18). Britton and his teacher Percival Gurrey became founding members in 1947 of the London Association for the Teaching of English (LATE). In 1963 LATE was swallowed up by the new National Association for the Teaching of English, NATE, which provided a succession to the then more or less moribund English Association. LATE became a truly major force not just numerically (by 1968, 4000 members and forty-nine branches) but qualitatively with the launching of the 'English as language' concept.

By the late 1950s, two traditions dominated English teaching: one linked to the selective grammar schools, and one to the non-selective secondary moderns, with its roots in elementary schooling (Medway, 1990, p. 4). At the same time,

> the Cambridge position was well on its way to becoming an alternative normalcy. The core of English, in this view, was the reading of literature as an active, creative and essentially moral pursuit through which the degeneracy of contemporary mass society might be combated. (*ibid*, p. 5)

The two challenges to the grammarian tradition represented very different climates of change and constituencies of support. The difference is well captured in Ball's polarities of Cambridge and London English.

Grammar Schooling	**Comprehensive Schooling**
Literature	Language
Elite	Mass
Cultural heritage	Cultural relevance
Transmission	Participation
Cambridge	London

Cambridge English grew up in the inter-war period a time of rigid class division into different schools — the public schools, the grammar schools (upper and middle class) and the secondary moderns (working class). This subject tradition was conceived of, and defined in, an elite university and was concerned with the transmission of a cultural heritage to passive and initially unknowing learners. Cambridge English then replaced the abstract/decontextualized grammar text with a series of texts of the literary and cultural heritage. It represented, however, the first powerful, high status opposition to the grammarian tradition.

In the late 1950s and 1960s, Cold War fears propelled a boom in education funding, spurring the development of new topics and approaches in English. The NATE School critique grew up and flourished at a time of change over to comprehensive schooling. By the 1960s, NATE was more concerned with a critique of the emergent Cambridge School of English as the social and political conditions of state schooling changed. The NATE position was built around an alternative view of experience and its relation to meaning, linked to a concern with the immediacy of language rather than canonical literary texts. In the lead in this critique was James Britton but there was a common link in the critique which applied both to the grammarian tradition and the literary tradition. Above all was the desire 'to replace the emphasis on second hand meaning in the text, with first hand meaning, in the daily life and authentic culture of the child'.

A key event in the emergence of a cluster of traditions from scholars associated with NATE was the 1966 Dartmouth seminar. At this conference both the classical grammarian and the Cambridge versions of cultural heritage were rejected and the notion of 'language and personal growth' was sponsored (Christie, 1993, p. 94). Language then is employed to order our experiences and issue of personal and social relevance become major foci for curriculum development.

From 1966 onwards a range of research projects emanated from the London Institute which sought to articulate and extend the paradigm of 'growth', as a central ingredient in the movement for 'English as language'. The work of Britton, of Masters, of Rosen, all extended this project. But to a degree the work began to bifurcate. One tendency focussed on *social relevance*. For Dixon (like Rosen, a teacher from Walworth Comprehensive in the working class East end of London) developed an influential collection of materials published under the title *Reflections*.

The development of these materials by teachers of ordinary working class children led a common front with a good deal of social studies material. The implications of this were substantial with regard to the hierarchies not only of curriculum definition but of curriculum delivery also. One writer saw this as 'a pedagogic version of social realism' because of the 'explicit and continuous discussion of social and moral issues'. Indeed the pedagogic implications are considerable, seeking as they do to redirect if not destroy the 'transmission process that binds knowledge, teacher, and pupil into a more traditional and more hierarchial set of relationships' (Ball, 1985a, p. 71).

A second tendency sought to build upon the linguistic stress of language in use. This tradition is epitomized in Doughty, Pearce and Thornton's language in use programme launched by Edward Arnold in 1971. In many ways, however, this works with notions of social relevance and grounds its materials in the pupils' lives. Moreover any severe sense of bifurcation between the social and linguistic was mediated by James Britton's work which always stressed the embeddedness of language within the child's own experience and cultural environment. This integrated sense of language in use and use in familiar cultural and personal environments, became the major ideology on curriculum orthodoxy of NATE. Medway (1990) has defined this version of English as follows:

> The version of English which now became dominant had great strengths. The purpose of full personal development (regardless of students' assigned destinations) lent a new dignity and seriousness to English teachers' work with the full range of abilities. An approach based on personal experience and social issues did indeed motivate many pupils, with the result that impressive new achievements in writing and drama were recorded. Ordinary lives of ordinary children were dignified as worthy matter for the English lesson. English became more enjoyable and less redolent of a stuffy official culture. Of all the school subjects except perhaps art, English was most in tune with the styles and preoccupations of youth culture. (p. 25)

Whilst not a total picture

> at the heart of the dispute between Cambridge and London, literature and language, there is not simply two views of the subject, but more profoundly, and politically of importance, two conceptions of the 'good society', and of the nature of civilization and citizenship. In crude terms the positions rest upon commitment to two opposed knowledge bases, one elite knowledge and the other the knowledge of the masses. In the Cambridge vision the English teacher and the great literary heritage, with which they are entrusted, are to stand against the depredations of the machine age. The Leavisites hark back to a better time before the coming of the mass industrial society, when social order and morality were invested in and maintained

by the community. In contrast the London vision celebrates the immediate life, culture and language of the school student. And for many teachers, especially those in the urban centres, that has meant primarily the lives, culture and language of the working class. (Ball, Kenny and Gardiner, 1990, p. 59)

The Cambridge School is as decontextualized as the classical grammarian tradition in one specific and vital sense: it most commonly presents life, culture and subjectivity as transcendent givens, independent of politics and history. Eagleton attacked the Cambridge version of English in his keynote speech to NATE in 1985:

Why does it insist so dogmatically on abstracting personal values and qualities from the whole concrete context — political society — in which they are embedded? Why does it continually offer us the cerebral abstraction of something called 'interpersonal relationships' or 'personal growth' or 'immediate experience', when a moments thought is enough to reveal that such things gain their concrete significance only in the whole political and historical context which shapes them. (*ibid*, p. 83)

This very abstract decontextualized modality opened the way to the new more assertive versions of English which grew up, particularly through the work of NATE in the 1960s and 1970s. Speaking of Eagleton's assertions Ball claims:

it was precisely this 'disinterested' way of looking at and presenting the world that enabled Leavis and his cohorts — his 'preachers of culture' — to champion the spontaneous, creative, inner life evinced by D.H. Lawrence whilst at the same time ignoring his virulent sexism, racism and rigid authoritarianism. In order to address issues of class, gender and race the assertive versions of English teaching that emerged in the 1960s and 70s needed to pose a direct challenge to the very notions of cultural heritage and literary canon, and also, by implication the critical discourse in which they are embedded. (*ibid*)

But the Cambridge School was decontextualised in another specific sense. The classical tradition 'had its origins and its plausibility structure in the universities in the early decades of the century'. Likewise, Cambridge English from the inter-war period onwards was defined by scholars working in university departments notably at Sussex and Bristol as well as the 'home base' at Cambridge.

The language and personal growth movement though often led from the University of London Institute of Education always, involved many practising teachers through the large NATE membership. The result was a very substantial shift of power in defining the subject towards classroom teachers. Speaking of the sixties, we have stated elsewhere, 'This was a time when, in Britain certainly, teachers' priorities and purposes appeared to have a greater than normal influence over the English curriculum resulting in the emergence of the version of English teaching which has come to be known by the label "personal growth"' (Goodson and Medway, 1990b, p. xiii). Medway has argued cogently that this reformulation of English represented a 'crisis of mission' on behalf of English teachers in the comprehensive school. He points out that many Cambridge English graduates went on to do their postgraduate certificate in education (teacher training year) at the London Institute. Hence he agreed that the polarities of Cambridge English and English as personal growth began, to some extent, to intermingle and cross-fertilize as comprehensivization gained strength after 1965. He therefore follows Goodson (1993 and 1995b) and Doyle in seeing curriculum change very much in terms of the defence of professionals' (i.e. teachers') material interests:

> It may be that the survival of English as a well-endowed core subject with generous capitation, a large share of the schools' salary points, access to sixth form work and good prospects of promotion to headships, depended on the invention of a new version of the subject as a single unified and distinct enterprise which was readily justifiable as a central component in the education of the entire population. (Medway, 1990, p. 27)

The promotion of the language and personal growth tradition therefore placed the English teacher at the centre of the definition, development and direction of the subject. In this way, partially breaking an established hierarchical pattern in the definition of English as a school subject. This factor above all marks the break from the Cambridge tradition and earlier the grammarian tradition. Here was a move from English defined by an elite for an elite to an attempt, often by teachers, to define and develop English as a vehicle of mass education.

Students wrote assignments which concentrated on 'subjectivity — what it feels like to be the unique experiencing subject' (*ibid*, p. 19).

> Younger students were learning to dramatise texts (and improvise on their themes); to write in emulation of them (and from oral traditions); and to choose, discuss and study them without the expectations of going on to produce a formulaic type of 'essay'. A renaissance in 'children's literature' stimulated and responded to this new tradition, from the 1960s on. By the later 1970s many of its leading writers were women, some black, some working class in origin. And within the schools some teachers were including modern media production alongside print. (Dixon, 1991, pp. 203–4)

Indeed some tendencies within English went one step further in the late sixties and early seventies.

> They felt the need to incorporate an extra dimension in their practice which faced the conflicts at the heart of a model of personal development which the rest of the school and society at large had no time for except in the case of a very small minority of pupils. It went beyond the reflections-style

interest in social issues; it tried to inject into the English curriculum the kinds of knowledge and experience which would give working class pupils an understanding of inequality and its causes; the emphasis would be of solidarity rather than upward mobility. (Ball, Kenny and Gardiner, 1990, p. 60)

The new 'assertive' English which spelled out connections to the wider society and dealt with issues of class genders and race only existed for a very brief moment. For new tendencies in British society were seeking to redirect such 'progressive' forces and rehabilitate old patterns for definition and delivery of school subject knowledge.

In 1975 the Bullock Report spelt out some of the arguments for redirection. Bullock, it has been claimed, 'served as a vehicle for restructuring English. Its role was symbolic in giving public censure to significant aspects of the "new wave" English and in creating space for the insertion of alternative concepts of the role and purpose, and form and content, of English teaching. It gave credibility to those voices which said "things have gone too far"' (*ibid*, p. 69). Yet Bullock was only the beginning of a redirection pointing the subject back to the literary tradition, to definition by scholars at Cambridge and elsewhere. In 1979 a Conservative Government was elected and this has presaged attempts not only to further weaken the role of teachers in subject definitions but to reembrace and reinstate grammar as an important element of English teaching and in doing so reinscribe a particular version of what constitutes teaching (and 'the teacher'). As we have argued elsewhere, from the mid-1970s in England and Wales (a salient moment was the Prime Minister's Ruskin College speech of 1976) the tide of change at system level turned, with a move to restructure schooling for more utilitarian purposes. English did not spontaneously change itself in sympathy for a time, versions of English more in harmony with the earlier democratic moment persisted and were unchecked, relations between the levels being characterized by a loosely-coupled apparent autonomy.

Now, however, with the introduction of the National Curriculum, we are witnessing a move towards a tighter coupling and imposition of government wishes down to the detail of classroom transactions. For example, MacLure and Elliott (1993) refer to the curriculum alignment effects of commercial publishers as they introduce course book schemes, especially at the primary school level and exert a reciprocal influence on further development of the National Curriculum, 'by promoting exemplars of good practice they shape what is possible and by casting it within the familiar textbook format they "domesticate" it' (pp. 91–113).

This tighter coupling, however, is not simply a matter of bringing English into line with the demands of the economy as rationally conceived (Reid, 1993, p. 21). Certainly, the justifications are expressed in the neutral language of 'the needs of society' and 'closer attention to the needs of industry', yet the relevance of the changes to these needs is by no means always obvious. Indeed, the British Government's education policy differs in significant ways from the recommendations of leading industrial and business bodies. It is not simply that the learning of grammar has dubious relevance to the language *competence* which industry requires; requirements for the study of English literary classics and the learning by heart of poetry appear to reflect a different order of purposes. More lies behind current attacks on approaches deriving from the sixties and early seventies, when concerns with social justice and common schooling were running strongly, than worries about their economic dysfunctionality. As we noted earlier, commentators have drawn the connection between the reinstatement of grammar and the reinstatement of discipline, 'punctiliousness in other matters'. As the leader of the National Association for the Teaching of English has said, 'The teaching of grammar seems to be associated in the prime minister's mind with picking up litter'[2] (this theme is echoed elsewhere, see Green, 1995b).

The new curricular prescriptions are consistent with a broader cultural reversal, a concern not with enabling more pupils to gain access to higher levels of education and work but with early division and exclusion, despite the emergence and clamouring of a post-modern educational culture (Green, 1995a, pp. 391–410). The underlying intention appears to be about reestablishing hierarchy and social discipline and restoring the older social configurations which had been partially disrupted. Effects of the emphasis on grammar on standard English and on the English 'national heritage' will clearly be to increase once again the relative disadvantage and sense of exclusion of pupils from working class and ethnic minority backgrounds, and it is hard not to conclude that this may be part of the intention. Doyle (1989) notes two developments which are interesting in their juxtaposition.

> By the 1970s, all of the familiar themes associated with the post-war new-critical programme had been appropriated by the new right and the humanistic sense that English departments might play a central and autonomous role in the transformation of the general 'quality of life' in society had all but collapsed. (p. 120)

> But in the 1970s students were flooding into English studies in previously unparalleled numbers across the range of relatively diverse institutions of higher education including the ancient and newer 'civic or provincial' universities, the post-war 'plateglass' universities, and the polytechnics. It would be true to describe the discipline as having achieved an astounding success if such success is measured in terms of the establishment of English literature as the central arts subject at 'A' level, and thus at the basis of the constant demand for undergraduate places. Furthermore, at the levels of teaching and research, the discipline was now able to offer wide and attractive career opportunities to its most successful graduates. (*ibid*, p. 121)

In the 1980s, English was caught up in the debates which presaged the launch of the National Curriculum in 1987–8. The original 'consensus' around the English National Curriculum subject outlines was not to the liking of the Prime Minister,

Margaret Thatcher. Among other things, she argued teaching grammar would help solve the problem of litter on the streets — one assumes she was making the established argument linking grammar and moral discipline. Hence, in the early 1990s the Prime Minister 'packed the education quangos with right-wingers determined to rewrite (the) 1989 consensus curriculum into a version promoting their own vision' (Hofkins, 1995, p. 5). Brian Cox, in a recent book on this period has seen that their version sought to overthrow the 1989 outline with which he was so centrally involved.

> The National Curriculum Council group who took over the English curriculum was deeply afraid of modern society, trapped in fantasies of a lost golden age of Victorian childhood, and desperate to prevent young children today from being subjected to the realities of the modern world. (Cox, 1995, p. 91)

Cox calls the version they agreed the 'curriculum for little England'. It was published in April 1993. 'Since then it has gone through much chopping and changing, tweaking and pulling, through a political tug of war and then Dearing's[3] diet' (Hofkins, 1995, p. 5).

English in North America

The emergence of English in colonial contexts was related initially to attempts to secure cultural hegemony in the newly-colonized territories of the British Empire. In due course, as we shall see as the links with imperial centre were weakened or broken, English came to develop its own indigenous characteristics. Of the imperial period, Morgan (1990) has argued that:

> in a colonial situation it arose out of the perceived needs of an English elite attempting to secure their cultural hegemony by extending and revitalizing a normalizing language curriculum in the unstable circumstances of late nineteenth-century immigration, growing nationalism, and the shifting class relations of early industrialization. An ironic offshot of this formative period has been a claim of ideological innocence, the belief that somehow English studies transcends politics, a myth which has plaqued English pedagogy to the present day. This fiction is harder to maintain given the historical facts of English's constitutive relation to state and empire formation, as well as the explicit statements of founding figures that the study of 'higher' English was 'Englishness', a racial and imperial positioning, not merely advanced language training. (p. 229)

A particularly interesting study of this intersection is Gerald Burns work on Benjamin Franklin's American text *Idea of the English School*. He argues

In this 1751 pamphlet Franklin not only devised a programme of vernacular linguistic and literary instruction which anticipated the subject of 'English' that would fully emerge in American secondary schools only a century and a half later; he also articulated a rationale for that programme that carries us to the heart of the social process by which the modern discipline was originated. The *Idea* answers Archer's questions of constituency, immediate educational result, and extra-educational aim, in terms, respectively, of class, language and power. Moreover, under these heads more specific identifications are made: of a commercially-oriented 'middle class' as the natural constituency for advanced vernacular study: of a type of enhanced linguistic competence, mainly associated with that constituency's social superiors, but also keyed to the technology and culture of print, as the immediate benefit of that study; and of access to positions in a power structure normally closed off to those of middle-class status, as the longer-term advantage. The text thus points, first to the general social parameters, then to the particular social historical dynamic, behind the eventual establishment of 'English' at the secondary level in the United States. (Burns, 1990, p. 88)

Franklin's curricula was piloted in the Philadelphia English School and this school developed a commercial and middle class clientele for its 'English' curricula. Hence, in the mid-1750s, ten of the thirteen boys in the English School were either artisans or merchants, by contrast twenty-six of the thirty-six pupils in the Latin and Greek School were the sons of upper class parents (*ibid*, p. 113). Burns judges that Franklin's programme marked

a quantum leap over contemporary practice in this area and foreshadowing in much of its content and some of its methods the modern secondary subject of English. The programme provides for much vigorous work in reading, especially reading of a critical kind, begun with fables and stories, continued with periodical essays, and carried over into the study of actual works of English literature. Spelling and English grammar are included, and also rhetoric, with attention to polite speaking and formal declamation. Further, two full years of vernacular study are earmarked for composition, first of letters, then of essays, with an ingenious series of exercises . . . (*ibid*)

In spite of the pioneering importance of Franklin's *Idea* it received only partial implementation at the Philadelphia School and always remained much smaller and provided with less resources than the Latin and Greek School. Nonetheless, when the School became a college in 1755, Ebenezer Kinnersley became the first professor of the English tongue and oratory (Harvard later established just such a professorship in 1806).

But elsewhere, English studies were beginning to emerge in opposition to Latin or Greek. A course in rhetoric was included for instance in the courses of study at Boston English High School from 1821. As in Britain, the subject had substantial initial appeal for young women. Applebee (1974) notes:

Girls' schools during this period were almost all finishing schools, and English studies did find an early place in some of them; the belles lettres were considered an appropriate subject for polite conversation, if nothing else. Thus it was not entirely accidental that many English textbooks were for 'young ladies' or prepared by schoolmasters in girl's finishing schools. Lacking a rigorous academic cachet, these 'appreciative' studies of English carried a certain stigma, an air of being a second-best choice for those it was presumed could not handle the rigor of classical studies. (p. 13)

Applebee has argued that in the late nineteenth century English school curriculum three traditions were intertwined: an *ethical tradition* which emphasized moral and cultural development, a *classical tradition* comprising intellectual discipline and close textual study and a *non-academic tradition* move concerned with enjoyment and appreciation (and often found in girls' finishing schools). He judges that by 1865 schools patchily recognized a variety of studies of English — rhetoric, oratory, spelling, grammar, literary history and appreciation; and 'reading'. 'Rhetorical and grammatical studies often included literary texts, but instruction was designed and carried out in the service of composition, not literature. Literary history, though the schools called it the teaching of literature, was biographical in emphasis and often involved no literature at all' (*ibid*, pp. 13–14). In fact it was the non-academic tradition which mostly stressed literary ready and this tradition was almost by definition without a place in colleges and preparatory schools.

By 1865, English was then an amalgam of tendencies and traditions

English studies had become a part of all three major traditions. Though in each case the study of English was subordinate to other goals, there was for the first time the possibility that all these traditions might be united within the teaching of a single subject. And this is in fact what happened in the following decades: English studies increasingly found ways to claim the intellectual strength of the classical tradition, the moral strength of the ethical tradition and the utilitarian strength of the non-academic tradition. It was a fruitful alliance, though sometimes a confusing one, and led in the end to a subject whose content and goals had no real counterpart in any of the traditions from which it arose. (*ibid*, p. 14)

Applebee begins his chapter on the 'birth of the subject' in the USA in 1865. He argues that

Before it could emerge as a major school study, English and in particular English literature, had to develop a methodology rigorous enough to win academic respect. It also had to overcome the supposition that imaginative literature posed a real threat to the moral well-being of its readers. The Romantic era brought a solution to both problems: that of methodology through the new techniques of the German philologists; that of moral well-being through a redefinition of culture and of the artist's role. Together these two movements made it *possible* for English to become a major subject, but they did not insure the success of the venture. This success depended upon institutional changes in the American system of education, changes begun through the influence of college education requirements, and consolidated by the report of the Committee of Ten. (*ibid*, p. 21)

In fact the definitions of English accepted for college entrance and enshrined in the Committee of Ten Report in 1894 had been systematically constructed and negotiated in the preceding period. The rapid success of the efforts to promote English can be judged by Applebee's statement that 'in 1800 formal instruction in literature was unknown; by 1865 it had made its way into the curriculum as a handmaiden to other studies; by 1900 literature was almost universally offered as an important study in its own right' (*ibid*, p. 30). Whilst Applebee is using the phrase 'literature' as we shall see this was largely a rhetorical devise which covered a range of institutionalized practices and contents.

College admission presented rather a different problem for preparatory schools during the nineteenth century than it does for schools today. Instead of facing secondary school graduation requirements, candidates for admission were assessed on the basis of entrance examinations set by each college. The topics for these examinations were announced in advance and had a way of dictating the preparatory school curriculum for the year. As the requirements changed, the curriculum changed with them.

Typically enough, literature gained its foothold in the requirements through the nonliterary uses to which readings could be put . . . the real milestone was the Harvard requirement for 1873–74: literature was to be studied, not for itself or even for philology, but as a subject for composition.

English Composition. Each candidate will be required to write a short English composition, correct in spelling, punctuation, grammar, and expression, the subject to be taken from such works of standard authors as shall be announced from time to time. The subject for 1874 will be taken from one of the following works: Shakespeare's *Tempest, Julius Caesar*, and *Merchant of Venice*; Goldsmith's *Vicar of Wakefield;* Scott's *Ivanhoe*, and *Lay of the Last Minstrel*.

This requirement institutionalized the study of standard authors and set in motion a process which eventually forced English to consolidate its position within the schools. (*ibid*, p. 30)

The Harvard model proved attractive to a wide range of other colleges and universities each of which produced their own version. Applebee contends that the Harvard model 'offered an easy way to recognize literary studies without raising different questions about standards and methods: the subject tested would be composition nor literature'. But the problem, of course proliferation, followed from this original compromise since 'there was no agreed canon of texts on which to base the examinations, and the lists changed yearly. Each college set its own examinations, quickly confronting the high schools with a flood of titles in which they were to prepare their students' (*ibid*, pp. 30–1).

This was not a situation which could continue for long as high schools were confused as to how to prepare their students for college entrance. As Burns (1990) has described it, it was the National Educational Association (NEA) which moved to clarify the position of English, 'It was this professional teacher's organization founded shortly after mid-century, which sponsored the major committees on secondary instruction in the 1890s whose reports gave quasi-official definition to the subject of "English"' (p. 121).

In 1892 the National Council of Education of the NEA called for the appointment of a 'Committee of Ten' to consider the general problems of secondary school subjects and entrance requirements. For English the recommendations of the Committee were a watershed in the acceptance of the subject.

Its report represented a summary and a reconciliation of the contemporary points of view about the teaching of English. It began with a statement of the purpose of such studies:

The main objects of the teaching of English in schools seem to be two: (1) to enable the pupil to understand the expressed thoughts of others and to give expression to thoughts of his own; and (2) to cultivate a taste for reading, to give the pupil some acquaintance with good literature, and to furnish him with the means of extending that acquaintance.

This simple two-art statement presented the necessary unification of the many disparate studies which go beneath the rubric English. Communication and appreciation were the focal points, and if English in later years was to lose some of its vigor because of the diversity of activities which it would be forced to assimilate, in the 1890s that same breadth allowed the various minor studies to be brought together into one far more vigorous whole.

This unification of the many parts of English was one of the most important effects of the *Report* of the Committee of Ten. The other major effect was to accord the new subject a status at least as important as that of the classical subjects. The Conference on English recommended that a total of five periods a week for four years be devoted to the various aspects of English studies, and the committee as a whole went so far as to accept four a week for the four years in its general recommendations. In the suggested programs of study, however, English is contracted a bit further. Out of the four years of study described for four alternate programs, English receives a full five periods a week in only the third year of the 'English' course, and is cut to three and even two at various points in all other programs. Nevertheless, English is the *only* subject recommended for definite inclusion in the program of study for every student during each of the four high school years. (Applebee, 1974, p. 33)

At the turn of the century, English educators, having for the moment established their subject in the school curriculum, had to adjust to a new form of high school, as the progressive movement sought to bring secondary schooling to all. The widening clientele, and the concurrent change in pedagogical theory (away from faculty psychology and towards child study), pushed school English away from university definitions. College influence remained, though, in the 'uniform lists' — lists of readings used for entrance exams, which thus had to be taught to university-bound students at all high schools. The movement to eliminate this vestige obtained its first success in 1916, with the introduction of a comprehensive exam as an alternative to the list-based one; the uniform list itself was abandoned in 1931 (*ibid*, pp. 46–54).

As Applebee points out, the period also saw a movement away from the dominance of philology:

> Almost all changes offered began out of a rejection of the earlier, analytic approach to literary studies, moving instead toward an emphasis on the work as a whole, and of the ideas or values embodied in it. Even during the period in which philological studies were at their strongest, there had been a dissenting tradition which claimed that the proper goal for the teaching of literature should be 'appreciation'. (*ibid*, p. 55)

Teachers of English organized their courses to emphasize genres, or reflect psychological principles.

> The concern with the child led almost inevitably to a new emphasis on modern writings. If teachers were really to start 'where the student is', they would have to start with the dime novel, the newspaper, and the magazine. This concern was reinforced by those who saw the magazine and newspaper as legitimate genres replete with their own conventions and characteristics to analyze and tabulate. Through most of the enthusiasm, however, there ran a curiously ambiguous undercurrent: the majority of the teachers who championed current works hoped in the end to lead their students away from them, toward what the teachers saw as the real riches of the literature of the past. (*ibid*, p. 58)

They now defended the study of literature on the grounds of moral examples, which depended on reading a complete work. This approach bore fruit during World War One, when 'literature became a way to instill a sense of national heritage and to encourage patriotism', and led to a long-term interest in teaching American literature (*ibid*, p. 65).

Between the wars, the movement for scientific efficiency did not threaten English — a cheap and functionally important subject. It did, however, lead to differentiation by student ability.

The concurrent move to experience as the justification of literature had even greater impact on the curriculum. At first teachers turned to the 'Project Method,' based on the 'purposeful act' as a unit of learning (*ibid*, pp. 107–9). Then came the Depression.

> In a time when established institutions did seem to be faltering, and just distant enough from the previous world war for the disillusionment it had generated to have faded, the original progressive concern with social progress could reemerge, if anything more radical for its long suppression. (*ibid*, p. 115)

The result was a series of publications on experience-based curriculum for English. In some ways these developments foreshadow the 'growth' movement in England in the 1960s. The most successful of these, Louise Rosenblatt's *Literature as Exploration* (1938), placed the focus squarely on student response.

> The Depression also damaged the ability of schools to provide books, so that by the end of the 1930s, the teaching of literature was to a large extent dominated by the literature anthology rather than by statements of goals or courses of study. (Applebee, 1974, p. 128)

Applebee sums up:

> The decades that fell between the two world wars were a time of change and experiment within the teaching of English. The period began with the liberation of the subject from overt control by the colleges; but that very liberation, as the leaders of the profession came to realize, raised problems of even greater magnitude than the ones it solved. When the teaching of literature had first come into the schools, it had a coherent — if somewhat circumscribed — function, and it had a methodology, albeit a borrowed one, that had given it the aura of a systematic study. (*ibid*, p. 130)

In the 1940s and 1950s, American high school English retreated to an even more narrow concern with helping adolescents deal with the transition to adulthood. This represented English's answer to the life adjustment movement, and its demands for a 'fused curriculum'; it also meant that English at this time passed over the arguments of the 'new critics', who emphasized wholistic readings (*ibid*, pp. 139–66). Meanwhile, language skills were starting to be emphasized over, and divorced from, the teaching of literature (*ibid*, pp. 160–1).

The failure of life adjustment to provide a meaningful framework for the study of English contributed to the subsequent academic campaign of the late 1950s and 1960s. Anxious when the curriculum revolution brought about by Sputnik knocked English to the sidelines, some reformers turned to the Ford Fund's Advanced Placement Program.

> From the beginning English was one of the most popular advanced placement subjects, and the emphases in its examination were those that characterized the next wave of reform. Textual analysis and literary criticism on the model of the new critics was the most important aspect of the exam; very little attention was given to the philosophical or ethical dimensions of literature. (*ibid*, p. 190)

Concerned that the life adjustment approach had left the 'academically talented' unchallenged, the new academic formation of English shifted the focus from the student back to the subject (*ibid*, pp. 189–93). University professors reentered the fray, and assumed some of the power to define the curriculum.

> The most important assertion was that English must be regarded as a 'fundamental liberal discipline', a body of specific knowledge to be preserved and transmitted rather than a set of skills or an opportunity for guidance and individual adjustment. As such, the importance of specific works, of the technical vocabulary of the literary critic, and of sequence determined by the logic of the subject matter could be opened for debate in a way that was impossible when the subject was defined in terms of the needs or interests of the student. (*ibid*, p. 193)

Applebee and Purves (1992) judge that:

> The first attempt to define a new, academic curriculum for English grew out of a 1958 conference cosponsored by NCTE, the Modern Language Association, and the College English Association. The widely distributed conference report, *The Basic Issues in the Teaching of English*, asserted that English is a 'fundamental liberal discipline' with a body of specific knowledge to be preserved and transmitted. By identifying this subject matter as the core of English, the conference also rejected the needs of the child and the accompanying metaphors of experience and exploration as the basis of the English curriculum. Instead, the attention of the profession turned to identifying the specific knowledge that best reflected the 'core' of the discipline of English in each of its three components: language, literature, and composition. (p. 736)

Working from this standpoint, teachers chose works which they felt exhibited high intellectual standards. Applebee and Purves note that this 'academic resurgence was relatively short-lived'.

Attention in curriculum had shifted toward more socially relevant programs. The shift had many causes, including the general social upheaval generated by the civil rights movement and the Vietnam War as well as new views of the nature of schooling. In the English language arts, major changes occurred through acquaintance with child-centred models of teaching that had been developed in British schools, where the emphasis was on personal and linguistic 'growth through English' (Dixon, 1967) and where Piaget rather than Chomsky dominated the view of structuralism. The Dartmouth Conference, an international gathering of educators from Australia, Canada, the United Kingdom, and the United States, was particularly influential, both through its influence on the participants, many of whom had been leaders in the development of the academic model, and through its widely distributed conference reports. (*ibid*, p. 737)

So in the middle of the 1960s, opposition to the academic approach sprang up.

In response to the national agony over the Vietnam war, student unrest, escalating problems in the inner city, and a widespread malaise even among academically talented students, the emphasis in educational thought shifted gradually but unmistakably away from knowledge of an academic discipline toward the process of knowing and the dignity of the individual. Men who had once led the attack on the progressives shifted their ground, now attacking the dehumanization of the school that seemed to have accompanied the academic approach. (Applebee, 1974, p. 236)

American critics cited British courses (see earlier in this chapter) which emphasized student response and interests, and reflected concerns with child development. This tendency was echoed in other subjects (and indeed other cultures) but in the pendulum swings of curriculum change began to be reversed in the 'Back to Basics' period of the 1980s. At the same time, however, major attacks were being launched on the whole 'canon' of English in the universities and this presaged a new battle for the 'high ground' within the subject. English departments were seen as major battle grounds for the definition of patterns of political correctness and deviation. This pattern has now reasserted itself forcefully in the 1980s and 1990s as the moral cleansing projects of the New Right lap around the moats of the university ivory tower.

The current initiatives to develop national standards is part of the pattern. To date specific standards for teaching and learning English, together with classroom vignettes are being produced by the National Council of Teachers, the International Reading Association and the University of Illinois' Centre for the Study of Reading (O'Neil, 1993, pp. 4–8). An English Language Arts Performance Standards package for the elementary school has been produced and is being trialled across a number of school districts and states (Borthwick, 1994).

Conclusion

As noted with regard to science and mathematics, conflicts occurred and recurred over the decades in the UK between English as a school subject and English as a university discipline as well as between English as literature or as language. The promotion of particular orthodoxies over the decades was attributable to particular groups and bases (Cambridge and London English, National Association for the Teaching of English). The introduction of the National Curriculum is now creating new prescriptions and partially reconstituting previous hierarchies and social configurations.

In North America similar traditions emerged in the eighteenth and nineteenth centuries. The Report of the Committee of Ten in 1892 produced a landmark decision about the importance of English as a school subject but various pressure groups created changing priorities over the decades for literary studies, personal growth (life adjustment movement) literary criticism and functional English. The balance between Language and Literature study was often distinctively different at particular times to patterns in Britain.

At the end of the day we are left realising the centrality of English as both a specific category within, and a general symbolic carrier of, schooling and curriculum. As Bill Green (1993c) has noted

we can productively refer to *the insistence of the letter* in curriculum and schooling. This is to be understood not only as a matter of language (and the symbolic order, more generally), conceived as absolutely crucial to considerations of curriculum and schooling, but also more particularly of *written* language and its associated cultural politics, social relations and epistemological effects. Hence, 'literacy' becomes a curriculum issue *par excellence* and a particularly significant 'topic' in and for curriculum history and theory, particularly with regard to the semiotic possibilities and curriculum politics associated with the all-important 'oral'/'literate', 'speech'/'writing' relationships and dichotomies. (pp. 1–2)

In general, social histories of the curriculum provide important antidotes to the presentism of many political and ideological claims about curriculum and schooling. As Allan Luke (1993) writes of the studies on the *Insistence of the Letter* 'many of the studies here indicate that the effects of the social technology of literacy are not natural and universal, but are contingent on historic and culture-specific institutional practices and contexts, discourses and ideologies. If indeed this is the case, we need to be wary of claims and guarantees of universal effectiveness which accompany modern instructional approaches to literacy' (p. ix). John Willinsky's elegant work on English in the secondary school curriculum has shown just how powerful historical work can be in problemisizing ideological claims for literacy and literature. Particularly valuable has been his work on the social history of literacy before schooling particularly in the period 1800–1850.

The drama and history of those earlier days, when literacy was at the forefront of the battle for democracy, are a lesson about literacy that often goes missing in schools today. These scenes from the nineteenth century throw considerations of current literature-based English programs into relief, as if to meet the inevitable question, 'the teaching of literature compared to what?' After all, what else could an English class be if not the study of the best that has been thought and said? In order to appreciate what we have made of English teaching over the course of the last hundred years, we need to realize what an education in literacy and literature was like prior to the rise of public schooling and the triumph of literature. It had been promised, after all, that state-sponsored education in Great Britain, which finally became law in 1870, would discipline, among other things, the unruly ways of this earlier interest in reading and writing. (Willinsky, 1993, p. 59)

There could be no better epilogue for the role of sociohistorical studies of school subjects in posing questions about the kind of 'political settlements' which present particular version of English as 'timeless' givens. In studying school subjects in this way we see how a subject represents a range of choices and priorities which intersect with social and economic histories.

Reflections and Issues

1   Explain why English was commonly taught in elementary schools but less so in secondary Schools in the United Kingdom up until the end of the nineteenth century.

2   Give reasons why the National Association of Teachers of English (NATE) had a major influence on school English in the United Kingdom during the 1960s and 70s.

3   Consider the advantages and disadvantages of a college admission test in the US requiring aspirants to write an English composition based upon set literary texts, as described by Applebee (1974).

4   In the US over the last three decades there have been shifting orthodoxies which can be defined as life adjustment (personal growth), literary criticism and functional English. Explain why these changing priorities occurred. What are some possible effects of the national standards movement in terms of school English?

5   Some recent writers argue that English teaching must draw on critical pedagogy and take into consideration recent developments in feminism and post structuralism. Present a case for or against this stance.

6   How have the balance between language and literature changed in English teaching since the Second World War? Is there evidence for the 'triumph of literature' discerned by Willinsky at an earlier stage? Compare the British and American developments.

Suggested Reading

Useful articles include:

Ball, S.J. (1985) 'English for the English Since 1906', in Goodson, I.F. (Ed) *Social Histories of the Secondary Curriculum: Subjects in Study*, London and Washington, DC: Falmer Press.

Ball, S.J., Kenny, A. and Gardiner, D. (1990) 'Literacy, Politics and the Teaching of English', in Goodson, I.F. and Medway, P. (Eds) *Bringing English to Order*, London and Washington, DC: Falmer Press.

Court, F. (1988) 'The Social and Historical Significance of the First English Literature Professorship in England', *PMLA*, **103**, 5, pp. 796–807.

Christie, F. (1993) 'The "Received Tradition" of English Teaching: The Decline of Rhetoric and the Corruption of Grammar', in Green, B. (Ed) *The Insistence of the Letter: Literacy Studies and Curriculum Theorizing*. Pittsburgh: University of Pittsburgh Press, pp. 75–106.

Goodson, I.F. (1996) '"Nations at Risk" and "National Curriculum": Ideology and Identity', in Goodson, I.F. with Anstead, C.J. and Mangan, J.M., *Subject Knowledge: Readings for the Study of School Subjects*. London and Washington, DC: Falmer Press.

Green, B. (1993) 'Literacy Studies and Curriculum Theorizing; or, The Insistence of the Letter', in Green, B. (Ed) *The Insistence of the Letter: Literacy Studies and Curriculum Theorizing*. Pittsburgh: University of Pittsburgh Press, pp. 195–225.

Green, B. (1995) 'Post-curriculum possibilities: English teaching, cultural politics and the post modern turn', *Journal of Curriculum Studies*. **24**, 4, pp. 391–410.

Green, B. (1995) 'Born Again Teaching? Governmentality, "Grammar" and Public Schooling', in Popkewitz, T.S. and Brennan, M. (Eds) *Governmentality through Education: Foucault's Challenge to the Institutional Production and Study of Knowledge*. New York: Teachers College Press.

Willinsky, J. (1993) 'Lessons from the Literacy Before Schooling 1800–1850', in Green, G. (Ed) *The Insistence of the Letter: Literacy Studies and Curriculum Theorizing*. Pittsburgh: University of Pittsburgh Press, pp. 58–74.

Useful books include:

Court, F. (1992) *Institutionalizing English Literature*. Stanford, California: Stanford University Press.

Doyle, B. (1989) *English and Englishness*, London and New York: Routledge.

Goodson, I.F. and Medway, P. (Eds) (1990) *Bringing English to Order*, London and Washington, DC: Falmer Press.

Shayer, D. (1972) *The Teaching of English in Schools 1900–1970*, London and Boston: Routledge & Kegan Paul.

Willinsky, J. (1991) *The Triumph of Literature — The Fate of Literacy: English in the Secondary School Curriculum*. New York and London: Teachers College Press.

Notes

1 Our thanks to Jane King for pointing out this and other valuable references.
2 *The Observer*, 2 April 1989.

3 This refers to Sir Ron Dearing who was brought in to develop a report which sought to defuse a general crisis over the National Curriculum. The argument about the little England views has been echoed in the battle over the history curriculum (see Crawford, 1995, pp. 433–56).

Chapter 9

School Subjects: Patterns of Change

Historical studies of school subjects show that the secondary school curriculum, far from being a stable and dispassionately constructed unity, is in fact a highly contested, fragmented and endlessly shifting terrain. The school subject is socially and politically constructed and the actors involved deploy a range of ideological and material resources as they pursue their individual and collective missions.

Behind this focus of inquiry lies an alternative conceptualization to mainstream views of schooling. In many ways, this conceptualization accords with the views of Meyer and Rowan (1983) who describe education systems as 'the central agency defining personnel — both citizen and elite — for the modern state and economy' (p. 83). In this view of schooling, standardized categories of graduates are produced through the use of standardized types of teachers, students, topics and activities. These graduates are allocated places in the economic and stratification system on the basis of their certified educational background. Through this certification role the 'ritual classifications of education' (i.e. student, teacher, topic, school, grade, etc.) have value as currency on the 'social identity market'. This market calls for a standard, stable currency of social typications. 'The nature of schooling is thus socially defined by reference to a set of standardized categories, the legitimacy of which is publicly shared' (*ibid*, p. 84). This is a constraint on what is possible in education and what will be accepted as conforming to the norm of schooling. But on the other hand 'the rewards for attending to external understandings are, an increased ability to mobilize societal resources for organizational purposes' (*ibid*, p. 86).

The social function of schooling by this view sets parameters, perspectives and incentives for those actors involved in the construction of school subjects. In our investigation, the activities of these actors can best be understood as individuals or collectives with 'careers' and 'missions' who are dependent for resources and ideological support on external sources. The interface between 'internal' subject actors and their external relations is mediated through the pursuit of resources and ideological support. Resource dependency has two faces: it is experienced as a constraint on strategies of action but can also be viewed as a mode of promoting and facilitating particular versions and visions of school subjects.

The great strength of Meyer and Rowan's characterization of schooling and of linking it to an analysis of resource allocation is that our study can focus on aspects of stability and conservation as well as on aspects of conflict and change. This provides an antidote to the dangers of internalism and givenness noted earlier. It also provides a response to Steven Lukes' critique of what he describes as 'one-dimensional' or pluralist views of power that focus only on conflict. He argues that the most effective and insidious use of power 'is to prevent conflict arising in the first place'. Hence to focus solely on conflict is to miss crucial dimensions of power, moreover 'conflict, according to that view, (i.e. pluralism) is assumed to be crucial in providing an experimental test of power attributions: without it the exercise of power will, it seems to be thought, fail to show up'. A further problem relates to issues of consciousness for pluralists 'are opposed to any suggestion that interests might be inarticulated or unobservable, and above all, to the idea that people might actually be mistaken about, or unaware of, their own interests' (Lukes, 1974, p. 14). Lynd (1943) long ago addressed this issue in a foreword to Brady's book *Business as a System of Power*, a system which he argues is:

> an intensely coercive form of organization of society that cumulatively constrains men and all their institutions to work the will of the minority — who hold and wield economic power; and that this relentless warping of men's lives and forms of association becomes less and less the results of voluntary decisions by 'bad' or 'good' men and more and more an impersonal web of coercions dictated by the need to keep the system running. (p. xii)

By analogy, it is therefore important in our studies of curriculum conservation and change to monitor those 'impersonal webs' which keep the education system running and which provide parameters and maybe indeed 'coercions' as well as 'facilitations' for those involved in the construction and promotion of school subjects.

School Subjects: Internal Affairs and External Relations

The Bucher and Strauss (1976) model of professional change described in chapter 4 (see p. 33) suggests that the belief in a subject as monolithic and unified is unlikely to resonate with the reality of the underpinning subject 'community' (p. 19). The subject community should not be viewed as a homogeneous group whose members share similar values and definitions of role, common interests and identities. Rather, the subject community might be seen as a 'social movement' comprising a shifting range of distinct 'missions' or 'traditions' represented by individuals, groups, segments or factions. The importance of these factions will vary considerably over time. As with professions, school subject associations or more *ad hoc* defense groups often develop at particular points in time when conflict intensifies over the school curriculum, resources, recruitment and training. The introduction of the National Curriculum in Britain in the 1980s brought about just such an intensification of conflict and group advocacy and activity.

The internal affairs of each subject community might have been characterized as the 'relations of change' which Ball (1985b) has defined as: 'The power struggles between social groups, coalitions, and segments within the subject community each with their own "sense of mission" and differing and competing vested interests, resources and influence' (pp. 17–18). Goodson has previously argued that school subject communities might be viewed as a political 'coalition' with the constituent subject factions engaged in ongoing political struggle for resources and influence. But it is important to view the subject groups' competition for resources and influence as part of a much wider set of cultural influences. For a start, school subjects themselves were aspects of a 'world movement' which modernized school curricula around subject themes: each subject then has a broad cultural context. Moreover, how school subjects are located and organised is itself considerably influenced by the political culture of the country under consideration. The following instance illustrates a pattern of structuration for school subjects which was analyzed in some earlier work in curriculum history.

The Structural Context of School Subjects: An Example

In previous work, Goodson studied the promotion and definition of secondary school subjects in the 1960s and 1970s in England. His studies pointed up 'the importance of aspects of the structure of the educational system in understanding actions at individual, collective and relational levels'. In some ways he was following Giddens (1986) question 'in what manner can it be said that the conduct of individual actors reproduces the structural properties of larger collectivities' (p. 24). Goodson certainly shared the view that 'analyzing the structuration of social systems means studying the modes in which such systems, grounded in the knowledgeable activities of situated actors who draw upon rules and resources in the diversity of action contexts, are produced and reproduced in action' (*ibid*, p. 25). In studying school subjects such structuration is evidential: 'These structures, which might be viewed from the actors standpoint as the "rules of the game", arise at a particular point in history, for particular reasons: until changed they act as a structural legacy constraining, but also enabling, contemporary actors' (Goodson, 1995b, p. 187). In England and Wales, a major historical period when the salient structure emerged was 1904–1917.

The period of course pre-dates the National Curriculum but as we shall see later bears an uncanny resemblance to it. The 1904 Secondary Regulations listed and prioritized those subjects suitable for education in the secondary grammar schools. These were largely those that have come to be seen as 'academic' subjects, a view confirmed and consolidated by their enshrinement in the School Certificate examinations launched in 1917.

From 1917 onwards examination subjects, the 'academic' subjects, inherited the priority treatment in finance and resources directed at the grammar schools. It should be noted that the examination system itself had developed for a comparable clientele. The foundation of these examinations in 1858 'was the universities' response to petitions that they should help in the development of 'schools for the middle classes'.

The structure of resources linked to examinations has effectively survived the ensuing changes in the educational system (although currently these are now subject to challenge). Byrne (1974) for instance has stated 'that more resources are given to able students and hence to academic subjects', the two are still synony-mous 'since it has been assumed that they necessarily need more staff, more highly paid staff and more money for equipment and books'. The Dearing Report (1996) on new patterns for advanced work may challenge this pattern of hierarchy.

The material interests of teachers — their pay, promotion and conditions — are, at present, intimately interlinked with the fate of their specialist subject as described in some detail in chapter 5. School subjects are organized within schools in departments. The subject teacher's career is pursued within such departments and the department's status depends on the subject's status. The 'academic' subject is placed at the top of the hierarchy of subjects because resource allocation takes place on the basis of assumptions that such subjects are best suited for the 'able' students (and vice versa of course) who, it is further assumed, should receive favourable treatment.

Thus in secondary schools the material and self-interest of subject teachers is interlinked with the status of the subject, judged in terms of its examination status. Academic subjects provide the teacher with a career structure characterized by better promotion prospects and pay than less academic subjects. The conflict over the status of examinable knowledge, as perceived and fought at individual and collective level, is essentially a battle over material resources and career prospects. This battle is reflected in the way that the discourse over school subjects, the debate about their form, content and structure, is constructed and organized. 'Academic' subjects are those which attract 'able' students, hence 'the need for a scholarly discipline' characterizes the way in which the discourse on curriculum is structured and narrowed (*ibid*, pp. 188–9).

Between the 'internal' missions of subject groups and the external 'publics' stands the bureaucracy vested with the task of operating local and central state systems of education. Ball (1985b) has described these 'structures of change' as they applied in the context of English teaching in the mid 1980s where they constituted

> the institutions, organisations, procedures, roles and persons that constitute the formal channels of educational policy making and administration through which or in relation to which must be accomplished, mediated, fought for and negotiated. These would include the Department of Education and Science, Her Majesty's Inspectorate, the Schools Council (perhaps now the Schools Curriculum Development Committee) the Examination Boards and other examining agencies (RSA, BTEC, CGLI), the Further Education Unit and the Manpower Services Commission, also committees of en-quiry. (p. 18)

He adds that these structures lay outside of the subject community but 'maybe influenced or captured by community members' or the structure may at particular points 'impinge directly upon the constitution of subjects by influence, authority or legislation'.

In the post-war British context the notion of 'partnership' between national agencies like the Department of Education and Science and local groups and agencies was paramount. Judge (1984) has noted both that by the mid-1970s the DES was finding it increasingly difficult to hold a restricted view of its responsibilities within the context of a partnership, and also that at the same time HM Inspectorate was redefining its historic function by what he termed a campaign of 'sustained and intelligent aggression'. Pauline Perry of Her Majesty's Inspectorate saw the possibility of breaking partnership constraints as a political initiative:

> So when ministers finally decided, for whatever political or economic reasons . . . at that point they look for the people who are saying the right kind of things willing to pick up the baton and run with it and I think the Inspectorate was riding high and has continued to ride high because we were there and there were enough of us around who were willing to pick up the baton and run with it and do something. We were certainly in a position to respond. (Ball, 1990)

Fletcher (1995) judges that the DES 'appears to have attempted to extricate itself from the constraints of a partnership, and to have been prepared to advance and implement contentious policies' exploiting what has been described as the 'window of opportunity' (p. 142) which emerged in the mid-1970s:

> In part the 'window of opportunity' has been exploited by putting the DES, since 1981, in the political hands of ministers with either a flair for publicity, or an unfortunate aptitude to attract it. John MacGregor's apparent willingness to consult, and to listen, places him beyond this generalisation and may go some way to explaining the brevity of his tenure. If the 'place in the sun' that the DES enjoyed in the late 1980s (Hennessy, 1990) has since been replaced by much less hospitable terrain and a more unflattering spotlight, this may in no small measure result from its iconoclastic presentation of education reform. Heralded as providing the most fundamental reform of the education service for decades, and one which would roll back the powers of the providers of education, in favour of its clienteles, the Education Reform Act 1988 epitomized the Thatcher governments' challenges to post-war consensus social welfare policy. (*ibid*)

In analyzing the place within the British context, of the educational state in promoting educational change Salter and Tapper (1985) have argued that the Department of Education and Science (which became the Department for Education in 1992 and the Department for Education and Employment in 1995) was 'an ambitious bureaucracy' long before it launched the 1988 goals for power code — named the National Curriculum (see chapter 10):

> the central educational bureaucracy, the DES, is an important part of the State because it is the main arena in which attempts are made to translate pressures from the economic base into educational policy. As such it acts as a focus for the exercise of educational power. (p. 22)

The Department took a range of important agenda-setting initiatives, for it

> is best placed to initiate and orchestrate the discussions which will lead to
> the formation of educational goals, to create those committees which carry
> the process one step further, to disseminate the findings that emerge from
> these committees, and to present the official response to the wider public
> reaction. At the same time it can put pressure on the local education
> authorities, schools and teachers to push the experience of schooling in the
> desired direction. (Salter and Tapper, 1981, p. 43)

Whilst the Department, as the most central agent of the educational state is
therefore very powerful, it is not at all clear that this will lead to management or
policy which is in harmony with those dominant interest groups linked to the
economic base. This is because of the nature of bureaucracy itself (let alone an
'ambitious bureaucracy'). Max Weber noted that 'once it is fully established bureaucracy is among those social structures which are hardest to destroy'. In quoting
this line Tapper and Salter argue that this permanence of a bureaucracy:

> is enhanced by its technical advantages (precision, speed, continuity etc.),
> the cult of the objective and indispensable expert; its hoarding and control
> of specialised knowledge; its use of secrecy to increase the superiority of
> the 'professionally informed'; and its general protective cloak of rational
> organisation and operation. (*ibid*, pp. 57–8)

Hence a bureaucracy can come to have its own interest and mission in the same
manner as subject groups. These interests can be loosely coupled with the political
regime in government and with the economic structure of the country. Once again
therefore, as with subject groups, we need to understand internal affairs and the
missions and agendas of particular bureaucratic factions. Hence with the DES

> as an established bureaucracy it has goals, needs and ideology which may
> well run counter in educational policy terms to the demands of the economy.
> Thus the emergence of policy is conceived of as the result of the interplay
> between the economic and bureaucratic dynamics; an interplay which can
> take time to draw to a conclusion given both the shifting nature of eco-
> nomic pressures and the internal inefficiencies in the Department's policy-
> making procedures. (Such as tensions between long-term planning and
> Public Expenditure Survey Committee (PESC) requirements, and inter-
> branch rivalry). (Salter and Tapper, 1985, pp. 22–3)

To put the matter in the simplest terms

> There is no guarantee that the bureaucratic dynamic will work harmoni-
> ously with the economic dynamic, no guarantee that it is able to ensure the
> appropriate policies concerning the organisation of knowledge, certification

and the attitudes and values inculcated in school will duly serve the capitalist order. For like all institutions the Department has over time developed
its own momentum, and its own inertia, which means that its exercise of
educational power runs in certain policy grooves. (*ibid*, p. 24)

Beyond the built-in internal constraints of the bureaucratic dynamic the educational state also collides with the range of constraints at school level we have
noted earlier. For in the schools there already exist structured and institutionalized
practices which may be defused rather than transformed by self-managing schools.
It is therefore true with regard to the curriculum of the schools that 'curricular
contests won in any one sphere may be lost in another, opening up the possibility
of wide variations between sites in their dominant definitions of curricula' (Bates,
1989, p. 228).

The bureaucratic apparatus of the educational state has degrees of autonomy
and the capacity to service its own internally-generated demands. In many ways,
however, the bureaucratic dynamic does take account of those demands related to
the economic base. In more recent times in both Britain and the USA this has not
been unrelated to the increasing participation of businessmen and representatives
of the 'enterprise culture' on advisory boards, committees, governing bodies and ad
hoc groups. But direct participation is not the major explanation.

Dougherty (1988) has spoken of a modality of power which works with and
accepts the bureaucratic dynamic and which 'operates when policies that benefit
private interest groups are enacted by government officials with little or no prior
articulation by the groups of their interests and policy preferences'. He argues that
such action occurs for two reasons: either the officials share the attitudes of the
private interest groups (ideological hegemony) or the Government officials believe
that the private interest groups control resources that they need to realize their own
bureaucratic and self interests (inducements):

The inducement side of the power of constraint has lain in the fact that
Government officials sphere of autonomous action is limited by their subordination to a democratic polity and a capitalist economy. Government
officials are ultimately dependent for their authority on the assent of the
people, as expressed by their votes. But those votes are strongly condi-
tioned by the state of the economy and government provision of politically
popular programs. And in a capitalist economy, economic growth and tax
revenues to finance government programs are dependent on business's
willingness to invest capital. (pp. 409–10)

In short the bureaucratic missions, similarly to the subject missions, afford
primacy to the pursuit of resources. In their common resource dependency lies the
interface with the economic base. We need to distinguish between domination (the
direct exercise of power by dominant groups) and mediation (the exercise of power
by mediating, normally professional or bureaucratic groups.) In the following section
we shall employ this distinction to reconceptualize power and the operation of the
education system as it is evidenced in the terrain of the school curriculum.

School Subjects and Political Process

The foregoing section provides some insight into how the allocation of resources, financial distribution, the attribution of status and the construction of career are both *structured practices* and *institutionalized practices*. For example, Goodson (1995b) has argued:

> The structure of the system, and its material and concrete form, is associated with the way that particular patterns of curriculum are constructed and reconstructed. In this way, certain priorities and parameters are set for local authorities, educators and practitioners. The political economy of the curriculum particularly of the school subject, is then of vital concern for it is a 'heartland' for the patterning and prioritizing which establishes a particular 'character' for schooling. (p. 8)

In this regard, John Meyer distinguishes between *institutional* and *organizational* categories.

> 'institutional' connotes a 'cultural ideology and is contrasted with 'organizational', meaning cushioned within unique and tangible structures such as schools and classrooms. Institutional categories comprise schooling levels (such as primary), school types (such as comprehensive) educational roles (such as college principal) and importantly for our purpose curricular topics (such as reading, the Reformation or 'O' level mathematics). In each of these instances, the organizational form as created and maintained by teachers and others is paralleled by an institutional category which is significant for some wider public or publics. (summarised in Reid, 1984, p. 68)

The institutional categories Meyer defines are the vital currency in the educational market place. In this market place identifiable and standard social typications are necessary: for students because they are constructing school careers connected to desired social and occupational destinations and for teachers who wish to ensure successful futures for their students and high status, well-resourced careers for themselves. The mission of subject fractions links into the market place in the pursuit of those rhetorics which will ensure identifiable categories which have credibility in the public mind. For Reid:

> successful rhetorics are realities. Though teachers and administrators have to be careful that disjunctions between practice and belief do not escalate to the point where credibility collapses, nonetheless it remains true that what is most important for the success of school subjects is not the delivery of 'goods' which can be publicly evaluated, but the development and maintenance of legitimating rhetorics which provide automatic support for correctly labelled activity. The choice of appropriate labels and the association of these in public mind with plausible rhetorics of justification can be seen

as the core mission of those who work to advance or defend the subjects of the curriculum. (*ibid*, p. 75)

We have also seen in the foregoing analysis of school subject missions and bureaucratic missions that beyond the internalistic pursuit of ideological support and resources lies the development of patterns of external support. The administration and definition of the institutional categories of schooling is often the task of the state bureaucracies. These institutional categories provide important parameters for the work of school subject missions. We have argued that these provide for the school subject groups discernible 'rules of the game' and that in examining the actions of subject groups in this way we are able to illuminate aspects of structuration.

The administrative operation and definition by state bureaucracies of institutional categories provides here the major terrain within which subject groups undertake their work in the English context. In other countries with varying but often greater effect the institutional categories of schooling both partially derive from and are sustained by groups and individuals external to the educational system. The ideologies and rhetorics of external constituencies are located in the sociocultural processes which label and support particular categories of the educational enterprise as valid and worthwhile. In this way 'external forces and structures emerge not merely as sources of ideas, prompting inducements and constraints, but as definers and carriers of content, role and activity to which the practice of schools must approximate in order to attract support and legitimation' (*ibid*, p. 68). The external constituencies are therefore vital actors in the ideological support for, and ongoing discourse around, the established institutional categories of schooling. In this sense there is a close ongoing alliance between the state bureaucracy who may formally define and administer institutional categories and the external constituencies who provide ideological support and resources. External relations cover the major constituencies not as formally organized special interest groups such as parents, employer and curious but more broadly concerned constituencies which cover these groups but include scholars, politicians, professionals and others:

> These interested publics which pay for and support education hand over its work to the professionals in only a limited and unexpected sense. For while it may appear that the professionals have power to determine what is taught (at school, district and national level, depending on the country in question) their hope is limited by the fact that only the forms and activities which have significance for external publics can, in the long run, survive. (*ibid*)

To win the continued support of external constituencies suitable categories or rhetorics must be defined and as we have seen this then becomes, as in the rules of the game, the core mission of subject groups. They must develop legitimating, rhetorics or mythologies which provide automatic support for correctly labelled activity.

The pursuit of ideological support and resources from educational bureaucracies and external constituencies provides one contextual framework for understanding subject group missions. This is not, however, to assert the singularity of *material interests* over all others with regard to the actions of subject groups. Clearly in the pursuit of financial resources per se these interests may have primacy but in the articulation of subject missions more *idealistic* and moral *interests* emerge. For instance 'I love my subject above all things' is a statement of ideal interests or 'I believe my subject is the major vehicle for human emancipation' is a moral version. Both of these statements provide legitimating rhetorics but they may be deeply held, internalized and believed in just the same way as more material interests are. Indeed the best legitimating rhetorics for subjects successfully merge material, idealistic and moral interests.

Moreover, these different 'interests' may impinge differently at different levels. The construction of a successful rhetoric for the subject may well concede primacy to material interests but once successfully established a subject has to be negotiated and realised at a number of subsequent levels. The subject may be *preactive* at the level of the guidelines, textbook or syllabus but is interactively negotiated at a range of subsequent levels: The subject *department*, the subject *subculture*, the daily *micropolitics* of the subject in the school and the *habitus* of the subject, the daily classroom routines of the subject teacher.

The subject group mission, however, is to promote the subject by winning over the legitimating constituencies to ideological support and resource provision. To achieve this task the subject's definition and rhetorics is in a very real sense a political *manifesto* or *slogan*. For the rationale of a particular version of the subject is in this sense political expediency. Successful school subjects must appear as unchallengeable and monolithic essences — (distillations of excellence in a particular form or field of knowledge to take a philosophical slant). The subject then becomes a mythologized monolith which exists regardless of its specific realization as structured or institutionalized practice.

The school subject then must 'have value as currency on the social identity market'. This market calls for a standard, stable currency of social typifications. In this sense the missions of school subject groups are just one aspect of the acceptance of the structures of the market and of the structuring of educational systems in the image of that market. The mythologization of school subject categories ensures a fixity in the public mind and an acceptance of the subject 'as currency'. This currency for the categorical subject remains until it is devalued by unsustainable contradictions at other levels or by major paradigm shifts, organizational shifts or changes in external constituency demands.

An interesting example to illustrate the above occurred in Queensland, Australia during the 1970s (Marsh and Stafford, 1988, pp. 181–4). During the 1970s in Australia, the influence of US national curriculum projects on Australian education was considerable, especially in such areas as mathematics, physics and biology. It was not surprising therefore than an integrated social science course, supervised by Jerome Bruner and entitled 'Man: A Course of Study' (MACOS) and which had gained considerable publicity and success in the USA, was accepted readily by several state education systems in Australia.

MACOS was seen to be a worthy alternative to traditional, dated primary social studies courses because it contained a wealth of stimulus materials including audio-visual materials, it espoused a values-oriented approach which was in vogue among educationalists during the 1970s, and it demonstrated the skills needed of social scientists, and especially the anthropologists. Furthermore, the Innovations Programme of the Commonwealth Schools Commission provided encouragement to schools to try innovative teaching programmes and provided financial support for this to occur.

In terms of Meyer's organizational categories there was considerable support for MACOS. The state education bureaucracy in Queensland supported the project. In particular, the Primary Curriculum Committee decided to trial it initially in fifteen pilot schools in 1973. Funds from the Commonwealth Schools Commission enabled teachers from the fifteen schools to receive an intensive five-day inservice training on key components of MACOS and its major sub-themes — What is human about human beings?

How did they get that way?

How can they be made more so?

The parents and citizens groups associated with the fifteen trial schools also attended in-service sessions where they were able to examine and interact with the attractive and enticing array of books, films, posters, records, games and other classroom materials which comprise the MACOS kit. The Queensland Teachers' Union was also very supportive of the project and saw benefits for their members to be involved.

In hindsight, it is apparent that the institutional categories, as defined by Meyer, were forces that were underestimated and which ultimately led to the banning of the subject.

The catalyst of the external forces which became marshalled to oppose MACOS was Mrs. Rona Joyner, the spokesperson for two fundamentalist pressure groups entitled Society to Outlaw Pornography (STOP) and the Committee Against Regressive Education (CARE). These organizations had invited a Texan fundamentalist textbook 'analyst' to their annual general meeting of the Festival of Light in July 1977.

During the latter months of 1977, Mrs Joyner and her STOP/CARE colleagues mounted an intensive lobbying campaign to abolish MACOS from Queensland State schools. Their tactics were direct and effective. State members of parliament, especially Cabinet ministers, were contacted frequently as additional information became available about the 'anti-Christian, anti-family, socialist-humanist cells active within the Education Department'.[1] Members of Parliament were encouraged to address local community meetings in their respective constituencies. The meetings were usually arranged by STOP/CARE to ensure that the banning of MACOS was kept alive as an issue. It was also part of the strategy to have newsworthy events occurring so that local press and daily press representatives could be given appropriate press releases. In addition, Mrs. Joyner kept up a steady stream of letters to the editor of regional and daily papers, made guest appearances on radio and television, and undertook a personal tour of many outlying regions of Queensland.

The message of STOP/CARE was designed to appeal to parents by playing on their emotions about what was 'good' and 'evil' for their children as future citizens. Reference was constantly made to two areas which were undermining Queensland society, namely sexual permissiveness and political conspiracy, and these evils, according to STOP/CARE, could only be countered by rigorous censorship. (Scott and Scott, 1980). In true propagandist style, this message was repeated constantly via the various media outlets.

Taken out of context, statements by the STOP/CARE group appear to be superficial, if not ridiculous in the extreme. For example, in one newspaper statement, Joyner expressed the view that

> Children don't go to school to learn to think. They go to learn to read and write and spell correctly. They can start thinking when they're older and their minds are not being manipulated.[2]

Yet these same statements when communicated at meetings and interviews created 'appropriate' doubts and fears in the minds of parents about the MACOS materials. The plurality of values and cultural relativism orientation in the MACOS materials was an easy target for STOP/CARE proponents. Using emotive language they were able to heighten concern that children using MACOS materials might develop undesirable values and attitudes, and that the fabric of their stable society was indeed being threatened. Supporters of MACOS did not appear to provide counter arguments about the positive effects of the materials and the desirable values that might be developed. They also tended to discount the impact of the STOP/CARE propaganda on the general public.

Other groups and individuals ably supported the initiatives of STOP/CARE. The Community Standards Organization applied pressure at the teacher training level and issued various media statements attacking teacher education institutions which studied MACOS in their pre-service courses. At a time of chronic oversupply of teachers, their exhortations that graduates from these teacher education institutions should not be employed in the Queensland State education system were indeed threatening. The Association of Catholic Parents was fully supportive of the efforts of STOP/CARE to exclude social science courses such as MACOS as they did not conform to traditional Christian culture and standards (Scott and Scott, 1980, p. 60).

Even individuals from tertiary institutions came out strongly in support of STOP/CARE, although the majority from this education sector were pro-MACOS. A reader in education at the University of Queensland entered the debate as a strong supporter of STOP/CARE via letters to the daily newspapers, public addresses and a television interview. His rhetoric was equally emotive and on occasions misleading, such as his comments about the dissemination program for MACOS 'disowned by the American Congress and now peddled around the world by multi-national companies'.[3]

The ferocity of the attack upon MACOS and the strength of support from so many quarters was such that pro-MACOS pressure groups could muster little effective counter. For example, the Queensland Council of State School Organizations (QCSSO) took the common sense line that decisions about adopting curriculum materials should be made by individual school communities. This in fact was what had happened at the fifteen trial schools where parents and teachers had agreed to cooperate in trialing and subsequently implementing the MACOS materials. But a common sense approach did not appeal to the general public who were being constantly pump-primed by the emotive rhetoric of STOP/CARE and allied organizations. Further, the QCSSO, supposedly representative of all State school parents, was unable to muster the authority it desired because there were very many parents who were evidently supportive of the STOP/CARE directives. Suffering from this lack of representation, it is not difficult to comprehend why the QCSSO had a very limited influence upon the turn of events during 1977/78.

Most surprising, perhaps, was the very limited initiative undertaken by the Queensland Teachers' Union (QTU). Despite the vociferous denunciations of MACOS by STOP/CARE during the latter months of 1977, the QTU did not make public statements about its stand until after the Minister of Education had formally announced in January 1978 that MACOS was to be banned. The union quite properly denounced the political interference into what teachers should or should not teach. They also supported the QCSSO stance that parents and teachers in individual schools should make decisions about the selection of rejection of materials and that the Government decision was insulting to all the parents who had become vitally involved in the fifteen trial schools.

Their demonstration of resistance to the government move was tangible evidence of their displeasure, but far from a show of strength. A protest meeting was held, letters were sent to Cabinet ministers, and the QTU supported efforts by teachers at seven State primary schools to resist moves to have MACOS materials confiscated by senior education officials. The QTU clearly did not want the dispute to widen because, prior to the compulsory conference held before the State Industrial Commission in February 1978, the union instructed the teachers at the seven schools to cease their resistance. The stand taken by the QTU may have had some leverage on the Premier's decision to establish an inquiry into the Queensland education system (Ahern Committee), but even that is doubtful considering that no union representative was included on the Committee.

The Premier and his Cabinet clearly held the trump card and had a dominant influence over the events leading up to the banning of MACOS in Queensland State schools. The Government had on previous occasions showed its willingness to ride over the educational bureaucratic structure and censor the use of specific curriculum materials (for example, a booklet on uranium mining). The Cabinet, and especially the Premier, had developed their own pragmatic set of values which reflected the aspirations of their rural, conservative constituents. They came down on the side of moral protection of minors, of upholding standards and of stamping out purported incursions by humanists, socialists, and libertarians — and to weaken the effects of 'undesirable' initiatives being developed by Federal government agencies!

The Premier made it quite clear to teachers where he stood after the announcement that the MACOS materials would be banned. In reply to a question about what would happen to teachers who refused to discontinue using MACOS materials, he stated:

There are plenty of others around the ridges. There are 200 out of work. Ministers were in 100 per cent agreement that MACOS goes. Teachers will comply. This is Government policy. I know all responsible teachers recognise this point.[4]

It is apparent that the institutional forces representing religious groups, politicians and especially the Premier, developed appropriate legitimating rhetoric to win over support from the general public. Above all, the Premier was able to withhold resource provisions to teachers and schools, thereby ensuring that the decision to ban MACOS would be enforced. The example illustrates some of the forces at work in fostering change, but also the powerful forces which can retain stability and conservation. This latter topic is discussed further in the next chapter.

Curriculum Change as Sociopolitical Process

The Australian example illustrates the nature of curricula change as sociopolitical process — sometimes the political aspect remains somewhat covert, at other times, as in the case of the British National Curriculum, it is overt, almost triumphalist, in tenor and mode. But either way a political process of definition, evolution and negotiation can be discerned. Looking at England in the 1960s and 1970s Goodson defined four stages in the 'process of academic establishment' for a school subject. In subsequent forms and when taken up in other milieux this process sometimes begins at stage 2 with promotion, stage 3 with legislation, to implement that which has been invented elsewhere.

1 *Invention* may come about from the activities or ideas of educators; sometimes as a response to 'climates of opinion' or pupil demands or resistance or from inventions in the 'outside world':

> The ideas necessary for creation . . . are usually available over a relatively prolonged period of time in several places. Only a few of these inventions will lead to further action'. (Ben-David and Collins, 1966)

2 *Promotion* by educator groups internal to the educational system. Inventions will be taken up 'where and when persons become interested in the new idea, not only as intellectual content but also as a means of establishing a new intellectual identity and particularly a new occupational role'. Hence, subjects with low status, poor career patterns and even with actual survival problems may readily embrace and promote new inventions such as environmental studies. Conversely high-status subjects may ignore quite major opportunities as they are already satisfactorily resourced and provide existing desirable careers. The response of science groups to 'technology' or (possibly) contemporary mathematics groups to 'computer studies' are cases in point. Promotion of invention arises from a perception of the possibility of basic improvements in occupational role and status.

3 *Legislation* The promotion of new inventions, if successful, leads to the establishment of new categories or subjects. Whilst promotion is initially primarily internally generated, it has to develop external relations with sustaining 'constituencies'. This will be a major stage in ensuring that new categories or subjects are fully accepted, established and institutionalized. And further, that having been established, they can be sustained and supported over time. Legislation is associated with the development and maintenance of those discourses or legitimating rhetorics which provide automatic support for correctly labelled activity.

4 *Mythologization*. Once automatic support has been achieved for a subject or category, a fairly wide range of activities can be undertaken. The limits are any activities which threaten the legitimating rhetoric and hence constituency support. The subject at this point is mythological. It represents essentially a licence that has been granted, (or perhaps a 'patent' or 'monopoly rights'), with the full force of the law and establishment behind it (Goodson, 1995b, pp. 193–4).

It is interesting to assess the significance of the National Curriculum in such a process of subject establishment especially with regard to the stages of legislation and mythologization. The forces of the arguments for remythologizing and relegislating school subjects at a time of 'market-led' arguments has been powerful (Ball, 1994). But it is worth recalling the views of David Layton about the patterns of change in school subjects.

Layton (1972b) has analyzed the evolution of science in England from the nineteenth century and in a brief article has developed a tentative model for the evolution of a school subject in the secondary school curriculum. Layton defined three stages in this evolution. In the first stage:

> the callow intruder stakes a place in the timetable, justifying its presence on grounds such as pertinence and utility. During this stage learners are attracted to the subject because of its bearing on matters of concern to them. The teachers are rarely trained specialists, but bring the missionary enthusiasms of pioneers to their task. The dominant criterion is relevance to the needs and interests of the learners.

In the interim second stage:

> a tradition of scholarly work in the subject is emerging along with a corps of trained specialists from which teachers may be recruited. Students are still attracted to the study, but as much by its reputation and growing academic status as by its relevance to their own problems and concerns. The internal logic and discipline of the subject is becoming increasingly influential in the selection and organization of subject matter.

In the final stage:

the teachers now constitute a professional body with established rules and values. The selection of subject matter is determined in large measure by the judgements and practices of the specialist scholars who lead inquiries in the field. Students are initiated into a tradition, their attitudes approaching passivity and resignation, a prelude to disenchantment.

Layton's model warns against any monolithic explanation of subjects and disciplines. It would seem that, far from being timeless statements of intrinsically worthwhile content, subjects and disciplines may carry substantial 'downsides' which lead to new moves to reform and reconstitute the school curriculum. Hence subjects can be successfully invented, legislated and mythologised but even then carry within them the seeds of new cycles of reform, reconstitution and reaction.

Reflections and Issues

1   Describe the major educational bureaucracies that you consider affect subject teaching. What goals and ideology do they espouse and in what ways do they facilitate or hinder the development of school subjects?
2   What are some typical strategies used by subject groups (subject teachers, subject associations) to win over support and resources from legitimating constituencies? Use examples from a teaching subject with which you are familiar.
3   In *Studying Curriculum*, Goodson (1994) notes that the National Curriculum in the U.K. emerged because the elite and middle class groups were 'at risk'. Explain what is meant by this assertion. Which external constituencies in the UK have provided support for the National Curriculum.

Suggested Reading

Useful articles include:

Ball, S.J. (1985) 'Relations, Structures and Conditions in Curriculum Change: A Political History of English Teaching 1970–85', in Goodson, I.F. (Ed) *International Perspectives in Curriculum History*, London: Routledge.

Fletcher, J. (1995) Policy-making in DES/DfE via Consensus and Contention. *Oxford Review of Education*, **21**, 2, 133–148.

Layton, D. (1972) 'Science as General Education', *Trends in Education*, January.

Meyer, J.W. and Rowan, B. (1983) 'The Structure of Educational Organization', in Meyer, J.W. and Scott, W.R. (Eds) *Organisational Environments*, California: Sage.

Taylor, T. (1995) 'Movers and Shakers: High politics and the Origins of the Nation Curriculum', *The Curriculum Journal*, **6**, 2, pp. 161–84.

Useful books include:

Hargreaves, A. (1995) *Changing Teachers, Changing Times*. London: Cassell.

Reid, W.A. (1992) *The Pursuit of Curriculum*. Norwood, New Jersey: Ablex.

Notes

1   Joiner, R. (1978) newspaper article in the *National Times*.
2   Joiner, R. (1978) newspaper article in *Gold Coast Bulletin*.
3   Article in *Courier Mail* newspaper, 9 November 1977.
4   Article in *Courier Mail* newspaper, 3 February 1978.

Chapter 10

School Subjects: Patterns of Stability

The internal affairs and external relations of curriculum change should be interlinked aspects in any analysis of educational reform. Where the internal and external are in conflict or unsynchronized, then change tends to be piecemeal or ephemeral. Since harmonization across the arenas of educational change at the same point in time is difficult, curriculum stability or conservation is common. Often what happens is a divergence between Meyers 'institutional categories' and 'organizational changes' as noted in chapter 9. If change at one level does not happen or is unsuccessful then change at the other level may be inappropriate, unsuccessful, or ephemeral.

For instance, in English secondary schools in the 1960s there was widespread organizational change towards a 'comprehensive system'. These changes created a political climate or perception that general participation was to be a major organizational goal and that school subjects should be organizationally redefined so as to educate the widest possible student clientele. However, the organizational change was not echoed by a general change in institutional categories. The internal and external were therefore unsynchronized and unharmonized. Reid (1984) has summarized the results:

> In the event, it seems that, though politically sanctioned, the changes which took place were more properly organizational than institutional. The norms imposed by university entrance requirements and by GCE examining continue to set the parameters for educational categories which have proved remarkably resistant to attempts to 'democratise' them (notably the removal of the pass/fail boundary from GCE 'O' level has met with no response in terms of public categories: students, parents and most teachers still talk of 'passing "O" level'). Subjects such as science, which a few years ago were trying to develop topics accessible to a wide range of students are now once again stressing high status content and deemphasizing innovative teaching styles. (p. 73)

Essentially this episode exemplifies a situation where the internal affairs and external relations are unharmonized or, put more starkly, divergent. Thus organizational changes were implemented but institutional categories, dependent on sustaining external constituencies, proved resistant to change. Organizational change which is unsustained or unparalleled by a new institutional category (that is significant for wider public constituencies) or vice versa is unlikely to be of importance or durability in the long run.

At root, what is required to understand curriculum stability and change are forms of analysis which seek to scrutinize internal affairs *alongside* external relations, as a way of developing insights on both organizational change and changes in the more broadly-based institutional categories. Such analysis moves beyond the somewhat internalistic mode of some genres of curriculum inquiry. These modes of inquiry often develop medical analogies for what Miles has called the 'organizational health' of schools. In Hoyles work (1969), curriculum change fails to 'take' because of a sort of tissue rejection by schools which lack organizational health. The emphasis is on the internal constitution and operation of the school as a discrete and self-regulating body.

Webster has cogently argued against this medical analogy by developing some of the insights of Robert A. Nisbet which exhort us to concentrate on wider aspects of cultural change and conservation. He urges us to appreciate 'the mechanisms of fixity and persistence in society . . . the sheer power of conservatism in social life; the power of custom, tradition, habit and mere inertia'. As Webster (1971) notes:

In Nisbet's view, we are often deceived into thinking that radical social change is taking place because we do not take note of the significant distinction . . . between readjustment or individual deviance within a social structure (whose effects, although possibly cumulative, are never sufficient to alter the structure on basic cultural postulates of a society or institution) and the more fundamental, though enigmatic, change of structure, type, pattern or paradigm. (pp. 204–5)

Hence, Nisbet argues 'the moments of history are rare when, as a result of crisis, and some form of attention given the crisis by some elite or individual, a genuinely new way of life is the result'. Mostly 'the consequence proves to be a kind of weathering of the crisis and then a regression to the familiar and traditional' (*ibid*, p. 206). I think any scholar of curriculum change and innovation would recognize this outcome. Organizational change has to be paralleled by institutional category change (and by the birth of new institutionalized practices) to ensure Nisbet's 'fundamental change'. But the establishment of a new institutional category and associated institutionalised practices carries within it the seeds of new patterns of tradition and inertia. Fundamental change in short requires the 'invention of (new) traditions'.

In a pioneering study McKinney and Westbury (1975) established the systemic nature of curriculum change. They were researching 'stability and change' in the public schools of Gary, Indiana in the years 1940–70.

Intellectual discourses which are thought in a given period to be of cultural or instrumental value for the young, become, in the school, *subjects* which, in their turn, offer the intellectual organization for, and the vehicles by which teachers of known character and quality are deployed to teach their knowledge systematically to millions of students for the twelve or so years they are in school. Teachers leave the schools but students remain

— it is the existence of a program organized in routinized ways that makes it possible for one teacher to pick up where another leaves off, whether in mid-year or at year-end. It is the existence of these social institutions with their known character that makes possible the common endeavours of a school system — the training of teachers, the writing of texts and examinations, the construction of apparatus and buildings and the like. In other words, subjects and the forms of schooling which surround them are structural frames which specify the conditions and the meaning contexts within which teaching will take place and are the foci and the means of institutional collaboration by the agencies of schooling for the furtherance of their work. (pp. 8–9)

The school subject as an institutionalized system and practice therefore provides a structural frame for action. But the subject itself is part of a wider structural frame which embodies and defines the social purposes and possibilities of schooling. For the definition of the school subject as rhetorical discourse, content, organizational form and institutionalized practice is implicated in the practices of social distribution and reproduction.

We have therefore to begin to see the subject as one block in a mosaic painstakingly constructed over the centuries that it has taken to devise state schooling systems. Only then can we begin to understand the role of the school subject within wider social purposes: purposes which often relate closely to the mysterious 'mechanisms of fixity and persistence in society' noted earlier. The school subject is therefore one of a number of prisms through what we might glimpse the structural frame surrounding state schooling. It seems, however, a particular valuable terrain for inquiry for the subject sits at the intersection of the internal and external forces we have noted: moreover the actions of 'educational state' are often uncharacteristically visible at times of subject redefinition (for example, in the current case of the British national curriculum or in the current debate over the Australian curriculum).

The school subject stands in a sense as the archetype of the division and fragmentation of knowledge within our societies. Encapsulated within each subject microcosm broader debates about the social purposes of schooling are pursued, but pursued in an insulated manner and segmented (and indeed sedimented) in the range of different internal and external levels and public and private arenas of discourse. Harmonization across levels and arenas is an elusive pursuit: stability and conservation therefore remain the most likely result of the structuring of schooling of which subjects are such a critical ingredient.

Some scholars have recently argued that the system was from its early days built to ensure stability and to mystify and conceal the power relations which underpin all curriculum-making. For instance, speaking of Germany specifically and Europe generally, Haft and Hopmann (1990) have argued that:

Societies like ours are class societies, organized to provide for an uneven distribution of the resources needed for self-determination of one's way of life, and thus one's chances of education. Since such resources cannot be increased at will, every decision about distribution means taking from one and giving to another. Consequently, social struggle is on the national as well as on the international agenda. Problems arise whenever the losers refuse to give in. Thus, from the viewpoint of the dominant forces in the distribution fight, it is necessary, to organize the distribution in a way that it can ensure consensus by a majority, or at least not effectively be challenged.

The same holds for state-run curriculum making: The distribution of knowledge is socially secure as long as it is accepted as a rule, or at least not effectively challenged, however unequal it may be. (p. 159)

And further that:

curriculum making is the mode of producing curricula which makes sure that the structure of the social process conceals the underlying power relations, or at least prevents their being effectively interfered with.

This concealment is not as easy as it sounds. Simply keeping quiet will not do, unless Orwell's nightmare comes true with complete control of the social distribution of knowledge. Moreover, to keep quiet, all of those contributing to the existing structure of distribution would have to agree — something which is very unlikely in a society like ours. Hence, what is needed is an elaborate system able to provide *legitimation* of the desired distribution. At its best, such a system can itself produce or organize the legitimation it needs. Frictions that may occur during the process of legitimation must not affect the underlying balance of power, but have to be neutralized in other areas (making them appear as technical problems of, for instance, the structure of knowledge or the method of teaching). (*ibid*, p. 160)

In scrutinizing the emergence of their own system in Germany from the first Prussian Normal plan of 1816, they note that the division of syllabi according to school level and school type further entailed divisions into timetables, examination and promotion regulations, instructions concerning textbooks etc. In its final version these divisions are augmented by the overall syllabus which is reduced to a subject-based catalogue of goals and contents. Haft and Hopmann argue that:

For the administration the practical returns of this differentiation of the curricular framework serve a double purpose. First, the separation of syllabus editing from decisions about structural as well as educational principles relieves planners from pressure which would otherwise arise from the curricular discourse where basic structures of knowledge distribution are touched upon. Proposals to change that distribution by curriculum reform can thus almost always be rejected with reference to other levels of regulation (such as laws, examination rules, or timetables). The exclusion of fundamental school organization and subject canon questions has become so self-evident for syllabus authors that today suggestions to treat such questions in curriculum commissions are met with incomprehensibility. On the other hand, all attempts to eliminate once initiated differentiation, for example, to have structural and subject planning questions solved by one and the same commission, have failed and thus proved the necessity of compartmentalization.

The second advantage of continuing differentiation lies in its creation of a clear framework of reasoning for the planning of distinct sections of subject-matter. Thus, there is no discussion at all about the purpose of schooling as a whole, but narrowly defined issues, such as whether optics should be taught in the seventh or in the ninth grade, or which type of literature should dominate in tenth grade lessons. Such detailed questions are obviously questions for experts, and not for the general public. Tying syllabus work to subjects opens up ways of justification which are hardly possible at a more comprehensive level. As for the rest, the subject constraints in syllabus work are reflected in parallel differentiations in school administration, teacher training, and employment, and thus create a consistent network of cross-reference elements in which all curricula quarrels can be taken care of. (*ibid*, p. 162)

The structuring of schooling into subjects represents at once a fragmentation and an internalization of the struggles over state schooling. Fragmentation because conflicts take place through a range of compartmentalized subjects; internalization because now conflicts take place not only within the school but also within subject boundaries. Giving primacy to the 'school subject' in the resourcing of schooling is therefore to finance and to promote a particular narrowing of the possible discourse about schooling.

The symbolic enshrinement of subjects as the basis of the secondary school curricula is perhaps the most successful principle in the history of curriculum making. However, as we have seen, it is not a neutral, bureaucratic or rational/educational device, it is a perfect device for conservation and stability and stands to effectively frustrate any more holistic reform initiatives. Comprehensive innovations such as those suggested by Dewey stand little chance of long-term implementation. In Nisbet's terms they inevitably remain within a subject-structured world 'readjustments or individual deviances' fundamental change is essentially unattainable within such a structured frame.

New initiatives in curriculum-making have to be scrutinized at this level of symbolic action. A segmented subject-centred model of schooling acts to effectively silence or marginalize alternative models. Yet often the symbolic significance of subject-centredness is itself unrecognized in much of the debate over new initiatives. In the debate over the English National Curriculum there has been a deafening silence on this aspect of the proposals.

Reinscribing the 'Traditional': The English National Curriculum

Each new subject initiative has been the site of furious debate about the purposes and parameters of schooling. But by accepting the structural frame, the discussants have accepted an initiative which as symbolic action is likely to make stability and conservation more pervasive and enduring. This is the enduring appeal of subject-centred models of curriculum to dominant groups: they allow endless debate about purposes and parameters but fragmented and internalized within boundaries that make any pervasive change all but impossible:

> a fragmented curriculum structure allows for new concepts to be at least partially adopted, provided borders between disciplines are not blurred past recognition. Permission to leave the given framework of subject administration is by no means easily obtained, and always confined to closely related areas of subject-matter. The 'coalition', . . . which makes up a particular subject must be weakened from within. Hence, the English effort to realize an integrated science approach succeeded only where it was supported by a combination of incentives and a severe shortage of science teachers. . . . To establish the integrated approach as the regular form of science instruction seems quite impossible unless corresponding programs materialize on the levels of both administration and schooling itself (which might, of course, prove difficult, given the social division of disciplines).

> The fact that integrated approaches are not useful in compartmentalized systems does, however, not mean that there have to be different curriculum concepts in every compartment. The reverse is true. The limits of the system as a whole curtail the degree of change a single effort can achieve. In compartmentalized systems no level has been left accessible where curriculum making could be organized as an effort of social construction of a completely changed structure and distribution of knowledge. Given dependencies and ruling ideas cannot be challenged in general. So, if there is a predominant curriculum concept for the system as a whole to rely on, this has to be accepted as the name of the game within each compartment, i.e. changes have to respect the limit of variance imposed on it. (*ibid*, p. 167)

In recent years the debate over the school curriculum has reasserted and reconstituted patterns of tradition and stability which were briefly obscured by reform efforts in the late 1960s and early 1970s (Goodson with Anstead and Mangan, 1997, chapter 2). Standing out more clearly than ever on the new horizon is the school subject, the 'basic' or 'traditional' subjects. Throughout the Western world there is exhortation but also evidence about a 'return to basics', a reembrace of 'traditional subjects'. In England, for instance, the new National Curriculum defines a range of subjects to be taught as a 'core' curriculum in all schools. The subjects thereby instated bear an uncanny resemblance to the list which generally defined secondary school subjects in the 1904 Regulations. This curriculum was presented by the national Board of Education under the detailed guidance of Sir Robert Morant (1904):

> The course should provide for instruction in the English language and literature, at least one language other than English, geography, history, mathematics, science and drawing, with due provision for manual work and physical exercises, and in a girls' school for housewifery. Not less than 4^1/$_2$ hours per week must be allotted to English, geography and history; not less than 3^1/$_2$ hours to the language where one is taken or less than 6 hours where two are taken; and not less than 7^1/$_2$ hours to science and mathematics, of which at least 3 must be for science.

Traditionally in England and Wales those stressing 'the basics' have referred to the three Rs — reading, writing and arithmetic. In the 1980s it would be fair to say that those with curriculum power have been following a new version of the three Rs — rehabilitation, reinvention and reconstitution. Often the rehabilitation strategy for school subjects in the 1980s takes the form of arguing that good teaching is in fact good *subject* teaching. This is to seek to draw a veil over the whole experience of the 1960s, to seek to forget why many curriculum reforms were developed to try to provide antidotes to the perceived failures and inadequacies of conventional subject teaching. The rehabilitation strategy is itself in this sense quintessentially ahistorical but paradoxically it is also a reminder of the power of 'vestiges of the past' to survive, revive and reproduce.

In England the campaign for the 'reinvention' of 'traditional' subjects began in 1969 with the issue of the first collection of *Black Papers* (Cox and Dyson, 1969). The writers in this collection argued that teachers had been too greatly influenced by progressive theories of education like the integration of subjects, mixed ability teaching, inquiry, and discovery teaching. This resulted in neglect of subject and basic skill teaching and led to reduced standards of pupil achievement and school discipline; the traditional subject was thereby equated with social and moral discipline. The rehabilitation of the traditional subject promised the reestablishment of discipline in both these causes. The Black Papers were taken up by politicians and in 1976 the Labour Prime Minister, James Callaghan, embraced many of their themes in his Ruskin Speech. Specific recommendations soon followed. In 1979, for instance, Graham and Tytler (1993) say simply that in the speed 'he called for a core-national curriculum'(p. 3) and following a survey of secondary schools in England and Wales, Her Majesty's Inspectorate (HMI) drew attention to what they judged to be evidence of an insufficient match in many schools between the qualifications and experience of teachers and the work they were undertaking: later in a survey of middle schools they found that when they examined, the proportion of teaching which was undertaken by teachers who had studied the subjects they taught as main subjects in initial training . . . higher standards of work overall were associated with a greater degree of use of subject teachers. (HMI, 1983, para 3.19)

These perceptions provided a background to the Department of Education pamphlet *Teaching Quality*. The Secretaries of State for Education listed the criteria for initial teacher training courses. The first criteria imposed the following requirement:

That the higher education and initial training of all qualified teachers should include at least two full years' course time devoted to subject studies at a level appropriate to higher education.

This requirement therefore

would recognize teachers' needs for subject expertise if they are to have the confidence and ability to enthuse pupils and respond to their curiosity in their chosen subject fields. (DES, 1983)

This final sentence is curiously circular. Obviously if the pupils choose subjects then it is probable that teachers will require subject expertise. But this is to foreclose a whole debate about *whether* they should choose subjects as an educational vehicle. Instead, we have a practical *fait accompli* presented as choice. In fact the students have no choice except to embrace 'their chosen subject fields'. The political rehabilitation of subjects by political dictate is presented as pupil choice.

In *Teaching Quality*, the issue of the match between the teachers' qualifications and their work with pupils first raised in the 1979 HMI document is again employed. We learn that 'the Government attach high priority to improving the fit between teachers' qualifications and their tasks as one means of improving the quality of education'. The criteria for such a fit is based on a clear belief in the sequential and hierarchial pattern of subject learning.

All specialist subject teaching during the secondary phase requires teachers whose study of the subject concerned was at a level appropriate to higher education, represented a substantial part of the higher education and training period, and built on a suitable 'A' level basic.

The beginning of subject specialization is best evidenced where the issue of non-subject based work in schools is scrutinized. Many aspects of school work take place outside (or beside) subject work — studies of school process have indeed shown how integrated pastoral and remedial work originates because pupils for one reason or another do not achieve in traditional subjects. Far from accepting the subject as an educational vehicle with severe limits if the intention is to educate all pupils, the document seeks to rehabilitate subjects even in those domains which often originate from subject 'fall-out':

Secondary teaching is not all subject based, and initial training and qualifications cannot provide an adequate preparation for the whole range of
secondary school work. For example, teachers engaged in careers or remedial work or in providing group courses of vocational preparation, and
those given the responsibility for meeting 'special needs' in ordinary
schools, need to undertake these tasks not only on the basis of initial
qualifications but after experience of teaching a specialist subject and
preferably after appropriate post-experience training. Work of this kind
and the teaching of interdisciplinary studies are normally best shared among
teachers with varied and appropriate specialist qualifications and expertise.
(HMI, 1983, para 3.40)

The rehabilitation of school subjects was becoming the mainstay of Government thinking about the secondary school curriculum. The associated issue of increasingly centralized control is also raised in a DES publication (1985) on *Education
8 to 12 in Combined and Middle Schools*. Again, the rehabilitation of school subjects is rehearsed in a section on the need to 'extend teachers' subject knowledge'.
Rowland (1987) has seen the document as 'part of an attempt to bring a degree of
centralized control over education'. He states that:

Education 8 to 12 may well be interpreted by teachers and others as
recommending yet another means in the trend towards a more schematicized
approach to learning in which the focus is placed even more firmly on the
subject matter rather than the child.

He adds cryptically that 'the evidence it produces, however, points to the need to
move in quite the opposite direction'. His reservations about the effects of rehabili-
tating school subjects are widely shared. Another scholar has noted that one effect
of the strategy 'will be to reinforce the existing culture of secondary teaching and
thereby inhibit curricular and pedagogic innovation on a school-wide front' (*ibid*).

The various Government initiatives and reports since 1976 have shown a
consistent tendency to return to 'basics', to reembrace 'traditional' subjects. This
Government project which spans both Labour and Conservative administrations has
culminated in the 'new' National Curriculum. The curriculum was defined in a
consultation document, the *National Curriculum 5–16*. This was rapidly followed
in the wake of the Conservatives' third election victory in succession (in 1987) by
the passing of the Education Reform Act (in 1988) which introduced the National
Curriculum.

Whilst presented as a striking new political initiative, comparison with the
1904 Regulations shows a remarkable degree of historical continuity. The comparison with the Secondary Regulations in 1904 shows the extent to which a patterning
of schooling has been reconstituted in this new political settlement called the National
Curriculum.

1904	1987
English	English
Maths	Maths
Science	Science
History	History
Geography	Geography
Physical exercise	Physical education
Drawing	Art
Foreign language	Modern foreign language
Manual work	
Domestic subjects	Technology
(Music added soon afterwards)	Music (Goodson, 1995b, pp. 203–4)

Historical amnesia allows curriculum reconstruction to be presented as curriculum revolution, as Orwell noted he (or in this case she) 'who controls the past, controls the future' (see Goodson, 1989, pp. 131–41).

The similarity between 1904 and 1988 questions the rhetoric of 'a major new initiative' employed by the Government and points to some historical continuities in social and political purpose and priorities. The 1904 Regulations embodied that curriculum historically offered to the grammar school clientele of the middle classes as opposed to the curriculum being developed in the Board Schools and aimed primarily at the working classes: one segment or vision of the nation was being favoured at the expense of another. In the intervening period more equalitarian impulses brought about the creation of comprehensive schools where children of all classes came together under one roof. This in turn led to a range of curriculum reforms which sought to redefine and challenge the hegemony of the grammar school curriculum.

Seeking in turn to challenge and redirect these reforms and intentions the political right has argued for the rehabilitation of the 'traditional' (i.e. grammar school) subjects. The National Curriculum can be seen as a political statement of the victory of the forces and intentions representing these political groups. A particular vision, a preferred segment of the nation has therefore been reinstated, prioritised, legislated and remythologized as 'national'.

However, whilst a 'victory' for certain forces, this was only a victory in the first battle not the war and inevitably it was to prove a long war which continues to this day. Among the victors in the first battle were the Department of Education and Science now called under a 'cosmetic name change' the Department for Education (Graham and Tytler, 1993, p. 136). As we saw in chapter 9, the Department was an 'ambitious bureaucracy' and as early as 1981 had issued a circular to local education authorities instructing them to develop a curriculum policy. The extent of the power shift is made plain in Graham's insider-account of the development of the National Curriculum. He writes comparing the new Education Departments' Civil Servants with the old powers of advice of Her Majesty's Inspectorate (HMI):

> I became acutely aware that in its implementation and substance this was a Civil Service driven curriculum and not the property of HMI. This was

the first evidence of a huge *de facto* power shift in the way education was controlled in England and Wales. The HMI were adjuncts and the inspectors on the working group were extremely helpful, but they were not the driving force: that was the civil servants. The national curriculum was their baby, the first major education reform in Britain that had not been created by the educational professionals. (*ibid*, p. 30)

Graham goes on to detail the effect of these new powers on the attitudes of the educational bureaucrats

There was also a marked change in the attitude of civil servants after the introduction of the 1988 Education Reform Act, which they rightly saw as their first chance of having real power over state education. There was a volatile mixture of palpable fear of failing to deliver what was expected of them and a determination to run the whole programme. This was the first time ever that the DES had control of the curriculum and it was the beginning of the demise of HMI, although that was barely appreciated at the time. The fear of officials may well have come from being in the front line as never before. (*ibid*, p. 13)

Paradoxically, by the end of the first battle, the educational bureaucrats were also seen by the politicians as the enemy

As civil servants have come more and more into the front line of curriculum management, ministers have come to view them in the same suspicious way as they see educational professionals. (*ibid*, p. 138)

The obsessive and narrow focus of the intervention of politicians in the detail of the school curriculum has been evidenced in a range of accounts: Graham's remains the most authoritative because of his key position as Chairman and Chief Executive of the National Curriculum Council charged with introducing the new National Curriculum into the 24,000 state schools in England and Wales. This book is littered with evidence of the politicians' refusal to listen to a range of advice. As a working group in English steadfastly refused to accept the simplistic demand for reintroducing Standard English Grammar, Graham comments on the most recent working group chaired by Brian Cox, an assumed right-winger.

The working group had simply failed to grasp that nothing less than a firm commitment to grammar however it was described, would be acceptable to the Government. (*ibid*, p. 47)

Political prejudice therefore drove preferred curriculum definition but such reference did not always ensure delivery as the Cox Committee showed. The initial victory in the National Curriculum battle was followed by years of skirmishes and guerilla activity as the war dragged on.

After humiliating the Argentinean Army in the Falklands and seeing off the miners union in the miners strike, striding in to take over the 'secret garden of the curriculum', must have seemed a decidedly easy target for triumphal Thatcherism. It was not to be so. This was partly because Kenneth Baker, the Secretary of State, involved in the original framing of the legislation 'stood in the way' of the right-wing Thatcherite view. Hence, whilst Thatcher did "propose a narrow, hard-right core curriculum", she and her allies were thwarted in part by Baker 'who pushed through his own scheme' (Taylor, 1995, p. 164). But any government scheme, even the watered-down, over-complicated scheme devised by Baker has ultimately to confront the existing ecology of the secret garden of the curriculum. The flora and fauna of the secret garden proved less delicate than may have first appeared to be the case. Each school subject had its own ecology and political economy. The attempt to standardize and nationalize the curriculum by Government edict had ultimately to face the history and traditions, subject associations and sub-groups, multiple paradigms and pedagogies of each subject microworld. At first the Government simply legislated a victory for the chosen version of each subject and linked this with detailed assessment targets and strategies. Backed by the finances and power of 'an ambitious bureaucracy' in the Ministry this was expected to provide a final solution, a definitive landscape plan for the secret garden. But subjects have long histories and very carefully tended and varied ecologies. These need to be carefully studied and understood — as the National Curriculum exercise shows, they cannot be legislated away. The lesson of the National Curriculum is that school subjects have been painstakingly constructed and reconstructed over time. Only detailed and delicate negotiation can change the ecology of each subject microworld. As commonsense should tell us there are no cheap and easy solutions with such carefully constructed human creations — tread delicately in the secret gardens for if you tread on the plants you may not kill them but could be badly stung. Not so much a secret garden as a delicately laid minefield.

Bowe and Ball (1992) illustrate how the content of the subjects within the National Curriculum remain the subject of continuing debate and contestation. But the important point to grasp is that a subject-centred National Curriculum controls and narrows the discourse over the social purposes of schooling. A common response to the argument that the National Curriculum constitutes curriculum stability and control is 'Oh no you don't understand, it's all up for grabs, the subjects are being redrawn and changed'. But the debates over the purposes of schooling is fragmented by the national curriculum and contained and internalized *within* each subject discourse. More general discussion about the social purposes of schooling is thereby balkanized and substantially pre-empted.

Graham makes an interesting point about the victory of the subject-centred curriculum:

There must be what in Scotland would be a not proven verdict on the subject-centred structure of the National Curriculum. Academic theses abound on the origins, power, and longevity of the subject tradition. They are pretty well divided on the merits of the case. Do subjects exist to

enable learning or as a vehicle for vested interests, lobbies, and departmental baronies? (Graham and Tytler, 1993, p. 120)

This book is littered with evidence about the power-subject 'baronies' acting for
their own purposes. He admits history and geography are 'prime examples of
subject lobbies getting too much in, with their conclusions distorted for political
purposes' (*ibid*, p. 121).

Of the working group for geography, he writes, 'they saw their remit as being
perfectly clear: their task was to win the curriculum battle for geography' (*ibid*,
p. 71). This has led to many audacious episodes in the history of geography as
opportunism drives the desire for territory (a good geographical characteristic one
might think). The problem was that 'the geographers had a score to settle with the
scientists who in their view had stolen the earth sciences from them' (*ibid*, p. 70).
In a replay of an earlier struggle (see Goodson, 1993), they decided to try to win
back the environmental studies area partially lost to rural studies teachers in the
1970s. In their desperation it even dawned on the politicians in the Government
that the curriculum battle was less about dispassionate scholarship than passion-
ate acquisition of territory. Hence, 'it appeared to ministers that having lost earth
sciences, the geographers were pushed into finding something else to put in its
place' (Graham and Tytler, 1993, p. 71). Nonetheless, inspite of the patent opportunism of the move, the drive to carve up the environment as geographers' territory
went ahead. This time Government politics posed a problem:

> The ecological issue showed the Government's dilemma. In rapid succes-
> sion ministers were against the proposals because they were worried about
> expense and the possibility of encouraging pressure groups, and for them
> because of the growing public interest in green issues and forthcoming
> regulations from the European Community. (*ibid*, p. 74)

Subject groups or political groups, therefore, fought the curriculum battle for
their own political and instrumental purposes. The NUT document '*A Strategy for
Curriculum*' defines the outcome in seeing the National Curriculum as the 'result
of selective, controversial, and arbitrary judgements' (Edwards, 1992, p. 463). Gwyn
Edwards agrees with this view:

> Witness the way in which the Geographical Association has actively cam-
> paigned for the inclusion of its subject in the National Curriculum. Those
> subjects that have been given enhanced status and a guaranteed future as
> a consequence of their inclusion in the National Curriculum are unlikely
> to surrender willingly the monopoly they now possess. If change is to be
> brought about the implications of a constructionist perspective have to be
> acknowledged and incorporated into the strategy of change. The implica-
> tions are far-reaching. Most fundamentally, schools and their communities
> have to be understood for what they invariably are: sites of value plural-
> ism and potential conflict where power is unevenly distributed, not sites

of consensual harmony secured through democratic means. The pursuit of consensus as a democratic ideal has to be seen as practically problematic, if not logically contradictory, in situations characterized by plurality of values. In such circumstances procedures which legitimate only one version of 'the truth', however representative, are inherently undemocratic and, in relation to the curriculum, anti-educational. What emerges in reality is compromise and as compromise generally favours the powerful and privileged, the status quo is maintained. (*ibid*, p. 467)

But the symbolic victory of the National Curriculum was to define debate about schooling within the narrow parameters of subject territory. Only once was the whole curriculum issue raised:

The situation reached crisis level in the spring of 1989 when the Council set out to address the problem of what came to be known as the whole curriculum, a phrase that became politically unacceptable. The legally required curriculum, together with the preamble of the Act insisting on breadth and balance, raised simple questions: what is the moral justification for all this, what is education about, what is the whole curriculum into which this fits? (Graham and Tytler, 1993, p. 19)

Following these lines, five booklets were developed which looked at the issues of citizenship environment economics and industrial understanding, careering and health. By raising this issue the whole symbolic logic of the National Curriculum as a 'power cushion' to contain serious debate about schooling was being threatened. As a result remarkably rapid action was taken. Graham captures the sense of crisis.

Then the roof fell in. A posse of civil servants descended on York to tell NCC that it could not continue work on nor publish the five booklets. They were a dangerous distraction, funds were not available, and work would have to be delayed until 1993 when the National Curriculum was due to be fully implemented.

Clearly alarmed by what he had been told by the civil servants, Kenneth Baker wrote a detailed two-page letter to the Council in May 1989 in which he told it to abandon investigations into the whole curriculum and get on with the real work of introducing the curriculum. In the future nothing should go to formal meetings of the Council for approval until it had been seen and approved by the Secretary of State. Here was the question of independence in a nutshell. There was something that did not add up: industry was a favour of our whole curriculum approach and had representatives on the working groups. Baker was friendly with industry and yet he appeared to want to stop work which they approved and supported. (*ibid*, p. 20)

For good reason then Kliebard (1986) has called the subject base of the secondary school curriculum 'the impregnable fortress' (p. 269). Impregnable to substantial challenge over the basic assumptions of schooling in the general sense and impregnable to outside challenge in the specific subject sense.

Curriculum reform initiatives obscured this impregnability in the 1960s and 1970s and, optimists might even argue somewhat reduced, the predominance of the subject-centred curriculum. What is clear, however, is that the 1980s and 1990s have seen a substantial reconstitution of the subject-centred curriculum under the guise of a new educational reform initiative.

Developing National Goals in the USA

In the USA curriculum reform initiatives occurred during the 1980s, although because of a complicated set of historical and constitutional arrangements, it is more difficult to generalize about initiatives across all states.

A widely publicised report *A Nation at Risk* was produced in 1983 by a prestigious, federal-government sponsored policy panel, the National Commission on Educational Excellence. Various other commissions, task forces, study groups, committees, hearing and legislative reports were formed or issued within weeks of the release of this report (Task Force on Education for Economic Growth, 1983; Goodlad, 1983). According to Guthrie and Pierce (1990) public officials and political aspirants were quick to board the education reform bandwagon (p. 196).

The initial state-level reform responses that followed from these reports and commissions tended to focus upon such matters as extending the school day and school year, reviewing textbooks, and requiring teachers to assign and systematically correct more homework. It was only with subsequent state-level reform efforts that fundamental curriculum matters were addressed. In some states, especially California, curriculum frameworks reflecting the traditional subject areas were developed and strenuous efforts were made to align frameworks with textbook content and achievement tests. In the core areas of English, mathematics, science and social studies, rigorous treatment of knowledge and skills was established, and not dissimilar to the subject groupings or the content outlined by the Committee of Ten in 1893.

Other reform initiatives have focussed on national educational goals, led largely by the then President (Bush) in a State of the Union address in 1990. This address had led in turn to an agreement by most states to introduce national achievement testing in reading and mathematics at grade 4 and 8 levels, building upon and extending the National Assessment of Educational Progress (NAEP) testing programme which had produced data on national samples of students since 1966. The new national achievement tests planned for 1994 would be based on nominated curriculum areas and would report achievements levels for all students.

Despite the numerous problems associated with testing in the past in the USA, it is likely that the new national assessment tests will occur. Whether this will lead to a National Curriculum, as forecast by various educators such as Eisner (1991), is problematic. What does appear certain is that school subjects are likely to retain their ascendancy in state systems throughout the USA even though there is bound to be endless debate about the appropriateness of the national goals and which topics will be tested and by whom. It is possible that basic skills areas such as reading and mathematics could lead to a diminution in time available to other subjects, such as social studies and science. Some research studies indicate that this is already occurring (for example, Darling-Hammond and Wise, 1985, pp. 315–36; Rottenberg and Smith, 1990). Whether the new achievement tests will be able to deliver 'authentic' assessment (a term used recently in the literature to connote that assessment tasks are embedded in concepts central to the discipline and tied to curriculum goals or frameworks) is an admirable intention but it may require substantial effort and resources. (Shepard, 1991).

A National Curriculum in New Zealand

Initiatives undertaken by the New Zealand Government in 1988 have been far-reaching and contributed greatly to a reinforcement of subject-centred curriculum. The changes which occurred in the mid-1980s were considerable — Capper comments that 'it is not possible to describe the complexities of the enormous eruptions of reforms experienced by the New Zealand education system between 1984 and 1990' (p. 175).

The Picot Report released in May 1988 recommended a radical restructuring of the education system. Within seven weeks the Government released a White Paper, *Tomorrow's Schools*, incorporating major aspects of the Picot Report, to be implemented by October 1989 (Codd, 1991, p. 178). The White Paper and the Picot Report produced fundamental changes to decision-making — a devolution to schools and Boards of Trustees of resource allocation, administration, staff appointments, support services and staff development, but control of the curriculum was firmly invested in two central agencies, the Ministry of Education and an Educational Review Office.

Guidelines for a National Curriculum soon appeared in 1991 in which National Curriculum objectives, principles, essential learning areas, essential skills and assessment methods were carefully enunciated. With one exception, the seven learning areas followed traditional academic subjects, namely, language, mathematics, technology, social sciences, the arts, and physical and personal development. 'Science and environment' had a wider focus by the inclusion of 'environment' but in the long-term it may have minimal impact on the science courses taught under that rubric. The details provided in the 'National Curriculum of New Zealand' (1991) demonstrate a close affinity between the new learning areas and traditional subject offerings, and as a consequence, tend to make statements such as the following rather vacuous:

> The Essential Learning Areas are broad categories which are cross-curricular in nature and which enable the grouping of subjects similar in kind. (Minister of Education, 1991, p. 9)

The timetable is already well advanced in producing a curriculum document for each of the seven essential learning areas and for each, a comprehensive array of student outcomes has been planned using specific assessment measures. Despite a decentralization of control to the school level there has been a strong centralization of control of curriculum, largely due to economic and financial motivations.

The actions taken by the Government since 1989 reveal that they have used both organizational and institutional factors to ensure that changes did occur. The end result by the mid-1990s is far from clear. It is evident that school principals are finding ways to minimize the devolution of powers to parent bodies, yet the major organizational structures are likely to continue. The National Curriculum with its public airing of achievement standards in essential learning areas (largely traditional subjects) is likely to be reinforced by all parties.

National Curriculum Developments in Australia

Events during the late 1890s in Australia also revealed a thrust toward a National Curriculum, although it has been a complicated exercise as the Federal Government, like its American counterpart, has no constitutional responsibility for education.

To a large extent, the National Curriculum developments currently reaching a climax in Australia are due to the assertive leadership of John Dawkins who, as the then Federal Minister for Education in 1988 announced that:

What is required is the development of a common framework that sets out the major area of knowledge and the most appropriate mix of skills and experience for students in all the years of schooling.

There is a need for regular assessment of the effectiveness and standards of our schools. A common curriculum framework should be complemented by a common national approach to assessment. (pp. 4–5)

Through his personal energy and commitment Dawkins succeeded to a very large extent in implementing the national frameworks he had been espousing. The means by which the Federal Minister transformed rhetoric into action has been through the Australian Education Council (AEC), a body comprising the Federal Minister and State Ministers of Education.

The AEC made substantial progress with its national collaborative curriculum project during the period 1991–93, although some writers have judged the use of this Committee as a means of circumventing constitutional and financial requirements of Federation (Lingard, 1991, pp. 179–205).

Other initiatives also assisted National Curriculum endeavours. The establishing in 1990 of a Curriculum Corporation of Australia, a company of which all Ministers for Education (except New South Wales) are owners, and with the express purpose of engaging in commercial curriculum activities, has been another significant move. Over recent years, with the preparation of national statements and profiles, the Curriculum Corporation is playing an increasingly powerful role in furthering national curriculum developments.

The pace quickened over the period 1991–93 as committees of the AEC, especially the Standing Committee (Schools) composed of State Chief Executive Officers, and more recently, the Curriculum and Assessment Committee (CURASS), composed of Directors of Curriculum in State Education Departments and Directors of Assessment agencies, decided upon an extremely tight schedule to complete the National Curriculum project. The motivation since 1991 to complete the total array of national statements and profiles for the eight learning areas (mathematics, English, science, technology, the arts, languages other than English, health and physical education, studies of society and environment) may have been due partly to frustration about the time taken during 1988–91 to obtain collaborative support from the States and Territories on curriculum matters, but it also appears to have been a strategy to counteract pressures from industry and training groups who had high visibility in policy reports such as Finn (1991), Mayer (1992) and the Employment and Skills Formation Council (1992).

Seven out of the eight learning areas represent traditional subject areas. The combination of 'environment' with 'social studies' (studies of society and environment) is an attempt to provide a cross-disciplinary focus and is an interesting contrast to the New Zealand grouping described earlier. To a large extent, the learning areas represent typical groupings of subjects included in the curriculum in most schools throughout Australia although they have been criticized as being little more than 'a confusing amalgam of traditional subjects and pragmatic expediency' (Marsh, 1994).

The coupling of profiles (descriptive statements of learning outcomes arranged in progressive order of difficulty through eight levels, K-12) with each learning area could have the effect of requiring the nominated subjects to be taught in schools throughout Australia. Those subjects given minimal prominence (for example, business studies, home economics) will be downplayed in terms of timetabling allocations. There are interesting parallels here with the core and foundation subjects established under the National Curriculum in the United Kingdom.

It is not yet clear how national statements and profiles will be used by state education systems especially after an AEC rejection in mid-1993, orchestrated by several states with newly-elected governments opposed to the Federal Government. Yet, pressures for national reporting of profile levels in each of the eight learning areas are considerable and states and territories are developing profiles during 1995/96. The impact upon teachers in schools could be quite dramatic if they are put under some pressure to ensure that their students achieve a high standard in particular learning areas. Teachers might concentrate upon assessments related to the profiles and not stray into any other more interesting teaching areas. If, as appears likely, the profiles concentrate upon traditional areas of knowledge and forms of inquiry there will be little opportunity for students to undertake individual project work and areas of learning which are more student-centred.

The 'institutional' factors are being put into place through the concentrated energies of the AEC (subsequently reconstituted as the Ministerial Council on Education, Employment Training and Youth Affairs (MCEETYA)) and senior education officers in states and territories. What is problematic is whether 'organizational' factors at the school level will facilitate or impede the implementation of these National Curriculum developments. For example, the professional development implications for teachers are enormous but they have been barely addressed, despite recent grants being offered by the Federal agency, the Department of Education, Employment and Training (DEET) (Hughes, 1990). The force-fit procedures for establishing eight learning areas each with the same number of profile levels and similar numbers of outcome statements may be stifling the inherent needs of some subjects and learning areas.

Conclusion

Historical studies of curriculum stability and change provide valuable insights into the parameters and purposes of schooling. The study of school subjects is an especially valuable prism for this kind of scholarly enquiry. In particular, such historical study alerts us to how the continuing debate about curriculum is at times narrowed to a debate about subject matter and subject-centredness. Such narrowing of the discourse is naturally most visible after periods of more openness such as in the 1930s and 1960s; in these latter periods, somewhat more general curriculum categories or themes might be countenanced or advocated such as the social studies in the 1930s.

By analyzing the role of the 'subject', particularly the 'traditional' or 'basic' subject in the discourses and legitimating rhetorics of schooling we often gain insights into the forces of 'fixity and persistence'. Moreover, we are provided with an access point form with which to scrutinize contemporary possibilities for action from reproduction through to transformation and for cultural politics generally.

Reflections and Issues

1 Reflect upon an educational change that you have recently witnessed and consider especially the organizational and institutional elements. Were these organisational and institutional elements developed in harmony with each example? Was the educational change enduring and successful? Give details.

2 Do you agree that school subjects are a perfect device for conservation and stability? What has been the impact of new groupings of knowledge such as integrated, multidisciplinary, or interdisciplinary courses? If you consider that they have not been successful, give reasons.

3 To what extent has the stability of traditional school subjects impeded efforts to reduce discrimination against disadvantaged groups such as girls and ethnic minorities?

4 It is argued that debates over the National Curriculum are largely internalised within individual subjects and that little attention has been paid to the wider, social purposes of schooling? Use examples to support or refute this statement.

Suggested Reading

There are several useful articles including:

Edwards, G. (1992) 'A Strategy for the Curriculum: A Response', *Journal of Curriculum Studies*, **24**, 5.

Goodson, I.F. (1997) 'Becoming a school subject', in Goodson, I.F. with Anstead, C.J. and Mangan, J.M. *Subject Knowledge: Readings for the Study of School Subjects*. London and Washington, DC: Falmer Press.

Goodson, I.F. (1997) "Nations at Risk" and "National Curriculum": Ideology and Identity', in Goodson, I.F. with Anstead, C.J. and Mangan, J.M. *Subject Knowledge: Readings for the Study of School Subjects*. London and Washington, DC: Falmer Press.

Rowland, S. (1987) 'Where is primary education going?', *Journal of Curriculum Studies*, **19**.

Webster, J.R. (1971) '"Curriculum Change" and "Crisis"', *British Journal of Educational Studies* **26**.

Useful books include:

Ball, S.J. (1994) *Education Reform. A critical and post-structural approach*. Buckingham: Open University Press, see especially chapter 3.

Bowe, R. and Ball, S. with Gold, A. (1992) *Reforming Education and Changing Schools*, London: Routledge.

Goodson, I.F. (1994) *Studying Curriculum: Cases and Methods*. Buckingham: Open University Press/New York: Teachers College Press/Toronto: OISE Press.

Goodson, I.F. (1995) *The Making of Curriculum: Collected Essays*. 2nd Edition. London and Washington, DC: Falmer Press.

Goodson, I.F. (1993) *School Subjects and Curriculum Change*, 3rd Edition, London and Washington, DC: Falmer Press.

Haft, H. and Hopmann, S. (1990) 'Curriculum Administration as Symbolic Action', in Haft, H. and Hopmann, S. (Eds) *Case Studies in Curriculum Administration History*, London and Washington, DC: Falmer Press.

Marsh, C.J. (1994) *Producing a National Curriculum: Plans and Paranoia*. Sydney: Allen & Unwin.

Meyer, J.W. and Rowan, B. (1983) 'The Structure of Educational Organization', in Meyer, J.W. and Scott, W.R. (Eds) *Organisational Environments*, California: Sage.

Reid, W.A. (1984) 'Curricular Topics as Institutional Categories: Implications for Theory and Research in the History and Sociology of School Subjects', in Goodson, I.F. and Ball, S. (Eds) *Defining the Curriculum: Histories and Ethnographies*, London and Washington, DC: Falmer Press.

Reid, W.A. (1992) *The Pursuit of Curriculum*. Norwood, New Jersey: Ablex.

Bibliography

AICHELE, D.B. (1988) 'Historical overview' in CAMPBELL, P.J. and GRINSTEIN, L.S. (Eds) *Mathematics Education in Secondary Schools and Two-year Colleges: A Sourcebook*, New York, Garland.

ANGUS, M.J., BECK, T.M., HILL, P.W. and McATTEE, W.A. (1979) *Open Area Schools: An Evaluative Study of Teaching and Learning in Primary Schools of Conventional and Open Area Design in Australia*, Canberra, ERDC.

ANSTEAD, C. and GOODSON, I.F. (1993) 'Subject status and curriculum change: Commercial education in London, Ontario, 1920–1940', *Paedagogica Historica*, **29**, 2.

APPLE, M.W. (1990a) 'The politics of official knowledge in the United States', *Journal of Curriculum Studies*, **22**, 4.

APPLE, M.W. (1990b) *Ideology and the Curriculum* (2nd edn), London, Routledge.

APPLEBEE, A.N. (1974) *Tradition and Reform in the Teaching of English: A History*, Illinois, National Council of Teachers of English.

APPLEBEE, A.N. and PURVES, A.C. (1992) 'Literature and the English language arts' in JACKSON, P.W. (Ed) *Handbook of Research on Curriculum*, New York, Macmillan.

ARGLES, M. (1964) *South Kensington to Robbins: An Account of English Scientific and Technical Education Since 1851*, London, Longmans.

BALL, N. (1964) 'Richard Dawes and the teaching of common things', *Educational Review*, **17**.

BALL, S.J. (1981) *Beachside Comprehensive*, Cambridge, Cambridge University Press.

BALL, S.J. (1985a) 'English for the English since 1906' in GOODSON, I.F. (Ed) *Social Histories of the Secondary Curriculum: Subjects in Study*, London and Washington, DC, Falmer Press.

BALL, S.J. (1985b) 'Relations, structures and conditions in curriculum change: A political history of English teaching 1970–85' in GOODSON, I.F. (Ed) *International Perspectives in Curriculum History*, London, Routledge.

BALL, S.J. (1987) *The Micropolitics of the School*, London, Methuen.

BALL, S.J. (1990) *Politics and Policymaking in Education: Explorations in Policy Sociology*, London, Routledge.

BALL, S.J. (1994) *Educational Reform: A Critical and Post-structural Approach*, Buckingham, Open University Press.

BALL, S.J. and BOWE, R. (1992) 'Subject departments and the "implementation" of the National Curriculum', *Journal of Curriculum Studies*, **24**, 2, pp. 97–116.

BALL, S.J., KENNY, A. and GARDINER, D. (1990) 'Literacy, politics and the teaching of English' in GOODSON, I.F. and MEDWAY, P. (Eds) *Bringing English to Order*, London and Washington, DC, Falmer Press.

BALL, S.J. and LACEY, S.C. (1980) 'Subject disciplines as the opportunity for group action: A measured critique of subject sub-cultures' in WOODS, P. (Ed) *Teacher Strategies*, London, Croom Helm.

BARON, D. (1986) *Grammar and Gender*, New Haven, CT, Yale University Press.

BATES, I. (1989) 'Versions of vocationalism: An analysis of some social and political influences on curriculum policy and practice', *Journal of Sociology of Education*, **10**, 2.

BEN-DAVID, T. and COLLINS, R. (1996) 'Social factors in the origins of a new science: The case of psychology', *American Sociological Review*, **31**, 4.

BENNETT, N. (1976) *Teaching Styles and Pupils Progress*, London, Open Books.

BENTLEY, D. and DROBINSKI, S. (1995) 'Girls, learning and science in the framework of the National Curriculum', *The Curriculum Journal*, **6**, 1, pp. 79–100.

BERGONZI, B. (1990) *Exploding English*, Oxford, Oxford University Press.

BERNSTEIN, B. (1971) 'On the classification and framing of educational knowledge' in YOUNG, M.F.D. (Ed) *Knowledge and Control*, London, Macmillan.

BISHOP, G.C. (1961) *Physics Teaching from Early Times up to 1850*, London, RPM Pubishers.

BLYTH, W.A.L. (1965) *English Primary Education: A Sociological Description*, Vol 2, London, Routledge and Kegan Paul.

BOLI, J. (1989) *New Citizens for a New Society — The Institutional Orgins of Mass Schooling in Sweden*, Oxford, Pergamon Press.

BORTHWICK, A. (1994) 'English language arts performance standards for elemenatry school', unpublished paper, Pennsylvania State University.

BOWE, R. and BALL, S. with GOLD, A. (1992) *Reforming Education and Changing Schools*, London, Routledge.

BOYLE, A. (1990) 'Science in the National Curriculum', *The Curriculum Journal*, **1**, 1.

BRITTON, J. (1973) 'How we got there' in BAGNALL, N. (Ed) *New Movements in the Study and Teaching of English*, London, Temple Smith.

BROCK, W.H. (1979) 'From Leibig to Nuffield: A bibliography of the history of science education, 1839–1974', *Studies in Science Education*, **2**.

BROWNE, G.S. (1932) *The Case for Curriculum Revision*, Melbourne, Melbourne University Press.

BRUCKERHOFF, C. (1991) *Between Classes: Faculty Life at Truman High*, New York, Teachers College Press.

BUCHER, R. and STRAUSS, A. (1976) 'Professions in process' in HAMMERSLEY, M. and WOODS, P. (Eds) *The Process of Schooling: A Sociological Reader*, London, Routledge and Kegan Paul.

BURGESS, T. (1993) 'Returning history: Literacy, difference and English teaching in the post-war period' in GREEN, B. (Ed) *The Insistence of the Letter: Literacy Studies and Curriculum Theorizing*, Pittsburgh, PA, University of Pittsburgh Press.

BURNS, G.T. (1990) 'The social origins of English' in GOODSON, I.F. and MEDWAY, P. (Ed) *Bringing English to Order*, London and Washington, DC, Falmer Press.

BURTON, L. (1992) 'Evaluating and "entitlement curriculum": Mathematics for all', *The Curriculum Journal*, **3**, 2.

BUTTS, R.F. (1955) *Assumptions Underlying Australian Education*, Melbourne, ACER.

BYBEE, R.W. (1977) 'The new transformation of science education', *Science Education*, **61**, 1, pp 85–97.

BYRNE, E.M. (1974) *Planning and Educational Inequality*, Slough, NFER.

CANE, B.S. (1959/60) 'Scientific and technical subjects in the curriculum of English schools at the turn of the century', *British Journal of Educational Studies*, **8**.

CAPPER, P. (1991) 'Curriculum policy in New Zealand: A search and rescue exercise', *Journal of Curriculum Studies*, **23**, 3.

CHEUNG, K.C. and TAYLOR, R. (1991) 'Towards a humanistic/constructivist model of science learning', *Journal of Curriculum Studies*, **23**, 1, pp. 21–40.

CHRISTIE, F. (1993) 'The "received tradition" of English teaching: The decline of rhetoric and the corruption of grammar' in GREEN, B. (Ed) *The Insistence of the Letter: Literacy Studies and Curriculum Theorizing*, Pittsburgh, PA, University of Pittsburgh Press, pp. 75–106.

CODD, J. (1991) 'Curriculum reform in New Zealand', *Journal of Curriculum Studies*, **23**, 2.

COHEN, P.C. (1982) *A Calculating People: The Spread of Numeracy in Early America*, Chicago, IL, University of Chicago Press.

COLLINS, R. (1979) *The Credential Society: An Historical Sociology of Education and Stratification*, London and New York, Academic Press.

CONNELL, R.W., ASHENDEN, D.J., KESSLER, S. and DOWSETT, G.W. (1982) *Making the Difference*, Sydney, Allen and Unwin.

COOPER, B. (1985) *Renegotiating Secondary School Mathematics: A Study of Curriculum Change and Stability*, London and Washington, DC, Falmer Press.

COOPER, B. (1992) 'Testing National Curriculum mathematics: Some critical comments on the treatment of "real" contexts for mathematics', *The Curriculum Journal*, **3**, 3.

COOPER, B. (1995) 'Exploring children's interpretation of Key Stage 2 National Curriculum tests in mathematics', unpublished paper, University of Sussex.

COURT, F. (1988) 'The social and historical significance of the first English literature professorship in England', *PMLA*, **103**, 5.

COURT, F. (1992) *Institutionalizing English Literature*, Stanford, CA, Stanford University Press.

COX, B. (1995) *Cox on the Battle for the English Curriculum*, London, Hodder and Stoughton.

COX, C.B. and BOYSON, R. (1975) *The Black Paper 1975*, London, Dent.

COX, C.B. and DYSON, A.E. (Eds) (1969) 'Fight for education: A Black Paper London', *The Critical Quarterly Society*.

CRAWFORD, K. (1995) 'A history of the right: The battle for control of National Curriculum history 1989–1994', *British Journal of Educational Studies*, **XXXXIII**, 4.

CREMIN, L.A. (1968) *The Transformation of the School: Progressivism in American Education, 1876–1957*, New York, Knopf.

CUBAN, L. (1984) *How Teachers Taught*, New York, Longman.

CUSICK, P.A. (1983) *The Egalitarian Ideal and the American High School*, New York, Longman.

DARLING-HAMMOND, L. and WISE, A.E. (1985) 'Beyond standardisation: State standards and school improvement', *The Elementary School Journal*, **85**.

DAWKINS, J. (1988) *Strengthening Australia's Schools: A Consideration of the Focus and Content of Schooling*, Canberra, AGPS.

DE BRABANDER, C.J. (1993) 'Subject conceptions of teachers and school culture' in KIEVIET, F.K. and VANDENBERGHE, V. (Eds) *School Culture, School Improvement and Teacher Education*, Leiden, University of Leiden.

DE VAULT, M.V. and WEAVER, J.F. (1970) 'Forces and issues related to curriculum and instruction, K-6' in National Council of Teachers of Mathematics *A History of Mathematics Education in the United States and Canada*, Washington, DC, National Council of Teachers of Mathematics.

DES (1965) *Organization of Secondary Education* (Circular 10/65), London, HMSO.

DES (1967) *Children and Their Primary Schools* (The Plowden Report), London, HMSO.

DES (1983) *Teaching Quality*, London, HMSO.

DES (1985) *Education 8 to 12 in Combined and Middle Schools: An HMI Survey*, London, HMSO.

DEWEY, J. (1915) 'Education vs. trade training — Dr Dewey's reply', *The New Acpaslic*, 3.

DEWEY, J. (1916) *Democracy and Education 1946: An Introduction to the Philosophy of Education*, New York, Macmillan.

DIXON, J. (1991) *A Schooling in English*, Milton Keynes, Open University Press.

DOBB, W.J. (1913) *A School Course of Geometry*, London, Longman.

DODD, T. (1978) *Design and Technology in the School Curriculum*, London, Hodder and Stoughton.

DOUGHERTY, K. (1988) 'Educational policy making and the relative autonomy of the state: The case of occupational education in the community college', *Sociological Forum*, **3**, 3.

DOYLE, B. (1982) 'The hidden history of English studies' in WIDDOWSON, P. (Ed) *Re-reading English*, London and New York, Methuen.

DOYLE, B. (1989) *English and Englishness*, London and New York, Routledge.

DYER, K.G. (1976) 'Crisis in biology: An examination of the deficiencies in the current expansion of biological education', *Journal of Biological Education*, **1**, 2.

DYHOUSE, C. (1976) 'Social Darwinistic ideas and the development of women's education in England, 1880–1920', *History of Education*, **5**, 1.

DYHOUSE, C. (1981) *Girls Growing up in Late Victorian and Edwardian England*, London, Routledge and Kegan Paul.

EDWARDS, G. (1992) A strategy for the curriculum: A response', *Journal of Curriculum Studies*, **24**, 5.

EGGLESTON, J. (1977) *The Sociology of the School Curriculum*, London, Routledge and Kegan Paul.

EISNER, E.W. (1991) 'Should America have a National Curriculum?', unpublished paper, Stanford University, CA.

EMPLOYMENT AND SKILLS FORMATION COUNCIL (1992) *The Australian Vocational Certificate Training System*, Canberra, AGPS.

FENSHAM, P.J. (1988) 'Physical science, society and technology: A case study in the sociology of knowledge', *Australian Journal of Education*, **32**, 3, pp. 375–86.

FENSHAM, P.J. (1993) 'Academic influence on school science curricula', *Journal of Curriculum Studies*, **25**, 1, pp. 53–64.

FINN, B. (1991) *Young People's Participation in Post-Compulsory Education and Training*, Report of the Australian Education Council Review Committe (Chair: Finn, B.), Canberra, AGPS.

FISHER, G.P. (1866) *Life of Benjamin Silliman, MD, LLD*, New York,

FLETCHER, J. (1995) 'Policy-making in DES/DFE via consensus and contention', *Oxford Review of Education*, **21**, 2, pp. 133–48.

GIDDENS, A. (1986) *The Constitution of Society*, California, University of California Press.

GINGRAS, Y. (1986) 'The institutionalization of scientific research in Canadian universities: The case of physics', *Canadian Historical Review*, **LXVII**, 2.

GOODLAD, J.I. (1983) *The Dynamics of Educational Change*, New York, McGraw Hill.

GOODSON, I.F. (Ed) (1985) *Social Histories of the Secondary Curriculum: Subjects for Study*, London and Washington, DC, Falmer Press.

GOODSON, I.F. (Ed) (1988) *International Perspectives in Curriculum History* (2nd edn), London, Routledge.

GOODSON, I.F. (1989) 'Curriculum reform and curriculum theory: A case of historical amnesia', *Cambridge Journal of Education*, **119**.

GOODSON, I.F. (1990) 'Studying curriculum: Towards a social constructionist perspective', *Journal of Curriculum Studies*, **22**, 4.

GOODSON, I.F. (Ed) (1993) *School Subjects and Curriculum Change* (3rd edn), London and Washington, DC, Falmer Press.

GOODSON, I.F. (1994) *Studying Curriculum: Cases and Methods*, Buckingham/New York/Toronto, Open University Press/Teachers College Press/OISE Press.

GOODSON, I.F. (1995a) 'The context of cultural invention: Learning and curriculum' in COOKSON, P. and SCHNEIDER, B. (Eds) *Transforming Schools*, New York and London, Garland Press.

GOODSON, I.F. (1995b) *The Making of Curriculum: Collected Essays* (2nd edn), London and Washington, DC, Falmer Press.

GOODSON, I.F. (1997a) 'Becoming a school subject' in GOODSON, I.F. with ANSTEAD,

C.J. and MANGAN, J.M. *Subject Knowledge: Readings for the Study of School Subjects*, London and Washington, DC, Falmer Press.

GOODSON, I.F. (1997b) 'The micropolitics of curriculum change: European studies' in GOODSON, I.F. with ANSTEAD, C.J. and MANGAN, J.M. *Subject Knowledge: Readings for the Study of School Subjects*, London and Washington, DC, Falmer Press.

GOODSON, I.F. (1997c) '"Nations at Risk" and "National Curriculum": Ideology and identity' in GOODSON, I.F. with ANSTEAD, C.J. and MANGAN, J.M. *Subject Knowledge: Readings for the Study of School Subjects*, London and Washington, DC, Falmer Press.

GOODSON, I.F. and ANSTEAD, C.J. (1993) *Through the Schoolhouse Door*, Toronto, Garamond Press.

GOODSON, I.F. with ANSTEAD, C.J. (1997a) 'Subject status and curriculum change: Local commercial education 1920–1940' in GOODSON, I.F. with ANSTEAD, C.J. and MANGAN, J.M. *Subject Knowledge: Readings for the Study of School Subjects*, London and Washington, DC, Falmer Press.

GOODSON, I.F. with ANSTEAD, C.J. (1997b) 'On explaining curriculum change: Beal, H.B. Organizational categories and the rhetoric of justification' in GOODSON, I.F. with ANSTEAD, C.J. and MANGAN, J.M. *Subject Knowledge: Readings for the Study of School Subjects*, London and Washington, DC, Falmer Press.

GOODSON, I.F. with ANSTEAD, C.J. (1997c) 'Subjects and the everyday life of schooling' in GOODSON, I.F. with ANSTEAD, C.J. and MANGAN, J.M. *Subject knowledge: Readings for the Study of School Subjects*, London and Washington, DC, Falmer Press.

GOODSON, I.F. with ANSTEAD, C.J. and MANGAN, J.M. (1997) *Subject Knowledge: Readings for the Study of School Subjects*, London and Washington, DC, Falmer Press.

GOODSON. I.F. and DOWBIGGIN, I. (1991) 'Vocational education and school reform', *History of Education Review*, **20**, 1, pp. 36–60.

GOODSON, I.F. with MANGAN, J.M. (1997) 'Subject cultures and the introduction of classroom computers' in GOODSON, I.F. with ANSTEAD, C.J. and MANGAN, J.M. *Subject Knowledge: Readings for the Study of School Subjects*, London and Washington, DC, Falmer Press.

GOODSON, I.F. and MEDWAY, P. (Eds) (1990a) *Bringing English to Order*, London and Washington, DC, Falmer Press.

GOODSON, I.F. and MEDWAY, P. (Eds) (1990b) 'Bringing English to order: Introduction' in GOODSON, I.F. and MEDWAY, P. (Eds) *Bringing English to Order*, London and Washington, DC, Falmer Press.

GORDON, P. and LAWTON, D. (1978) *Curriculum Change in the Nineteenth and Twentieth Centuries*, London, Hodder and Stoughton.

GRAMHAM, D. and TYTLER, D. (1993) *A Lesson for Us All*, London and New York, Routledge.

GREEN, B. (1993a) 'Literacy studies and curriculum theorizing; or the insistence of the letter' in GREEN, B. (Ed) *The Insistence of the Letter: Literacy Studies and*

Curriculum Theorizing, Pittsburgh, PA, University of Pittsburgh Press, pp. 195–225.

GREEN, B. (Ed) (1993b) *The Insistence of the Letter: Literacy Studies and Curriculum Theorizing*, Pittsburgh, PA, University of Pittsburgh Press.

GREEN, B. (1993c) 'Introduction' in Green, B. (Ed) *The Insistence of the Letter: Literacy Studies and Curriculum Theorizing*, Pittsburgh, PA, University of Pittsburgh Press.

GREEN, B. (1995a) 'Post-curriculum possibilities: English teaching, cultural politics and the postmodern turn', *Journal of Curriculum Studies*, **24**, 4, pp. 391–410.

GREEN, B. (1995b) 'Born again teaching? Governmentality, "grammar" and public schooling' in POPKEWITZ, T.S. and BRENNAN, M. (Eds) *Governmentality Through Education: Foucault's Challenge to the Institutional Production and Study of Knowledge*, New York, Teachers College Press.

GROSSMAN, P.L. and STODOLSKY, S.S. (1995) 'Content as context: The role of school subjects in secondary school teaching', *Educational Researchers*, **24**, 8.

GUTHRIE, H.W. and PIERCE, L. (1990) 'The international economy and national education reform: The comparison of education reforms in the United States and Great Britain', *Oxford Review of Education*, **16**, 2.

HAFT, H. and HOPMANN, S. (1990) 'Curriculum administration as symbolic action' in HAFT, H. and HOPMANN, S. (Eds) *Case Studies in Curriculum Adminstration History*, London and Washington, DC, Falmer Press.

HAMILTON, D. (1980) 'Adam Smith and the moral economy of the classroom system', *Journal of Curriculum Studies*, **12**, 4.

HAMILTON, D. (1989) *Towards a Theory of Schooling*, London and Washington, DC, Falmer Press.

HARGREAVES, A. (1990) 'Teachers' work and the politics of time and space', *Qualitiative Studies in Education*, **3**, 4.

HARGREAVES, A. (1995) *Changing Teachers, Changing Times*, London, Cassell.

HER MAJESTY'S INSPECTORATE (1983) *A Survey of Schools*, London, HMSO.

HEWITSON, M., MCWILLIAM, E. and BURKE, C. (1991) 'Responding to teacher education imperatives for the nineties', *Australian Journal of Education*, **35**, 3.

HIGHFIELD, M.E. and PINSENT, A. (1952) *A Survey of Rewards and Punishments*, London, Newnes.

HODSON, D. (1988) 'Science curriculum change in Victorian England: A case study of the science of common things' in GOODSON, I.F. (Ed) *International Perspectives in Curriculum History*, London and New York, Routledge.

HODSON, D. and PROPHET, R.B. (1983) 'Why the science curriculum changes: Evolution or social control?', *School Science Review*, **230**, September, pp. 5–18.

HOFKINS, D. (1995) 'Battles still to be fought', *Times Educational Supplement*, 13 October.

HOLT, M. (1981) 'Core curriculum: Some problems and possibilities', *Curriculum Perspectives*, **1**, 2.

HORD, S.H. and DIAZ-ORTIZ, E.M. (1987) 'Beyond the principal: Can the department head supply leadership for change in high schools' in VANDENBERGHE, R. and HALL, G.E. (Eds) *Research on Internal Change Facilitation in Schools*, ACCO, Leuven, p. 130.

HORWOOD, J. (1992) 'Reflections on the development of mathematics curriculum — An historical perspective', unpublished paper, Melbourne, Victoria University of Technology.

HORWOOD, J. (1994) 'Towards control of a mathematics curriculum', *Curriculum Perspectives*, **14**, 1, pp. 11–16.

HOWEY, K.R. (1990) 'Changes in teacher education: Needed leadership and new networks', *Journal of Teacher Education*, **41**, 1.

HOWSON, A.G. (1982) *History of Mathematics Education in England*, Cambridge, Cambridge University Press.

HOYLES, E. (1969) 'How does the curriculum change? A proposal for inquiries', *Journal of Curriculum Studies*, 1.

HUBERMAN, M. (1990) 'The social context of instruction in schools', paper presented at the annual meeting of the American Educational Research Association, Boston.

HUGHES, P.W. (1990) 'A National Curriculum: Promise or warning', Occasional Papers No 14, Canberra, Australian College of Education.

HUNTING, R.P. (1987) 'Issues shaping school mathematics curriculum development in Australia', *Curriculum Perspectives*, **7**, 1, pp. 29–38.

HYAMS, B.K. and BESSANT, B. (1972) *Schools for the People?*, Melbourne, Longman.

INGLIS, F. (1995) *Raymond Williams*, London and New York, Routledge.

JENKINS, E.W. (1979) *From Armstrong to Nuffield: Studies in Twentieth Century Science Education in England and Wales*, London, John Murray.

JENKINS, E.W. (1980) 'Some sources for the history of science education in the twentieth century, with particular reference to secondary schools', *Studies in Science Education*, **7**.

JENKINS, E.W. (1992) 'School science education: Towards a reconstruction', *Journal of Curriculum Studies*, **24**, 3, pp. 229–46.

JENKINS, E.W. (Ed) (1993) *School Science and Technology: Some Issues and Perspectives*, Leeds, Centre for Studies in Science and Mathematics Education.

JENKINS, E.W. (Ed) (1994) 'Public understanding of science and science education for action', *Journal of Curriculum Studies*, **26**, 6, pp. 601–12.

JONES, P.S. and COXFORD, A.F. JR (1970) 'Mathematics in the evolving schools' in NATIONAL COUNCIL OF TEACHERS OF MATHEMATICS *A History of Mathematics Education in the United States and Canada*, Washington, DC, National Council of Teachers of Mathematics.

JUDGE, H.G. (1984) *A Generation of Schooling*, Oxford, Oxford University Press.

KILPATRICK, V.E. (1905) 'Departmental teaching in the elementary schools', *Educational Review*, pp. 468–85 quoted in Siskin (1994), p. 40.

KLIEBARD, H. (1982) 'Education at the turn of the century: A crucible for curriculum change', *Educational Researcher*, **11**, 1.

KLIEBARD, H. (1986) *The Struggle for the American Curriculum 1893–1958*, Boston, MA, London and Henley, Routledge and Kegan Paul.

KLIEBARD, H.M. (1992) *Forging the American Curriculum: Essays in Curriculum History and Theory*, New York/London, Routledge/Chapman and Hall.

KRUG, E. (1969) *The shaping of the American High School*, New York, Harper and Row.

KUSLAN, L.I (1969) 'The founding of the Yale School of Applied Chemistry', *Journal of the History of Medicine and Applied Sciences*, **24**.

KUSLAN, L.S. (1982) 'Chemistry in some 19th century New England normal schools', *Journal of Research in Science Teaching*, **19**, 1.

LABAREE, D. (1984) 'Academic excellence in an early US high school', *Social Problems*, **31**, 5.

LABAREE, D. (1986) 'Curriculum, credentials, and the middle class: A case study of a nineteenth century high school', *Sociology of Education*, **59**.

LABAREE, D. (1987) 'Shaping the role of the public high school: Past patterns and present implications', paper presented at the annual meeting of the American Educational Research Association, Washington, DC.

LABAREE, D. (1988) *The Making of an American High School: The Credentials Market and the Central High School of Philadelphia, PA, 1838–1939*, New Haven, CT, Yale University Press.

LACEY, C. (1970) *Hightown Grammar: The School as a Social System*, Manchester, Manchester University Press.

LAYTON, D. (1972a) 'Science in the schools: The first wave — A study of the influence of Richard Dawes (1793–1867)', *British Journal of Educational Studies*, **20**.

LAYTON, D. (1972b) 'Science as general education', *Trends in Education*, January.

LAYTON, D. (1973) *Science for the People: The Origins of the School Science Curriculum in England*, London, George Allen and Unwin.

LINGARD, B. (1991) 'Policy-making for Australian schooling: The new corporate federalism', *Journal of Education Policy*, **6**, 1.

LITTLE, J.W. (1982) 'Norms of collegiality and experimentation: Workplace conditions of school success', *American Educational Research Journal*, **19**, pp. 325–40.

LITTLE, J.W. (1993) 'Professional community in comprehensive high schools: The two worlds of academic and vocational teachers' in LITTLE, J.W. and McLAUGHLIN, M.W. (Eds) *Teachers' Work*, New York, Teachers College Press.

LITTLE, J.W. (1995) 'Subject affiliation in high schools that restructure' in SISKIN, L. and LITTLE, J.W. (Eds) (1995) *The Subjects in Question: The Department Organization of the High School*, New York, Teachers College Press.

LITTLE, J.W. (forthcoming) 'Contested ground: The basis of teacher leadership in restructured high schools', *Elementary School Journal*, p. 7.

LITTLE, J.W. and McLAUGHLIN, M.W. (Eds) (1993) *Teachers' Work*, New York, Teachers College Press.

LUKE, A. (1993) 'Foreword' in GREEN, B. (Ed) *The Insistence of the Letter: Literacy*

Studies and Curriculum Theorizing, Pittsburgh, PA, University of Pittsburgh Press.

LUKES, S. (1974) *Power: A Radical View*, London and Basingstoke, Macmillan.

LYND, R. (1943) Foreword to R.A. Brady *Business as a System of Power*, Columbia, NY, Columbia University Press.

MCCULLOCH, G. (1993) 'Towards a social history of school science and technology?' in JENKINS, E.W. (Ed) *School Science and Technology: Some Issues and Perspectives*, Leeds, Centre for Studies in Science and Mathematics Education.

MCKILLOP, A.B. (1979) *A Disciplined Intelligence*, Montreal, McGill-Queens University Press.

MCKINNEY, W.L. and WESTBURY, I. (1975) 'Stability and change: The public school of Gary, Indiana 1940–1970' in REID, W.A. and WALKER, D.F. (Eds) *Case Studies in Curriculum Change, Great Britain and the United States*, London and Boston, MA, Routledge and Kegan Paul.

MACLURE, M. and ELLIOTT, J. (1993) 'Packaging the primary curriculum: Textbooks and the English National Curriculum', *The Curriculum Journal*, **4**, 1.

MANN, H. (1957) '3rd annual report 1841', quoted in CREMIN, L. (Ed) *The Republic and the School. Horace Mann and the Education of Free Man*, Columbia, NY, Teachers' College Press.

MARIS, D. (1907) *A School Course of Mathematics*, Oxford, Oxford University Press.

MARSH, C.J. (1990) 'Recent development in primary initial training in Wales: An outsider's perspective', *Journal of Education for Teaching*, **16**, 2.

MARSH, C.J. (1994) *Producing a National Curriculum: Plans and Paranoia*, Sydney, Allen & Unwin.

MARSH, C.J. and STAFFORD, K. (1988) *Curriculum: Practices and Issues* (2nd edn) Sydney, McGraw Hill.

MATHIESON, M. (1975) *The Preachers of Culture*, London, George Allen & Unwin.

MAYER, E. (1992) *Putting General Education to Work: The Key Competencies Report* (Chair: E. Mayer), Melbourne, Australian Education Council.

MAYO, C. and MAYO, E. (1849) *Practical Remarks on Infant Education*, London, Home and Colonial School Society.

MEDWAY, P. (1990) 'Into the sixties: English and English society at a time of change' in GOODSON, I.F. and MEDWAY, P. (Eds) *Bringing English to Order*, London and Washington, DC, Falmer Press.

MESSER-DAVIDOW, E. (Ed) (1993) *Knowledges: Historical and Critical Studies in Disciplinarity*, Charlottesville and London: University Press of Virginia.

MEYER, J.W., KAMENS, D.H. and BENAVOT, A. (1993) *School Knowledge for the Masses*, London and Washington, DC, Falmer Press.

MEYER, J.W. and ROWAN, B. (1983) 'The structure of educational organization' in MEYER, J.W. and SCOTT, W.R. (Eds) *Organisational Environments*, California, Sage.

MICHAEL, I. (1987) *The Teaching of English: From the Sixteenth Century to 1870*, Cambridge, Cambridge University Press.

MINISTER OF EDUCATION (1991) *The National Curriculum of New Zealand: A Discussion Document*, Wellington, Ministry of Education.

MOON, B. (1986) *The 'New Maths' Curriculum Controversy*, London, Washington, DC and Philadelphia, PA, Falmer Press.

MORANT, SIR R. (1904) *Board of Education Secondary Regulations*, London, Board of Education.

MORGAN, R. (1990) 'The "Englishness" of English teaching' in GOODSON, I.F. and MEDWAY, P. (Eds) *Bringing English to Order*, London and Washington, DC, Falmer Press.

MUSGRAVE, P.W. (1992) *From Humanity to Utility, Melbourne University and Public Examinations 1856–1964*, Melbourne, ACER.

NARAYAN, N. and FRUGILL, B. (1996) 'Death of the comprehensives', *The Observer*, 7 January.

NATIONAL COUNCIL OF TEACHERS OF MATHEMATICS (1992) *The Road to Reform in Mathematics Education*, Washington, DC, National Council of Teachers of Mathematics.

NORMAN, L. (1983) *The Brown and Yellow: Sydney Girls' High School 1883–1983*, Melbourne, Oxford University Press.

OLSEN, J.P. (1979) 'University governance: Non-participation as exclusion or choice' in MARCH, J.G. and OLSEN, J.P. (Eds) *Ambiguity and Choice in Organizations*, Bergen, University Press.

O'NEIL, J.O. (1993) 'Can national standards make a difference', *Educational Leadership*, **50**, 5.

OSBORNE, A.R. and CROSSWHITE, F.J. (1970) 'Forces and issues related to curriculum and instruction, 7–12' in NATIONAL COUNCIL OF TEACHERS OF MATHEMATICS *A History of Mathematics Education in the United States and Canada*, Washington, DC, National Council of Teachers of Mathematics.

PARISH, M. (1993) 'Politics', *The Spectator*, 9 October.

PRICE, A. (1959/60) 'A pioneer of scientific education: George Combe (1786–1958)', *Educational Review*, **12**.

PRICE, M.H. (Ed) (1986) *The Development of the Secondary Curriculum*, London, Sydney and Dover, NH, Croom Helm.

RAMIREZ, F.O. and BOLI, J. (1987) 'The political construction of mass schooling: European origins and worldwide institutionalism', *Sociology of Education*, **60**, January.

REID, W.A. (1984) 'Curricular topics as institutional categories: Implications for theory and research in the history and sociology of school subjects' in GOODSON, I.F. and BALL, S. (Eds) *Defining the Curriculum: Histories and Ethnographies*, London and Washington, DC, Falmer Press.

REID, W.A. (1985) 'Curriculum change and the evolution of educational constituencies: The English sixth form in the nineteenth century' in GOODSON, I.F. (Ed) *Social Histories of the Secondary Curriculum: Subjects for Study*, London and Washington, DC, Falmer Press.

REID, W.A. (1992) *The Pursuit of Curriculum*, Norwood, NJ, Ablex.

REID, W.A. (1993) 'Literacy, orality and the functions of curriculum' in GREEN, B. (Ed) *The Insistence of the Letter: Literacy Studies and Curriculum Theorizing*, Pittsburgh, PA, University of Pittsburgh Press.

RODERICK, G.W. and STEPHENS, M.D. (1972) *Scientific and Technical Educa* *in Nineteenth Century England: A Symposium*, Newton Abbot, David S. Charl

ROMBERG, T.A. (1993) 'NCTM's standards: A rallying flag for mathematics teach ers', *Educational Leadership*, **50**, 5.

ROSENBLATT, L.M. (1938) *Literature as Exploration, for the Commission on Human Relations of the Progressive Education Association*, New York, D Appleton-Century Co.

ROTTENBERG, C. and SMITH, M.L. (1990) 'Unintended effects of external testing in elementary schools', paper presented at the annual meeting of the American Educational Research Association, Boston.

ROWLAND, S. (1987) 'Where is primary education going?', *Journal of Curriculum Studies*, **19**.

SALTER, B. and TAPPER, T. (1981) *Education Politics and the State: The Theory and Practice of Educational Change*, London, Grant Macintyre.

SALTER, B. and TAPPER, T. (1985) *Power and Policy in Education: The Case of Independent Schooling*, London and Washington, DC, Falmer Press.

SCOTT, A. and SCOTT, R. (1980) *The Paradox of Reform and Reaction in the 'Deep North': Education and Policy Making in Queensland*, Melbourne, University of Melbourne Press.

SEDDON, T.L. (1989) 'Coherence in the changing form of schooling: State and society: An analysis of Australian educational reform 1901–1907', *British Journal of Sociology of Education*, **10**, 2.

SHAYER, D. (1972) *The Teaching of English in Schools 1900–1970*, London and Boston, MA, Routledge and Kegan Paul.

SHEPARD, L. (1991) 'Will national tests improve student learning?', paper presented at the annual meeting of the American Educational Research Association, Chicago.

SHILLING, C. (1989) *Schooling for Work in Capitalist Britain*, London and Washington, DC, Falmer Press.

SHIPMAN, M. (1971) 'Curriculum for inequality' in HOOPER, R. (Ed) *The Curriculum: Context, Design and Development*, Edinburgh, Oliver and Boyd.

SILBERMAN, C.E. (1970) *Crisis in the Classroom*, New York, Random House.

SILBERMAN, C.E. (Ed) (1973) *The Open Classroom Reader*, New York, Vintage Books.

SISKIN, L. (1994) *Realms of Knowledge: Academic Departments in Secondary Schools*, London and Washington, DC and Falmer Press.

SISKIN, L. and LITTLE, J.W. (Eds) (1995) *The Subjects in Question: The Department Organization of the High School*, New York, Teachers College Press.

SIZER, T.R. (1964) *Secondary Schools at the Turn of the Century*, New Haven, CT, Yale University Press.

SMITH, R. (1994) 'Richer or poorer, better or worse? How has the development of primary science teaching been affected by National Curriculum policy?', *The Curriculum Journal*, **5**, 2, pp. 163–78.

SNEDDEN, D. (1911) 'International commission on the teaching of mathematics, mathematics in the elementary schools of the United States', Washington, DC, Government Printing Office, quoted in Stanic (1987).

NIAK, L.A., ETHINGTON, C.A. and VARCLAS, M. (1991) 'Teaching mathematics without a coherent point of view: Findings from the IEA second international mathematics study', *Journal of Curriculum Studies*, **23**, 2.

STANIC, G. (1986) 'A historical perspective on justifying the teaching of mathematics' in GOODSON, I.F. (Ed) *International Perspectives in Curriculum History* (2nd edn reprinted 1988), London, Routledge.

STANIC, G. (1987) 'Mathematics education in the United States at the beginning of the twentieth century' in POPKEWITZ, T. (Ed) *The Formation of School Subjects*, London and Washington, DC, Falmer Press.

SWETZ, F. (1987) *Capitalism and Arithmetic: The New Math of the 15th Century*, La Salle, IL, Open Court.

TASK FORCE ON EDUCATION FOR ECONOMIC GROWTH (1983) *Action for Excellence: A Comprehensive Plan to Improve Our Nation's Schools*, Denver, CO, Education Commission of the States.

TAYLOR, T. (1995) 'Movers and shakers: High politics and the origins of the National Curriculum', *The Curriculum Journal*, **6**, 2.

TOMKINS, G.S. (1986) *A Common Countenance: Stability and Change in the Canadian Curriculum*, Scarborough, Ont, Prentice Hall.

TRACEY, C.W. (1962) 'Biology: Its struggle for recognition in English schools during the period 1900–60', *School Science Review*, **XCIII**, 150.

TURNER, D.M. (1927) *History of Science Teaching in England*, London, Chapman and Hall.

TURNEY, C. (Ed) (1975) *Sources in the History of Australian Education*, Sydney, Angus and Robertson.

TYACK, D.B. (1974) *The One Best System*, Cambridge, MA, Harvard University Press.

UNIVERSITY OF CAMBRIDGE LOCAL EXAMINATIONS SYNDICATE (1958) *100th Annual Report to University*, University of Cambridge.

WARING, M. (1979) *Social Pressures and Curriculum Innovation: A Study of the Nuffield Foundation Science Teaching Project*, London, Methuen.

WARING, M. (1980) unpublished paper on 'History of biology'.

WATSON, F. (1909) *The Beginnings of the Teaching of Modern Subjects in England*, London, Pitman.

WEBSTER, J.R. (1971) 'Curriculum change and crisis', *British Journal of Educational Studies*, **26**.

WENHAM, M. (1992) 'Current concepts of science', *Journal of Curriculum Studies*, **24**, 6.

WILLIAMS, R. (1975) *The Long Revolution*, London, Penguin Books.

WILLINSKY, J. (1991) *The Triumph of Literature — The Fate of Literacy: English in the Secondary School Curriculum*, New York and London, Teachers College Press.

WILLINSKY, J. (1993) 'Lessons from the literacy before schooling 1800–1850' in GREEN, B. (Ed) *The Insistence of the Letter: Literacy Studies and Curriculum Theorizing*, Pittsburgh, PA, University of Pittsburgh Press, pp. 58–74.

WILLIS, S. (1988) 'Mathematics should be more "relevant": What do they mean?', *Education Australia*, issue 4.

WOODS, P. (Ed) (1980) *Teacher Strategies*, London, Croom Helm.

WOOLNOUGH, B. (1988) *Physics Teaching in Schools 1960–85*, London and Washington, DC, Falmer Press.

WOOTON, W. (1965) *SMSG: The Making of a Curriculum*, New Haven, CT, Yale University Press.

WRIGHT, E. (1986) 'English teaching: Classics in the vernacular' in PRICE, M.H. (Ed) *The Development of the Secondary Curriculum*, London, Sydney and Dover, NH, Croom Helm, p. 71.

WROTTESLEY, LORD J. (1860) *Thoughts on Government and Legislation*, London, John Murray.

YOUNG, M.F.D. (Ed) (1971) *Knowledge and Control*, London, Macmillan.

YOUNG, M.F.D. (1977) 'Curriculum change: Limits and possibilities' in YOUNG, M.F.D. and WHITTY, G. (Eds) *Society, State and Schooling*, Lewes, Falmer Press.

Index